BASIC COMPUTER PROGRAMS
in SCIENCE and ENGINEERING

BASIC COMPUTER PROGRAMS
in SCIENCE and ENGINEERING

JULES H. GILDER

HAYDEN BOOK COMPANY, INC.
Rochelle Park, New Jersey

To Jordan, Gayle, Evan and Scott—
children of the computer age

Library of Congress Cataloging in Publication Data

Gilder, Jules H.   1947–
   Basic computer programs in science and engineering.

   1. Electronics—Data processing. 2. Electronics—
Computer programs. 3. Mathematics. 4. Engineering
mathematics. I. Title.
TK7835.G48   620'.0028'542   80-7969
ISBN 0-8104-0761-2

			7	8	9	PRINTING
83	84	85	86	87	88	YEAR

Preface

This book is meant to serve two main purposes. First, it is a sourcebook of basic programs that can be referenced from time to time when the need arises. In this role, the book serves as an instant software library. It contains 114 programs related primarily to mathematics and engineering (mostly electronic). These programs represent hundreds of hours of work that you the reader can now take advantage of. To be honest, this book was a joy to put together because it gave me a legitimate excuse to spend many hours working on my computer.

The second purpose of this book is to serve as a guide for the computer newcomer by showing him or her how a particular problem has been solved. Many of the programs contained in the book are simple. In some cases, the supporting text built into the program actually takes up more space than the computational section. This has been done deliberately; these programs should be able to stand by themselves as much as possible.

Of course, programs that design circuits will require some additional documentation, such as a circuit diagram. Most other programs are meant to stand alone. A self-documenting program has a big advantage. You don't have to remember how to use it or where you put the instruction sheet that goes with it. Nevertheless, a brief explanation of each program is included with each listing.

In writing these programs, I have refrained from using any special machine-dependent functions so that the software can be used on virtually any home computer with little or no modification. The single exception to this is the first statement of each program, which is a "CALL –936." This is a statement that calls a machine-language subroutine to clear the video screen. It may be completely eliminated or replaced with the equivalent for your machine.

All the programs in this book were written and tested on an Apple II microcomputer using Applesoft II BASIC. This is a version of Microsoft BASIC that includes special graphics commands for the Apple computer. However, as mentioned earlier, since none of these special commands have been included, the programs should be usable on just about any computer.

I would like to take this opportunity to thank Steve Jobs, Steve Wozniak, and Mike Markkula of Apple Computer Inc. whose help made this book possible.

The programs represent about 100 K of code. For those of you who need practice typing, here's your chance. Program tapes are also available from the publisher for the Apple, Pet, Sorceror, and TRS-80 computers.

Happy computing.

Jules H. Gilder

Contents

1 General Mathematics

Most home computers come with a wide variety of built-in mathematical functions. There are, however, many occasions when these are not enough, and more capabilities are needed. The programs in this chapter are in part designed to extend your machine's capabilities.

In some of the programs (e.g., extended factorial and improved combinations), the computer is programmed to handle numbers whose size would ordinarily cause an overflow. By carefully analyzing this programming technique, it is possible to learn how it can be used in other applications.

In addition to the probability related programs (1.1 to 1.5), this section also shows how the special mathematics of vectors can be handled (1.6 and 1.7). Most BASIC interpreters do not contain base 1∅ logarithmic capability and can only handle natural logarithms (logs to the base e, which is 2.718). However, a simple program (1.8) will provide the ability not only to handle the evaluation of base 1∅ logarithms, but to deal with logarithms to any base.

Two of the programs in this chapter deal with coordinate systems. The first (1.9) provides the capability of translating and/or rotating a given coordinate system. This is very handy if you want to convert data or measurements from one frame of reference to another. The second coordinate related program is 1.10. This one converts data from Cartesian (rectangular) coordinates to polar coordinates, and vice versa.

Next are some programs that work on numbers. The first is 1.11, which finds the maximum and minimum of a given set of numbers, an absolute necessity if any plotting of data is to be done. Program 1.12 is simple and can be incorporated as a subroutine in a larger program so that the results produced will be of uniform accuracy. It illustrates a technique used in many of the programs in this book, that is, rounding-off numbers to a given decimal place.

If you've ever had to draw an object on a piece of paper accurately, you will quickly realize the value of the dimension scaling program (1.13). And if you want to do some plotting, the histogram program produces attractive output. As given (1.14), it is used to plot functions. However, with very little effort it can be used to plot individual data points. Try to do so by combining 1.14 with the max/min locator program.

Did you ever have three points through which you wanted to draw a circle? Try to do it. Draw three points on a piece of graph paper and try to draw a circle that will pass through all of them. It's not so easy, is it? Now enter the location of those three points into program 1.15. It will tell you the radius of the circle and where the center is located. The remaining programs produce normally distributed numbers, find any root of any number, and convert any number into a rational fraction.

1.1 FACTORIAL

The factorial of a number is an operation frequently used in probability calculations. It is arrived at by evaluating:

$$\text{n factorial} = n(n - 1)(n - 2) \ldots 1$$
$$\text{5 factorial} = 5(4)(3)(2)(1) = 120$$

The notation n! is often used to designate the factorial operation and is read "n factorial." There is one special case, for Ø!, which is defined as being equal to 1. The factorial calculation is carried out in lines 11Ø to 14Ø. A variable XF is initialized as 1. The number whose factorial is desired is n. This number is used to set up a FOR . . . NEXT loop in which the equation XF = XF*K is evaluated where K varies from 1 to n. This is where the factorial value is calculated. If n is equal to Ø, the program will go through the loop once with K equal to 1 and produce the answer 1, as it will do for 1!.

```
0   CALL  - 936
1   PRINT : PRINT : PRINT : PRINT "WRITTEN BY JULES H. GILDER"
2   PRINT : PRINT "COPYRIGHT (C)  HAYDEN BOOK CO. 1978"
3   FOR X = 1 TO 4000: NEXT X
10  PRINT : PRINT : PRINT : PRINT
20  PRINT "                 FACTORIAL"
30  PRINT : PRINT : PRINT
40  PRINT "THIS PROGRAM COMPUTES THE FACTORIAL OF"
50· PRINT "A GIVEN NUMBER. OPERATION IS LIMITED"
60  PRINT "BY THE LARGEST NUMBER YOUR COMPUTER CAN"
70  PRINT "HANDLE. ONLY INTEGERS ARE VALID."
80  PRINT : PRINT
90  INPUT "ENTER THE NUMBER  ";N
100  PRINT : PRINT : PRINT
110 XF = 1
120  FOR  K = 1  TO  N
130 XF = XF * K
140  NEXT  K
150  PRINT N;"! = ";XF
160  PRINT : PRINT : INPUT "DO YOU HAVE ANOTHER NUMBER? ";A$
170  IF  LEFT$ (A$,1) = "Y" THEN 80
180  END
```

```
             FACTORIAL


THIS PROGRAM COMPUTES THE FACTORIAL OF
A GIVEN NUMBER. OPERATION IS LIMITED
BY THE LARGEST NUMBER YOUR COMPUTER CAN
HANDLE. ONLY INTEGERS ARE VALID.

ENTER THE NUMBER  9


9! = 362880

DO YOU HAVE ANOTHER NUMBER? YES

ENTER THE NUMBER  35


?OVERFLOW ERROR IN 130
```

1.2 EXTENDED FACTORIAL[1]

A major problem with the previous program is that the limit of the computer's number-handling ability is quickly reached. Most home computers become overloaded with a calculation whose results produce a number larger than $10 \uparrow 39$. This program contains a separate routine that factors the answer into powers of 10 so that much greater capability is offered (lines 140 to 160).

As in the previous program, the factorial is calculated in line 130, and the factoring takes place thereafter. Thus numbers such as 121! can easily be evaluated, whereas in the previous program they would overload the computer.

```
0   CALL  - 936
1   PRINT : PRINT : PRINT : PRINT "WRITTEN BY JULES H. GILDER"
2   PRINT : PRINT "COPYRIGHT (C) HAYDEN BOOK CO. 1978"
3   FOR X = 1 TO 4000: NEXT X
4   REM    ADAPTED FROM "COMPUTER  PROGRAM EXTENDS COMPUTATION OF
        FACTORIALS",W.M. BUNKER, ELECTRONIC DESIGN 4/71,P.86
10  PRINT : PRINT : PRINT : PRINT
20  PRINT "      EXTENDED FACTORIAL CALCULATION"
30  PRINT : PRINT : PRINT
40  PRINT "THIS PROGRAM WILL PERFORM FACTORIAL"
50  PRINT "CALCULATIONS WHOSE RESULTS ARE MUCH "
60  PRINT "LARGER THAN 10↑39, A VALUE THAT OVER-"
70  PRINT "LOADS MOST HOME COMPUTERS. JUST ENTER"
80  PRINT "THE NUMBER WHEN ASKED."
90  PRINT : PRINT : PRINT : PRINT
100  INPUT "ENTER THE NUMBER: ";N
105  PRINT : PRINT : PRINT
110 E = 0
115 F = 1
120  FOR  I = 2  TO  N
130 F = F * I
140  IF  F < 1E5  THEN  170
150 F = F * 1E - 5
160 E = E + 5
170  NEXT  I
175  PRINT : PRINT : PRINT
180  PRINT N;" ! = ";F;" TIMES"
185  PRINT
190  PRINT "10 TO THE ";E;" POWER."
195  PRINT : PRINT
200  PRINT : PRINT : INPUT "DO YOU HAVE ANOTHER NUMBER? ";A$
205  PRINT : PRINT
210  IF  LEFT$ (A$,1) = "Y" THEN 100
220  END
```

---

[1] Adapted from W. M. Bunker, "Computer Program Extends Computation of Factorials," *Electronic Design* (April 1971): p. 86.

EXTENDED FACTORIAL CALCULATION

THIS PROGRAM WILL PERFORM FACTORIAL
CALCULATIONS WHOSE RESULTS ARE MUCH
LARGER THAN 10^{39}, A VALUE THAT OVER-
LOADS MOST HOME COMPUTERS. JUST ENTER
THE NUMBER WHEN ASKED.

ENTER THE NUMBER: 35

35 ! = 1.0333148 TIMES
10 TO THE 40 POWER.

DO YOU HAVE ANOTHER NUMBER? YES

ENTER THE NUMBER: 121

121 ! = 8.09429863 TIMES
10 TO THE 200 POWER.

DO YOU HAVE ANOTHER NUMBER? NO

1.3   PERMUTATIONS

In some probability problems, it is often necessary to calculate the number of ways that n objects can be arranged in order in groups of r objects. In figuring this out, we see that there are n ways of choosing the first object, n – 1 ways of choosing the second object, and so forth. This continues until the last object of the group is reached. For this object, there are n – r + 1 ways of choosing it. The different ways that these objects can be arranged are called permutations (P). Mathematically, the number of permutations can be calculated by multiplying the number of ways each object can be chosen by the next:

$$P = n(n-1)(n-2)(n-3)\ldots(n-r+1)$$

This expression can be written more simply as

$$P = n!/(n-r)!$$

The term n! is called "n factorial" and is equal to $n(n-1)(n-2)\ldots 1$. So 3! equals 3(2)(1) or 6.

The program uses the factorial approach to calculate the number of permutations. The factorials are calculated in a subroutine starting at line 220. After both factorials are calculated, the larger is divided by the smaller to get the final result.

The program contains two error detection tests. Located in lines 100 and 110, these will determine if an invalid input entry is made.

```
0    CALL   - 936
1    PRINT : PRINT : PRINT : PRINT "WRITTEN BY JULES H. GILDER"
2    PRINT : PRINT "COPYRIGHT (C)  HAYDEN BOOK COMPANY 1978"
3    FOR X = 1 TO 4000: NEXT X
10    PRINT : PRINT : PRINT : PRINT
20    PRINT "                PERMUTATIONS"
30    PRINT : PRINT : PRINT : PRINT
40    PRINT "THIS PROGRAM COMPUTES THE PERMUTATIONS"
50    PRINT "OF 'N' OBJECTS TAKEN 'R' AT A TIME."
60    PRINT : PRINT : PRINT
70    INPUT "ENTER NUMBER OF OBJECTS ";N
80    INPUT "ENTER NUMBER PER GROUP ";R
90    PRINT : PRINT : PRINT
100    IF  N < R  THEN    PRINT "INPUT ERROR - N<R": GOTO  60
110    IF  R < 0  THEN    PRINT "INPUT ERROR - R<0": GOTO  60
120  X = N
130    GOSUB  220
140  NN = XF
150  X = N - R
160    GOSUB  220
170  NR = XF
180  P =  INT (NN / NR)
185    PRINT : PRINT : PRINT
190    PRINT "THERE ARE ";P;" PERMUTATIONS OF "
195    PRINT
200    PRINT N;" OBJECTS TAKEN ";R;" AT A TIME."
210    GOTO 270
```

```
220 XF = 1
230  FOR  K = 1  TO  X
240 XF = K * XF
250  NEXT  K
260  RETURN
270  END
```

PERMUTATIONS

THIS PROGRAM COMPUTES THE PERMUTATIONS
OF 'N' OBJECTS TAKEN 'R' AT A TIME.

ENTER NUMBER OF OBJECTS 10
ENTER NUMBER PER GROUP 3

THERE ARE 720 PERMUTATIONS OF

10 OBJECTS TAKEN 3 AT A TIME.

1.4 COMBINATIONS

In the permutations program, the number of ways n objects could be arranged in order into groups of r was calculated. Sometimes the order of the objects in a group is not important—for example, the number of ways 12 people can be divided into groups of 3. Another application is found in error detection and correction codes for communication systems.

The number of ways items can be grouped into groups of r objects, where order is not important, is called the "combination."

The combination of 12 objects taken 2 at a time is equal to

$$C = 12!/(3!(12 - 3)!) = 22\emptyset$$

The generalized formula for calculating combinations is

$$C = n!/(r!(n - r)!)$$

The difference between this calculation and the one for permutations is the extra r! term in the denominator.

Once again, the factorial calculation is carried out by a subroutine located at line $22\emptyset$. The results of three calls to this subroutine are used to calculate the combinations. As in the permutations program, error detection tests are included.

```
0    CALL  - 936
1    PRINT : PRINT : PRINT : PRINT "WRITTEN BY JULES H. GILDER"
2    PRINT : PRINT "COPYRIGHT (C)  HAYDEN BOOK COMPANY 1978"
3    FOR X = 1 TO 4000: NEXT X
10   PRINT : PRINT : PRINT : PRINT
20   PRINT "              COMBINATIONS"
30   PRINT : PRINT : PRINT : PRINT
40   PRINT "THIS PROGRAM COMPUTES THE COMBINATIONS"
50   PRINT "OF 'N' OBJECTS TAKEN 'R' AT A TIME."
60   PRINT : PRINT : PRINT
70   INPUT "ENTER NUMBER OF OBJECTS.  ";N
80   INPUT "ENTER NUMBER PER GROUP.  ";R
90   PRINT : PRINT : PRINT
100  IF  N < R  THEN   PRINT "INPUT ERROR - N<R": GOTO  60
110  IF  R < 0  THEN   PRINT "INPUT ERROR - R<0": GOTO  60
120  X = N
130  GOSUB  220
140  NN = XF
150  X = N - R
160  GOSUB  220
170  NR = XF
172  X = R
174  GOSUB  220
176  RR = XF
180  C =  INT (NN / NR / RR + .5)
185  PRINT : PRINT : PRINT
190  PRINT " THERE ARE ";C;" COMBINATIONS OF"
195  PRINT
200  PRINT N;" OBJECTS TAKEN ";R;" AT A TIME."
210  GOTO 270
220  XF = 1
230  FOR  K = 1  TO  X
240  XF = K * XF
250  NEXT  K
260  RETURN
270  END
```

```
                    COMBINATIONS


THIS PROGRAM COMPUTES THE COMBINATIONS
OF 'N' OBJECTS TAKEN 'R' AT A TIME.


ENTER NUMBER OF OBJECTS.  12
ENTER NUMBER PER GROUP.  3



  THERE ARE 220 COMBINATIONS OF

12 OBJECTS TAKEN 3 AT A TIME.
```

1.5   IMPROVED COMBINATIONS[1]

The problem with the previous program is that it is limited in the magnitude of the numbers used to calculate combinations. If the number of objects is greater or equal to 34, the computer will indicate that the number is too large and give an overflow error message.

This program uses a method of calculation that prevents the overflow problem, unless the final answer itself is too large for the computer. First, the program determines if the number of objects n is less than twice the number of objects per group k. If it is, the program sets I = 1 and calculates:

$$\binom{k+1}{k} = \binom{k+1}{k} = k + 1$$

Then for $I = 2, 3, 4, 5, \ldots, n - k$, the following expression is recursively computed:

$$\binom{k+1}{k} = \binom{k+1-1}{k} \left(\frac{k+1}{1}\right)$$

If n is equal to or greater than twice k, the following recursive calculation is made for values of $j = 2, 3, 4, \ldots, k$:

$$\binom{n}{j} = \left(\frac{n}{j-1}\right) \left(\frac{n+1-j}{j}\right)$$

For the case when k is equal to 1, the combination is simply n.

```
0    CALL  -.936
1    PRINT : PRINT : PRINT : PRINT "WRITTEN BY JULES H. GILDER"
2    PRINT : PRINT "COPYRIGHT (C)  HAYDEN BOOK CO. 1978"
3    FOR X = 1 TO 4000: NEXT X
10   PRINT : PRINT : PRINT
20   PRINT "    IMPROVED COMBINATIONS CALCULATION"
30   PRINT : PRINT : PRINT : PRINT
40   PRINT "THIS PROGRAM WILL CALCULATE COMBINA-"
50   PRINT "TIONS WITHOUT CAUSING AN OVERFLOW UN-"
55   PRINT "LESS THE FINAL ANSWER ITSELF IS TOO BIG"
60   PRINT "FOR THE COMPUTER. 'N' AS LARGE AS 120"
65   PRINT "CAN BE USED."
70   PRINT : PRINT : PRINT
80   INPUT "ENTER NUMBER OF OBJECTS: ";N
85   INPUT "ENTER NUMBER OF GROUPS: ";K
90   PRINT : PRINT : PRINT : PRINT
100  IF  N < 2 * K  THEN  230
110  B0 = N
120  FOR  J = 2  TO  K
130  B1 = B0 * ((N + 1 - J) / J)
140  B0 = B1
150  NEXT  J
190  GOSUB 290
220  GOTO  310
230 L = N - K
```

---

[1]Adapted from R. Lambert, "Perform Large-Value Computations on a Computer," *Electronic Design.*

```
240 S0 = K + 1
250  FOR  I = 2  TO  L
260 S1 = S0 * (K + I) / I
270 S0 = S1
280  NEXT  I
285 B1 = S1: GOSUB 290
286  GOTO 310
290  PRINT "THERE ARE ";B1;" COMBINATIONS OF"
300  PRINT : PRINT N;" OBJECTS TAKEN ";K;" AT A TIME."
310  END
```

IMPROVED COMBINATIONS CALCULATION

THIS PROGRAM WILL CALCULATE COMBINA-
TIONS WITHOUT CAUSING AN OVERFLOW UN-
LESS THE FINAL ANSWER ITSELF IS TOO BIG
FOR THE COMPUTER. 'N' AS LARGE AS 120
CAN BE USED.

ENTER NUMBER OF OBJECTS: 120:
ENTER NUMBER OF GROUPS: 23

THERE ARE 2.69002945E+24 COMBINATIONS OF

120 OBJECTS TAKEN 23 AT A TIME.

1.6   SCALAR PRODUCT OF TWO VECTORS

The scalar product of two vectors, also called the "dot product," is defined as the product of the magnitudes of the two vectors multiplied by the cosine of the angle between them. The result of this calculation is a scalar (not vector) quantity.

While this approach can be used to calculate the scalar product, a much simpler method is to use the following formula:

$$A \cdot B = (XA)(XB) + (YA)(YB) + (ZA)(ZB)$$

where

$$A = XA + YA + ZA$$
$$B = XB + YB + ZB$$

This law is used to perform the calculation in line 100 of the program. An interesting feature of the scalar product is that if neither of the two vectors is zero but the scalar product is zero, the two vectors are perpendicular to one another.

```
0   CALL  - 936
1   PRINT : PRINT : PRINT "WRITTEN BY JULES H. GILDER"
2   PRINT : PRINT "COPYRIGHT (C)  HAYDEN BOOK CO. 1978"
3   FOR X = 1 TO 4000: NEXT X
10   PRINT : PRINT : PRINT : PRINT
20   PRINT  TAB( 13)"SCALAR PRODUCT"
30   PRINT : PRINT : PRINT : PRINT
40   PRINT  "THIS PROGRAM CALCULATES THE SCALAR PRO-"
50   PRINT "DUCT OF TWO VECTORS."
60   PRINT : PRINT : PRINT
70   INPUT "ENTER VECTOR 1 (X,Y,Z) ";X1,Y1,Z1
80   INPUT "ENTER VECTOR 2 (X,Y,Z) ";X2,Y2,Z2
90   PRINT : PRINT : PRINT
100 S = X1 * X2 + Y1 * Y2 + Z1 * Z2
110   PRINT "THE SCALAR PRODUCT IS ";S
120   END
```

```
          SCALAR PRODUCT


THIS PROGRAM CALCULATES THE SCALAR PRO-
DUCT OF TWO VECTORS.


ENTER VECTOR 1 (X,Y,Z) 2,3,4
ENTER VECTOR 2 (X,Y,Z) -3,5,0


THE SCALAR PRODUCT IS 9
```

1.7   CROSS PRODUCT OF TWO VECTORS

Unlike the scalar product of two vectors, the cross product of two vectors is itself a vector. The magnitude of this vector is defined as the product of the magnitude of the two original vectors multiplied by the sine of the angle between them.

The direction of the cross product vector is perpendicular to the plane that contains the two original vectors. The values of the cross product vector components can be calculated by using the following formulas:

$$X = Y1 * Z2 - Z1 * Y2$$
$$Y = Z1 * X2 - X1 * Z2$$
$$Z = X1 * Y2 - Y1 * X2$$

where the original vectors are

$$A1 = X1 + Y1 + Z1$$
$$A2 = X2 + Y2 + Z2$$

These calculations are performed in lines 100 to 120.

```
0   CALL  - 936
1   PRINT : PRINT : PRINT : PRINT "WRITTEN BY JULES H. GILDER"
2   PRINT : PRINT "COPYRIGHT (C)  HAYDEN BOOK CO. 1978"
3   FOR X = 1 TO 4000: NEXT X
10   PRINT : PRINT : PRINT : PRINT
20   PRINT  TAB( 13)"CROSS PRODUCT"
30   PRINT : PRINT : PRINT : PRINT
40   PRINT  "THIS PROGRAM CALCULATES THE CROSS PRO-"
50   PRINT "DUCT OF TWO VECTORS."
60   PRINT : PRINT : PRINT
70   INPUT "ENTER VECTOR 1 (X,Y,Z) ";X1,Y1,Z1
80   INPUT "ENTER VECTOR 2 (X,Y,Z) ";X2,Y2,Z2
90   PRINT : PRINT : PRINT
100 X = Y1 * Z2 - Z1 * Y2
110 Y = Z1 * X2 - X1 * Z2
120 Z = X1 * Y2 - Y1 * X2
130   PRINT "THE CROSS PRODUCT IS:"
140   PRINT
150   PRINT "X = ";X;"   Y = ";Y;"   Z = ";Z
160   END



        CROSS PRODUCT


THIS PROGRAM CALCULATES THE CROSS PRO-
DUCT OF TWO VECTORS.


ENTER VECTOR 1 (X,Y,Z) 2,3,4
ENTER VECTOR 2 (X,Y,Z) -3,5,0


THE CROSS PRODUCT IS:

X = -20   Y = -12   Z = 19
```

1.8 LOG TO ANY BASE

The logarithm of any number is the power to which the base of the logarithm must be raised to produce the number. This is a classic definition of logarithms. Generally, only two bases are used to calculate logarithms. The base 1∅ and the base e (where e = 2.71828). The latter is often referred to as the natural logarithm.

Sometimes to make calculations easier, it is desirable to calculate logarithms to bases other than these. In addition, most BASIC interpreters used in home computing systems do not even provide the elementary log-to-base-10 capability. They only permit calculation of the natural log (often written "ln").

This program makes it possible for your computer to calculate the log of any number to any base. For example, the log of 64 to the base 4 equals 3 and ln e equals 1. This can be helpful in computer applications for calculating what power of 2 a particular number is. For example, if the number 65536 is entered when this program is run and the base is 2, we discover that 65536 is equal to 2 to the 16th power.

The calculation is based on the definition of a logarithm stated above. From this definition, the following formula can be derived:

$$base \uparrow log = number$$

where the number is produced by raising the base to the log power. If the logarithm of both sides of this equation is taken, the result is

$$log\,(base \uparrow log) = log\,(number) \quad or \quad log\,(B \uparrow L) = log\,n$$

The left side of this last equation, however, is equal to $L * log\,(B)$ so that the final result is

$$L * log\,B = log\,n$$

If both sides of the equation are divided by log B, the formula used by the program to evaluate the log of any number to any base results. This formula is

$$L = (log\,n)/(log\,B)$$

```
0   CALL  - 936
1   PRINT : PRINT : PRINT : PRINT "WRITTEN BY JULES H. GILDER"
2   PRINT : PRINT "COPYRIGHT (C)  HAYDEN BOOK CO. 1978"
3   FOR X = 1 TO 4000: NEXT X
10    PRINT : PRINT : PRINT : PRINT
20    PRINT "          LOG TO ANY BASE"
30    PRINT : PRINT : PRINT : PRINT
40    PRINT "THIS PROGRAM WILL CALCULATE THE LOGA-"
50    PRINT "RITHM OF ANY NUMBER TO ANY BASE."
60    PRINT : PRINT
70    INPUT "ENTER THE NUMBER   ";N
80    INPUT "ENTER THE BASE   ";B
90    PRINT : PRINT : PRINT
100 LN =  LOG (N) /  LOG (B)
110   PRINT "THE LOG OF ";N;" TO THE BASE ";B
120   PRINT
130   PRINT "IS EQUAL TO ";LN
140   END
```

LOG TO ANY BASE

THIS PROGRAM WILL CALCULATE THE LOGA-
RITHM OF ANY NUMBER TO ANY BASE.

ENTER THE NUMBER 65536
ENTER THE BASE 2

THE LOG OF 65536 TO THE BASE 2
IS EQUAL TO 16

1.9 NEW COORDINATES

This program is helpful when it is necessary to convert data from one frame of reference to another. The operation is frequently necessary in the study of physics. If it is desired to translate the coordinate axis of a particular set of data, subtract the coordinates of the new origin from the old data point. If the axis is to be rotated as well, it has to be accounted for by multiplying by the sine and cosine of the angle involved.

The actual calculation of the new point is done in lines 160 and 170. Lines 165 and 175 simply round off the answer to the nearest hundredth.

A point of interest here is that BASIC does not recognize degrees as the argument for trigonometric functions such as sine and cosine. To overcome this inconvenience, the program is designed to accept degrees as the input and convert them to radians (line 130) so that BASIC can use the information.

```
0    CALL  - 936
1    PRINT : PRINT : PRINT : PRINT "WRITTEN BY JULES H. GILDER"
2    PRINT : PRINT "COPYRIGHT (C)  HAYDEN BOOK CO. 1978"
3    FOR X = 1 TO 4000: NEXT X
10   PRINT : PRINT : PRINT : PRINT
20   PRINT "          NEW COORDINATES"
30   PRINT : PRINT : PRINT : PRINT
40   PRINT "THIS PROGRAM WILL CALCULATE THE COORDI-"
50   PRINT "NATES OF DATA POINTS IN A RECTANGULAR"
60   PRINT "COORDINATE SYSTEM THAT HAS BEEN ROTATED"
70   PRINT "ABOUT ITS ORIGIN, OR TRANSLATED TO A"
80   PRINT "NEW ORIGIN.  ORIGINAL ORIGIN IS ASSUMED"
90   PRINT "TO BE AT THE POINT (0,0)."
100   PRINT : PRINT : PRINT
105   INPUT "HOW MANY DATA POINTS  ";N
110   INPUT "ENTER NEW ORIGIN (X,Y)  ";X1,Y1
120   INPUT "ENTER DEGREES ROTATION  ";D
130 D = D * 3.14159 / 180
140   FOR  K = 1  TO  N
150   INPUT "ENTER OLD LOCATION OF POINT (X,Y)  ";X(K),Y(K)
160 XN(K) = (X(K) - X1) *  COS (D) + (Y(K) - Y1) *  SIN (D)
165 XN(K) =   INT (100 * XN(K) + .5) / 100
170 YN(K) =  - (X(K) - X1) *  SIN (D) + (Y(K) - Y1) *  COS (D)
175 YN(K) =   INT (100 * YN(K) + .5) / 100
180   NEXT  K
185   PRINT : PRINT : PRINT
190   PRINT "DATA POINTS ON THE NEW AXIS ARE:"
200   PRINT
210   FOR  K = 1  TO  N
220   PRINT " X ";K;" = ";XN(K);"          Y ";K;" = ";YN(K)
230   NEXT  K
240   END
```

THIS PROGRAM WILL CALCULATE THE COORDI-
NATES OF DATA POINTS IN A RECTANGULAR
COORDINATE SYSTEM THAT HAS BEEN ROTATED
ABOUT ITS ORIGIN, OR TRANSLATED TO A
NEW ORIGIN.   ORIGINAL ORIGIN IS ASSUMED
TO BE AT THE POINT (0,0).

HOW MANY DATA POINTS   3
ENTER NEW ORIGIN (X,Y)   3,3
ENTER DEGREES ROTATION   0
ENTER OLD LOCATION OF POINT (X,Y)   3,3
ENTER OLD LOCATION OF POINT (X,Y)   0,0
ENTER OLD LOCATION OF POINT (X,Y)   5,2

DATA POINTS ON THE NEW AXIS ARE:

```
 X 1 = 0          Y 1 = 0
 X 2 = -3           Y 2 = -3
 X 3 = 2          Y 3 = -1
```

1.10 RECTANGULAR-TO-POLAR COORDINATE CONVERSION

Like the previous program, this one is also used to convert data from one frame of reference to another. This time, however, the data is converted from the conventional rectangular (or Cartesian) coordinates to polar coordinates. Conversions of this type are very common in the solving of problems in electrical engineering.

The program is actually two programs in one. It can accept either polar coordinate data and give rectangular coordinates, or vice versa. The segment of program used depends on the answer to the question posed by the input statement on line 5Ø. If "polar" is entered, the computer ignores the first part of the program and goes to line 2ØØ, where the polar-to-rectangular coordinate conversion takes place.

If "rectangular" is entered at line 5Ø, the rectangular-to-polar conversion is done. In line 9Ø the angle theta is calculated. However, its value is returned in radians, which must be converted to degrees. Radian-to-degree conversion takes place in line 97.

```
0    CALL  - 936
1    PRINT : PRINT : PRINT : PRINT "WRITTEN BY JULES H. GILDER"
2    PRINT : PRINT "COPYRIGHT (C) HAYDEN BOOK CO. 1978"
3    FOR X = 1 TO 4000: NEXT X
5    PRINT : PRINT : PRINT : PRINT
6    PRINT "RECTANGULAR/POLAR COORDINATE CONVERSION"
7    PRINT : PRINT : PRINT : PRINT
10   PRINT "THIS PROGRAM CONVERTS POINTS IN REC-"
20   PRINT "TANGULAR COORDINATES TO POLAR COORDI-"
30   PRINT "NATES AND VICE VERSA. ENTER THE TYPE"
40   PRINT "OF DATA YOU ARE SUPPLYING."
50   INPUT "(POLAR OR RECTANGULAR) ";A$
55   PRINT
60   IF  A$ = "POLAR"  THEN  200
70   PRINT
80   INPUT "ENTER X,Y ";X,Y
85   PRINT
90   THETA =  ATN (Y / X)
95   R = Y /  SIN (THETA)
97   THETA = THETA * 57.2958
100  THETA =  INT (THETA + .5)
110  R =  INT (100 * R + .5) / 100
120  PRINT "R = ";R;"  ANGLE = ";THETA;" DEGREES"
125  PRINT
130  INPUT "DO YOU HAVE MORE DATA (YES/NO) ";A$
135  PRINT
140  IF  A$ = "YES"  THEN  50
145  PRINT
150  END
200  INPUT "ENTER R,THETA (DEGREES) ";R,THETA
205  PRINT
210  THETA = THETA / 57.2958
220  X =  INT (100 * R *  COS (THETA) + .5) / 100
230  Y =  INT (100 * R *  SIN (THETA) + .5) / 100
240  PRINT "X= ";X;"   Y= ";Y
245  PRINT
250  GOTO 130
```

RECTANGULAR/POLAR COORDINATE CONVERSION

THIS PROGRAM CONVERTS POINTS IN REC-
TANGULAR COORDINATES TO POLAR COORDI-
NATES AND VICE VERSA. ENTER THE TYPE
OF DATA YOU ARE SUPPLYING.
(POLAR OR RECTANGULAR) R

ENTER X,Y 3,4

R = 5   ANGLE = 53 DEGREES

DO YOU HAVE MORE DATA (YES/NO) NO

1.11 MAX/MIN LOCATOR

When doing any type of data analysis, it is often necessary to know the largest and smallest numbers of the data set. This need is so widespread, in fact, that the FORTRAN computer language has special max and min functions built in. While no such capability exists in BASIC, it is a simple matter to write a program to find these numbers.

In this program, variable B is the largest number, and variable S is the smallest. To start, both B and S are assigned the same value, the value of the first number entered. Then each number is examined in turn to see if it is larger than B (line 15Ø) or smaller than S (line 16Ø). If the number is larger than B, B is set equal to the new number. Similarly, if the number is smaller than S, S is set equal to the number.

Since this program is so handy, you may want to use it as a subroutine in a larger program. Assuming that this larger program generates a list of numbers, it is only necessary for you to include lines 13Ø through 21Ø.

```
0    CALL  - 936
1    PRINT : PRINT : PRINT : PRINT "WRITTEN BY JULES H. GILDER"
2    PRINT : PRINT "COPYRIGHT (C) HAYDEN BOOK CO. 1978"
3    FOR X = 1 TO 4000: NEXT X
5    PRINT : PRINT : PRINT : PRINT
6    PRINT  TAB( 13 )"MAX/MIN LOCATOR"
7    PRINT : PRINT : PRINT : PRINT
10   PRINT "THIS PROGRAM FINDS THE LARGEST AND"
20   PRINT "SMALLEST NUMBERS IN A LIST OF NUMBERS"
30   PRINT : PRINT : PRINT
50   INPUT "HOW MANY NUMBERS IN LIST? ";N
60   DIM  A(N)
70   PRINT
80   PRINT "ENTER THE NUMBERS"
90   FOR  I = 1  TO  N
100    PRINT "A";I;" = ";
110    INPUT A( I )
120    NEXT I
130  S = A(1):B = S
140  FOR  I  = 1  TO  N
150    IF  A(I) > B   THEN   B = A(I)
160    IF  A(I) - S < 0   THEN   S = A(I)
170    NEXT  I
180  PRINT : PRINT : PRINT
190  PRINT "THE LARGEST NUMBER IS ";B
200  PRINT
210  PRINT "THE SMALLEST NUMBER IS ";S
220  END
```

```
            MAX/MIN LOCATOR


THIS PROGRAM FINDS THE LARGEST AND
SMALLEST NUMBERS IN A LIST OF NUMBERS


HOW MANY NUMBERS IN LIST? 5

ENTER THE NUMBERS
A1 = ?78
A2 = ?-9
A3 = ?0
A4 = ?3445
A5 = ?.01


THE LARGEST NUMBER IS 3445

THE SMALLEST NUMBER IS -9
```

1.12 NUMBER ROUNDER

Digital computers are great. They perform thousands of computations in almost no time at all and turn out results that are accurate to many decimal places. However, most of the time this accuracy is not necessary and, in fact, can be bothersome. If you're producing a list of numbers by computer and some have eight decimal places while others have only two, it really messes up the appearance of the number columns in your final output. To overcome those super-long numbers, it is convenient to round off.

This program will allow you to input any number and round off to any fewer number of decimal places (within the limits of your computer, of course). Most computers will not handle more than eight places after the decimal point. So if you enter a number with eleven places after the decimal point and try to round off to nine decimal places, don't be surprised when you find that your answer is rounded off to eight places. This is because the computer has automatically rounded off to the limit of its accuracy. There are, however, some BASIC interpreters that just truncate the extra decimal places. So pay attention to your computer's capabilities.

```
0    CALL  - 936
1    PRINT : PRINT : PRINT : PRINT "WRITTEN BY JULES H. GILDER"
2    PRINT : PRINT "COPYRIGHT (C)  HAYDEN BOOK CO. 1978"
3    FOR X = 1 TO 4000: NEXT X
10   PRINT : PRINT : PRINT : PRINT
20   PRINT  TAB( 13)"NUMBER ROUNDER"
30   PRINT : PRINT : PRINT : PRINT
40   PRINT "THIS PROGRAM WILL ROUND OFF ANY GIVEN"
50   PRINT "NUMBER TO ANY NUMBER OF PLACES."
60   PRINT : PRINT : PRINT
70   INPUT "ENTER NUMBER   ";N
75   PRINT
80   INPUT "ROUND TO HOW MANY-PLACES   ";R
90   PRINT : PRINT : PRINT
95 RR =  INT (10 ↑ R + .5)
96   IF  R = 6  THEN  RR = 1E6
98 N2 =  INT (RR * N + .5)
100 N1 = N2 / RR
110  PRINT N;" ROUNDED TO ";R;" PLACES IS"
120  PRINT : PRINT N1
130  END
```

NUMBER ROUNDER

THIS PROGRAM WILL ROUND OFF ANY GIVEN
NUMBER TO ANY NUMBER OF PLACES.

ENTER NUMBER   34.3086516
ROUND TO HOW MANY PLACES   4

34.3086516 ROUNDED TO 4 PLACES IS
34.3087

1.13 DIMENSION SCALER

Anyone who has made a scaled-down drawing of an object realizes the headaches involved in converting the dimensions of the object to a scaled-down size that will fit on the paper at hand. This program eliminates tedious work.

After entering the largest dimension of the object and the largest dimension of the drawing, the program calculates the scale factor. It then requests the units of measurement used in the drawing and the units of the object. Next it asks how many dimensions are going to be converted so that it can set aside memory space for them. Finally, it asks for the dimensions themselves.

A handy feature is the test on line 215 that checks the dimensions entered to make sure none of them are larger than the previously designated largest dimension. If a value is larger, an error message is generated and the user is asked to enter the dimension again.

```
0    CALL  - 936
1    PRINT : PRINT : PRINT : PRINT "WRITTEN BY JULES H. GILDER"
2    PRINT : PRINT "COPYRIGHT (C)  HAYDEN BOOK CO. 1978"
3    FOR X = 1 TO 4000: NEXT X
10   PRINT : PRINT : PRINT : PRINT
15   PRINT  TAB( 12)"DIMENSION SCALER"
17   PRINT : PRINT : PRINT
20   PRINT "THIS PROGRAM DETERMINES THE DIMENSIONS"
30   PRINT "REQUIRED TO DRAW TO SCALE GIVEN THE"
40   PRINT "LARGEST DIMENSION OF THE OBJECT AND THE"
50   PRINT "LARGEST DIMENSION THAT IS POSSIBLE ON"
60   PRINT "THE DRAWING. "
70   PRINT : PRINT
80   PRINT "WHAT IS THE LARGEST DIMENSION OF THE"
90   INPUT "OBJECT  ";P
100  PRINT
110  PRINT "WHAT IS THE LARGEST DIMENSION OF THE"
120  INPUT "DRAWING  ";Q
122  PRINT : PRINT : INPUT "WHAT ARE YOUR DRAWING UNITS (E.G INCH
     ES) ";Y$
125  PRINT : PRINT : INPUT "WHAT ARE YOUR OBJECT UNITS  ";Z$
130  PRINT : PRINT "HOW MANY DIMENSIONS DO YOU WANT"
140  INPUT "TO CONVERT  ";N
150  PRINT : PRINT : PRINT
160  DIM  D( N)
170  PRINT "ENTER ALL DIMENSIONS IN DECIMAL FORM"
180  PRINT : PRINT
190  FOR  X = 1  TO  N
200  PRINT "ENTER DIMENSION ";X;" ";
210  INPUT  D( X)
215  IF D(X) > P THEN  PRINT "DIMENSION TOO LARGE": GOTO 200
220  NEXT  X
230  PRINT : PRINT : PRINT
240  S = Q / P
250  PRINT "SCALE FACTOR = ";S
260  PRINT : PRINT : PRINT
270  FOR  X = 1  TO  N
280  PRINT D( X);" ";;Z$;" SCALES TO  "; INT (100 * S * D(X) + .5)
     / 100;" ";Y$
290  NEXT  X
300  END
```

```
DIMENSION SCALER


THIS PROGRAM DETERMINES THE DIMENSIONS
REQUIRED TO DRAW TO SCALE GIVEN THE
LARGEST DIMENSION OF THE OBJECT AND THE
LARGEST DIMENSION THAT IS POSSIBLE ON
THE DRAWING.

WHAT IS THE LARGEST DIMENSION OF THE
OBJECT   35

WHAT IS THE LARGEST DIMENSION OF THE
DRAWING   11

WHAT ARE YOUR DRAWING UNITS (E.G INCHES)
   INCHES

WHAT ARE YOUR OBJECT UNITS   FEET

HOW MANY DIMENSIONS DO YOU WANT
TO CONVERT   4


ENTER ALL DIMENSIONS IN DECIMAL FORM

ENTER DIMENSION 1 ?35
ENTER DIMENSION 2 ?12
ENTER DIMENSION 3 ?4036
DIMENSION TOO LARGE
ENTER DIMENSION 3 ?6
ENTER DIMENSION 4 ?23.75


SCALE FACTOR = .314285714


35 FEET SCALES TO   11 INCHES
12 FEET SCALES TO   3.77 INCHES
6 FEET SCALES TO   1.89 INCHES
23.75 FEET SCALES TO   7.46 INCHES
```

1.14 HISTOGRAM

This program will plot any function as a histogram. Instead of plotting a point as a single spot, the histogram approach plots everything up to and including the data point as a bar so that it stands out more clearly. The bar in this program is constructed of asterisks. Any other symbol can be used by simply changing line 160.

This program can be confusing if you don't examine it before use. At first glance, line 99 seems unnecessary because line 100 immediately changes the zero value assigned to J in line 99 to 1. This line, however, is essential to the proper operation of the program. The variable J is acting as a switch. If this is the first time the program is run, the final value of J is 1, and the computer prints out the operating instructions and then stops. If J is not set equal to 1 in line 100, the operating instructions will never be printed out.

When the user follows the instructions given by the computer, line 100 is replaced by a function definition. The next time the program is run, the final value of J is zero. With J equal to 0, the computer prints out the histogram, after which it skips the section containing the instructions and then stops.

The histogram is plotted with the Y-axis horizontal and the X-axis vertical. The resolution of the plot can be greatly improved by decreasing the value of delta X.

```
0   CALL  - 936
1   PRINT : PRINT : PRINT : PRINT "WRITTEN BY JULES H. GILDER"
2   PRINT : PRINT "COPYRIGHT (C)  HAYDEN BOOK CO. 1978"
3   FOR X = 1 TO 4000: NEXT X
10    PRINT : PRINT : PRINT : PRINT
20    PRINT "              HISTOGRAM"
30    PRINT : PRINT : PRINT : PRINT
99  J = 0
100 J = 1
105   IF  J = 1  THEN  200
108   INPUT "ENTER YMIN,YMAX  ";Y2,Y1
110   INPUT "ENTER XMIN, XMAX, DELTA X ";X2,X1,X3
115   PRINT : PRINT : PRINT
120   FOR  X = X2  TO  X1  STEP  X3
130 Y =  FN A(X)
140 YP =  INT (39 * (Y - Y2) / (Y1 - Y2) +  .5)
150   FOR  Z = 1  TO  YP
160   PRINT "*";
170   NEXT  Z
180   PRINT
190   NEXT  X
195   GOTO 260
200   PRINT "THIS PROGRAM PLOTS A HISTOGRAM. YOU "
210   PRINT "ENTER THE FUNCTION TO BE PLOTTED BY"
220   PRINT "TYPING:"
230   PRINT "        100 DEF FNA(X)=F(X)  EG SIN(X)"
240   PRINT "             RUN"
250   PRINT : PRINT : PRINT
260   END
```

HISTOGRAM

THIS PROGRAM PLOTS A HISTOGRAM. YOU
ENTER THE FUNCTION TO BE PLOTTED BY
TYPING:
```
        100 DEF FNA(X)=F(X)   EG SIN(X)
        RUN
```

```
]100 DEF FNA(X)=SIN(X)

]RUN
```


HISTOGRAM

ENTER YMIN,YMAX -1,1
ENTER XMIN, XMAX, DELTA X 0,4,.2

```
********************
*************************
****************************
*********************************
************************************
*****************************************
*******************************************
**********************************************
**********************************************
*********************************************
*******************************************
**********************************
**********************************
*****************************
************************
****************
*************
********
```

1.15 CIRCLE FINDER

One of the laws of geometry states that if three points are located in a plane and they do not form a straight line, it is possible to draw a circle that will pass through each of the three points. The equations for calculating the radius of that circle and the location of the X and Y coordinates of the center (below) are complex and difficult to handle:

$$Y = \frac{\dfrac{(X3\uparrow2 - X1\uparrow2) + (Y3\uparrow2 - Y1\uparrow2)}{2(X3 - X1)} - \dfrac{(X2\uparrow2 - X1\uparrow2) + (Y2\uparrow2 - Y1\uparrow2)}{2(X2 - X1)}}{\dfrac{Y3 - Y1}{X3 - X1} - \dfrac{Y2 - Y1}{X2 - X1}}$$

$$X = \frac{(X3\uparrow2 - X1\uparrow2) + (Y3 - Y1)((Y3 + Y1) - 2Y)}{2(X3 - X1)}$$

$$R = ((X3 - X)\uparrow2 + (Y3 - Y)\uparrow2)\uparrow\cdot5$$

This program takes these equations and uses them to calculate the required information. To make it easier to check, the equations have been broken down into two parts located in lines 130 to 190.

```
0    CALL  - 936
1    PRINT : PRINT : PRINT : PRINT "WRITTEN BY JULES H. GILDER"
2    PRINT : PRINT "COPYRIGHT (C)  HAYDEN BOOK CO. 1978"
3    FOR X = 1 TO 4000: NEXT X
10   PRINT : PRINT : PRINT : PRINT
20   PRINT "          CIRCLE FINDER"
30   PRINT : PRINT : PRINT : PRINT
40   PRINT "THIS PROGRAM WILL THE CENTER AND THE"
50   PRINT "RADIUS OF A CIRCLE THAT IS DETERMINED"
60   PRINT "BY ANY THREE POINTS IN A PLANE THAT DO"
70   PRINT "NOT FORM A STRAIGHT LINE."
80   PRINT : PRINT : PRINT
90   INPUT "ENTER FIRST POINT (X,Y)  ";X1,Y1
100  INPUT "ENTER SECOND POINT (XY)  ";X2,Y2
110  INPUT "ENTER THIRD POINT (X,Y)  ";X3,Y3
120  PRINT : PRINT : PRINT
130  L = ((X2 - X1) * (X2 + X1) + (Y2 - Y1) * (Y2 + Y1)) / (2 * (X
     2 - X1))
140  M = ((X3 - X1) * (X3 + X1) + (Y3 - Y1) * (Y3 + Y1)) / (2 * (X
     3 - X1))
150  N = (Y2 - Y1) / (X2 - X1)
160  P = (Y3 - Y1) / (X3 - X1)
170  Y = (M - L) / (P - N)
180  X = M - P * Y
190  R =  SQR ((X3 - X) ↑ 2 + (Y3 - Y) ↑ 2)
195  R =  INT (100 * R + .5) / 100
200  PRINT "THE CIRCLE DEFINED BY THE FOLLOWING"
210  PRINT "THREE POINTS:"
220  PRINT
```

```
230    PRINT "  X1 = ";X1;"    Y1 = ";Y1
240    PRINT "  X2 = ";X2;"    Y2 = ";Y2
250    PRINT "  X3 = ";X3;"    Y3 = ";Y3
260    PRINT : PRINT : PRINT
270    PRINT "HAS A RADIUS = ";R
280    PRINT : PRINT "AT A CENTER LOCATED AT:"
290    PRINT : PRINT "X = ";X;"    Y = ";Y
300    END



              CIRCLE FINDER


THIS PROGRAM WILL THE CENTER AND THE
RADIUS OF A CIRCLE THAT IS DETERMINED
BY ANY THREE POINTS IN A PLANE THAT DO
NOT FORM A STRAIGHT LINE.


ENTER FIRST POINT (X,Y)   3,0
ENTER SECOND POINT (XY)   0,3
ENTER THIRD POINT (X,Y)   6,3


THE CIRCLE DEFINED BY THE FOLLOWING
THREE POINTS:

  X1 = 3    Y1 = 0
  X2 = 0    Y2 = 3
  X3 = 6    Y3 = 3


HAS A RADIUS = 3

AT A CENTER LOCATED AT:

X = 3    Y = 3
```

1.16   NORMALLY DISTRIBUTED RANDOM NUMBERS [1]

Most BASIC interpreters have an RND function that generates a random number. The properties of these random numbers are not always clear, and some are, in fact, not even closely random. Very often, especially in statistical studies, it is necessary to have a series of random numbers that are normally distributed or, in other words, Gaussian distributed.

Among the properties of normally distributed numbers is that 68.27 percent of them will fall within one standard deviation, 95.45 percent within two standard deviations, and 99.73 percent within three standard deviations. If normally distributed numbers are plotted on an axis (Y-coordinate) versus standard deviation (X-coordinate), a bell-shaped curve will be formed.

This program uses the RND function available in BASIC and performs calculations on the resulting number produced by it so that the new numbers resulting will be normally distributed. The exact characteristics of the distribution (e.g., its standard deviation and average) are entered by the user along with a constant K. The value of K can vary from 1 to any higher number. The higher its value, the more accurate the results will be and the longer it will take to calculate the desired number. The quantity of random numbers to be generated is requested by the program in line 115.

```
0   CALL  - 936
1   PRINT : PRINT : PRINT : PRINT "WRITTEN BY JULES H. GILDER"
2   PRINT : PRINT "COPYRIGHT (C)  HAYDEN BOOK CO. 1978"
3   FOR X = 1 TO 4000: NEXT X
10    PRINT : PRINT : PRINT : PRINT
20    PRINT "  NORMALLY DISTRIBUTED RANDOM NUMBERS"
30    PRINT : PRINT : PRINT : PRINT
40    PRINT "THIS PROGRAM GENERATES NORMALLY DISTRI-"
50    PRINT "BUTED RANDOM NUMBERS.  YOU MUST ENTER"
60    PRINT "THE DESIRED STANDARD DEVIATION, MEAN"
70    PRINT "AND K (LARGE FOR ACCURACY, SMALL FOR"
75    PRINT "SPEED)"
80    PRINT : PRINT : PRINT
90    INPUT "ENTER STANDARD DEVIATION ";S
100   INPUT "ENTER K ";K
110   INPUT "ENTER THE MEAN ";M
115   INPUT "HOW MANY NUMBERS DO YOU WANT? ";NN
120   PRINT : PRINT : PRINT
130   FOR I = 1 TO NN
140 T = 0
150   FOR  J = 1  TO  K
160 R =  RND ( 1)
170 T = T + R
180   NEXT  J
190 N = S *  SQR (12 / K) * (T - K / 2) + M
200   PRINT  N
210   NEXT  I
220   END
```

---

[1] Adapted from M. Perlman, "Generate Normally Distributed Random Numbers with BASIC," *Electronic Design* 24 (Nov. 22, 1970): p. 62.

```
NORMALLY DISTRIBUTED RANDOM NUMBERS


THIS PROGRAM GENERATES NORMALLY DISTRI-
BUTED RANDOM NUMBERS.  YOU MUST ENTER
THE DESIRED STANDARD DEVIATION, MEAN
AND K (LARGE FOR ACCURACY, SMALL FOR
SPEED)


ENTER STANDARD DEVIATION 21
ENTER K 10
ENTER THE MEAN 85
HOW MANY NUMBERS DO YOU WANT? 10

65.2562827
80.9362216
78.2831784
80.7409763
113.860552
64.6222784
85.3722137
76.4160722
83.8775965
87.2776285
```

1.17 Nth ROOT OF A NUMBER

Some tiny BASICS that do not have the ability to calculate the Nth root of a number can easily be implemented to do so with the program below. The program calculates successively finer approximations of the root until a desired level of accuracy is reached. The accuracy is set in line 160. By changing the value of 1E - 8 to another number, the accuracy can be varied (within the limits of your computer, of course).

This program also contains a number rounding routine, which decreases accuracy. It is located at line 175. To get the full accuracy of the program, specify the number of decimal places as a number larger than your computer can handle (10 should be sufficient for most home computers).

```
0   CALL  - 936
1   PRINT : PRINT : PRINT : PRINT "WRITTEN BY JULES H. GILDER"
2   PRINT : PRINT "COPYRIGHT (C)  HAYDEN BOOK CO. 1978"
3   FOR X = 1 TO 4000: NEXT X
10  PRINT : PRINT : PRINT : PRINT
15  PRINT  TAB( 10 )"NTH ROOT OF A NUMBER"
17  PRINT : PRINT : PRINT
20  PRINT "THIS PROGRAM WILL FIND THE NTH ROOT OF"
30  PRINT "ANY NUMBER.  YOU MUST ENTER THE NUMBER"
40  PRINT "AND THE ROOT DESIRED."
50  PRINT : PRINT
60  INPUT "WHAT IS THE NUMBER  ";X
70  PRINT : INPUT "WHAT ROOT DO YOU WANT  ";R
75  PRINT : INPUT "TO HOW MANY DECIMAL PLACES  ";S
80  PRINT : PRINT
90  IF  R <  0  THEN  PRINT "THE ROOT MUST BE ZERO OR LARGER." :
        GOTO 190
100  IF  R = 0  THEN  P = 1: GOTO  180
110 P = X / R
120  FOR  Y = 1  TO  100
130 Z = P
140 RR = R - 1
150 P = (X / P ↑ RR + RR * P) / R
160  IF  ABS (Z - P) / ( ABS (A) +  ABS (P)) < 1E - 8  THEN  175

170  NEXT  Y
175 P =  INT (P * 10 ↑ S + .5) /  INT (10 ↑ S + .5)
180  PRINT : PRINT : PRINT "THE ";R;" ROOT OF ";X;" IS ";P
190  END


        NTH ROOT OF A NUMBER


THIS PROGRAM WILL FIND THE NTH ROOT OF
ANY NUMBER.  YOU MUST ENTER THE NUMBER
AND THE ROOT DESIRED.

WHAT IS THE NUMBER  65536

WHAT ROOT DO YOU WANT  8

TO HOW MANY DECIMAL PLACES  3


THE 8 ROOT OF 65536 IS 4
```

1.18   RATIONAL FRACTIONS[1]

Designers often find a need to express a number as a rational fraction, especially in frequency synthesizer and gear train design applications. This program takes any number (rational or irrational) and produces successively finer rational fraction approximations of it.

The output consists of the rough approximation, which is the integer part of the number, followed by finer and finer approximations. Since, for an irrational number, these approximations can go on until the accuracy of the computer is reached, the program asks for a limit to the number of iterations desired.

The input of a rational number results in a finite number of iterations followed by the word "EXACT," assuming that the exact fraction is reached in the number of iterations indicated.

```
0    CALL  - 936
1    PRINT : PRINT : PRINT : PRINT "WRITTEN BY JULES H. GILDER"
2    PRINT : PRINT "COPYRIGHT (C) HAYDEN BOOK CO. 1978 "
3    FOR X = 1 TO 4000: NEXT X
4    REM    ADAPTED FROM "BASIC PROGRAM EXPRESSES ANY NUMBER AS A RA
         TIONAL FRACTION",ELECTRONIC DESIGN 25,12/7/72, P.102
5    PRINT : PRINT : PRINT : PRINT
10   PRINT  TAB( 11)"RATIONAL FRACTIONS"
20   PRINT : PRINT : PRINT : PRINT
30   PRINT "THIS PROGRAM WILL ACCEPT ANY NUMBER AS"
40   PRINT "AN INPUT AND PRODUCE SUCCESSIVELY FINER"
50   PRINT "RATIONAL FRACTION APPROXIMATIONS OF IT."
60   PRINT "IF A RATIONAL NUMBER IS ENTERED, THE"
70   PRINT "PROGRAM WILL INDICATE THAT THE FINAL"
80   PRINT "ANSWER IS EXACT."
90   PRINT : PRINT : PRINT
100   INPUT "ENTER THE NUMBER: ";S
104   PRINT : INPUT "HOW MANY ITERATIONS? ";Q
105  NN = S
110  A1 = 0:B2 = 0
120  A2 = 1:B1 = 1
125   PRINT : PRINT : PRINT
126   FOR Z = 1 TO Q
130  N =   INT (S)
140  T = A2
150  A2 = N * A2 + A1
160  A1 = T
170  T = B2
180  B2 = N * B2 + B1
190  B1 = T
195   PRINT
200   PRINT A2;"/";B2;
210   IF S = N OR NN = A2 / B2 THEN 240
215   PRINT
220   PRINT :S = 1 / (S - N)
230   NEXT Z
235   GOTO 250
240   PRINT "    EXACT"
250   END
```

----

[1]Adapted from "BASIC Program Expresses Any Number As a Rational Fraction," *Electronic Design* 25 (Dec. 7, 1972): p. 102.

THIS PROGRAM WILL ACCEPT ANY NUMBER AS
AN INPUT AND PRODUCE SUCCESSIVELY FINER
RATIONAL FRACTION APPROXIMATIONS OF IT.
IF A RATIONAL NUMBER IS ENTERED, THE
PROGRAM WILL INDICATE THAT THE FINAL
ANSWER IS EXACT.

ENTER THE NUMBER: 6.12318
HOW MANY ITERATIONS? 15

6/1

49/8

398/65

845/138

4623/755

5468/893

21027/3434

47522/7761

306159/50000   EXACT

2 Engineering Mathematics

One of the major uses of computers today is in science and engineering. This chapter contains six programs that solve frequently encountered problems in the field of engineering. The first solves a set of simultaneous equations by using a process known as Gaussian elimination. Equations of this type crop up in every field from finance to physics.

The next program (2.2) evaluates polynomials by using an efficient algorithm that minimizes the number of computations to be performed. Quadratic equations are solved in 2.3, a general program that solves for real roots, repeating roots, and complex roots. The next program, Newton-Raphson roots, can be used to find one root of an equation. By combining this program with the previous one and factoring out the root it finds, third order equations can be solved. Try it.

The next two programs (2.5 and 2.6) perform functions that are a little more difficult. In order to write a program to do integration or differentiation, the theory underlying these operations must be understood. A quick look at the necessary details is provided in the text accompanying each of these programs.

2.1 SIMULTANEOUS EQUATIONS

One of the most common problems in science and engineering is finding the solution to a system of linear simultaneous equations. Many methods have been developed to solve such systems. One of the oldest and still most commonly used is known as Gaussian elimination. It replaces certain equations of the system by combinations of other equations. The system is then solved by back substitution.

The number of equations to be solved is designated by N, but statement 9 limits N to a maximum of 2Ø equations, more than enough for most applications. Lines 15 to 88 enter data from the keyboard, one equation at a time. The variable Z on line 9Ø is used as a flag to indicate whether or not a unique solution to the system can be found. When a unique solution cannot be found, Z will be given the value 1, and the program will indicate that no solution of the system has been found. This occurs, for example, when N = 1 and A(1,1) = Ø.

Lines 1ØØ to 15Ø take care of the case when N = 1. The remainder of the program solves for all other values of N. Back substitution to get the actual answer takes place in lines 49Ø to 58Ø. The results are printed in lines 64Ø to 69Ø.

The sample run solves the following system of equations:

$$3\ X1 + \ \ 7\ X2 + 32\ X3 = 12$$
$$9\ X1 + 43\ X2 + 21\ X3 = 31$$
$$2\ X1 + \ \ 8\ X2 + 19\ X3 = 32$$

It also shows a run for a system of equations that cannot be uniquely solved:

$$2\ X1 + 4\ X2 = \ \ 6$$
$$4\ X1 + 8\ X2 = 12$$

```
0    CALL  - 936
1    PRINT : PRINT : PRINT : PRINT "WRITTEN BY JULES H. GILDER"
2    PRINT : PRINT "COPYRIGHT (C) HAYDEN BOOK CO. 1978"
3    FOR X = 1 TO 4000: NEXT X
5    PRINT : PRINT : PRINT : PRINT
6    PRINT  TAB( 5)"SIMULTANEOUS EQUATION SOLVER"
7    PRINT : PRINT : PRINT : PRINT
9    DIM  A(20,20),B(20),X(20)
10   PRINT "THIS PROGRAM SOLVES A SET OF SIMULTA-"
11   PRINT "NEOUS EQUATIONS. YOU MUST ENTER THE"
12   PRINT "NUMBER OF EQUATIONS INVOLVED (N) AND"
13   PRINT "THE VALUE OF THE COEFFICIENTS A,B."
14   PRINT
15   INPUT "ENTER THE NUMBER OF EQUATIONS: ";N
20   PRINT
30   PRINT "ENTER THE VALUES FOR 'A' AND 'B' ONE"
40   PRINT "EQUATION AT A TIME."
45   PRINT
50   FOR  I = 1  TO  N
60   FOR  J = 1  TO  N
70   PRINT "A(";I;",";J;") = ";
75   INPUT  A(I,J)
80   NEXT  J
85   PRINT "B(";I;") = ";
87   INPUT  B(I)
88   NEXT  I
```

```
90 Z = 0
100   IF  N < > 0 THEN  160
110   IF  A(1,1) = 0   THEN  140
120  X(1) = B(1) / A(1)
130  GOTO  600
140 Z = 1
150  GOTO  600
160 M = N - 1
170  FOR  I = 1  TO  M
180 B =  ABS (A(I,I))
190 L = I
200 I1 = I + 1
210  FOR  J = I1  TO  N
220   IF   ABS (A(J,I)) < B   THEN  250
230 B =  ABS (A(J,I))
240 L = J
250  NEXT  J
260  IF  B < > 0 THEN  290
270 Z = 1
280  GOTO  600
290  IF  L = I   THEN  380
300  FOR  J = 1  TO  N
310 G = A(L,J)
320 A(L,J) = A(I,J)
330 A(I,J) = G
340  NEXT  J
350 G = B(L)
360 B(L) = B(I)
370 B(I) = G
380  FOR  J = I1  TO  N
390 T = A(J,I) / A(I,I)
400  FOR  K = I1  TO  N
410 A(J,K) = A(J,K) - T * A(I,K)
420  NEXT  K
430 B(J) = B(J) - T * B(I)
440  NEXT  J
450  NEXT  I
460  IF  A(N,N) < > 0 THEN  490
470 Z = 1
480  GOTO  600
490 X(N) = B(N) / A(N,N)
500 I = N - 1
510 S = 0
520 I1 = I + 1
530  FOR  J = I1  TO  N
540 S = S + A(I,J) * X(J)
550  NEXT  J
560 X(I) = (B(I) - S) / A(I,I)
570 I = I - 1
580  IF  I > 0   THEN  510
600  PRINT
610  PRINT
620   IF  Z < > 1 THEN  640
630  PRINT "NO SOLUTION TO THE SYSTEM HAS BEEN FOUND"
635  GOTO  700
640  PRINT "THE SOLUTION TO THE SYSTEM OF EQUATIONS"
650  PRINT "IS AS FOLLOWS:"
660  PRINT
670  FOR  I = 1  TO  N
680  PRINT "X(";I;") = ";X(I)
690  NEXT  I
695  PRINT
700  PRINT "DO YOU HAVE MORE DATA";
710  INPUT  Z$
720  PRINT
730  PRINT
740  IF   LEFT$ (Z$,1) = "Y"   THEN  15
750  END
```

SIMULTANEOUS EQUATION SOLVER

THIS PROGRAM SOLVES A SET OF SIMULTA-
NEOUS EQUATIONS. YOU MUST ENTER THE
NUMBER OF EQUATIONS INVOLVED (N) AND
THE VALUE OF THE COEFFICIENTS A,B.

ENTER THE NUMBER OF EQUATIONS: 3

ENTER THE VALUES FOR 'A' AND 'B' ONE
EQUATION AT A TIME.

A(1,1) = ?3
A(1,2) = ?7
A(1,3) = ?32
B(1) = ?12
A(2,1) = ?9
A(2,2) = ?43
A(2,3) = ?21
B(2) = ?31
A(3,1) = ?2
A(3,2) = ?8
A(3,3) = ?19
B(3) = ?32

THE SOLUTION TO THE SYSTEM OF EQUATIONS
IS AS FOLLOWS:

X(1) = -46.5218121
X(2) = 9.11912753
X(3) = 2.74161074

DO YOU HAVE MORE DATA?NO

SIMULTANEOUS EQUATION SOLVER

THIS PROGRAM SOLVES A SET OF SIMULTA-
NEOUS EQUATIONS. YOU MUST ENTER THE
NUMBER OF EQUATIONS INVOLVED (N) AND
THE VALUE OF THE COEFFICIENTS A,B.

ENTER THE NUMBER OF EQUATIONS: 2

ENTER THE VALUES FOR 'A' AND 'B' ONE
EQUATION AT A TIME.

A(1,1) = ?2
A(1,2) = ?4
B(1) = ?6
A(2,1) = ?4
A(2,2) = ?8
B(2) = ?12

NO SOLUTION TO THE SYSTEM HAS BEEN FOUND
DO YOU HAVE MORE DATA?NO

2.2 POLYNOMIAL EVALUATOR

Polynomials pop up in every field from engineering to finance. This program will compute the value of any polynomial. All you have to do is enter the coefficients of each term and the point at which the polynomial is to be evaluated.

The order of the polynomial, which is the first item asked for by the program, is equal to the highest power appearing in the polynomial. The program overcomes the inefficiency of evaluating each power separately by generating each power from the previous smaller one with a single multiplication. This can be a big time-saver if many evaluations of high-power polynomials are done. Thus, a polynomial,

$$F(X) = A(1) \, X{\uparrow}N + A(2) \, X{\uparrow}(N - 1) + A(3) \, X{\uparrow}(N - 3) + \ldots + A(N + 1)$$

can be expressed in a factored form as

$$F(X) = ((\ldots (A(1) \, X + A(2)) \, X + A(3)) \, X \ldots + A(N + 1)$$

This form of the equation is extremely easy to program in a FOR...NEXT loop, as is done in lines 14Ø to 17Ø. These few lines constitute the heart of the program, with the remainder concerned with inputting and outputting the information in a useful format.

```
0    CALL  - 936
1    PRINT : PRINT : PRINT : PRINT "WRITTEN BY JULES H. GILDER"
2    PRINT : PRINT "COPYRIGHT (C) HAYDEN BOOK CO. 1978"
3    FOR X = 1 TO 4000: NEXT X
4    DIM A(20),B$(20)
5    PRINT : PRINT : PRINT : PRINT
6    PRINT  TAB( 10)"POLYNOMIAL EVALUATOR"
7    PRINT : PRINT : PRINT
10   PRINT "THIS PROGRAM EVALUATES POLYNOMIALS"
20   PRINT "TO USE, YOU MUST ENTER THE COEFFICIENTS"
30   PRINT "OF THE POLYNOMIAL, THE ORDER (HIGHEST"
40   PRINT "POWER) OF THE POLYNOMIAL AND A VALUE "
50   PRINT "FOR X TO BE EVALUATED."
55   PRINT
60   INPUT "ENTER THE ORDER OF THE POLYNOMIAL: ";N
64   IF N < 1 THEN  PRINT : PRINT "INPUT ERROR": GOTO 55
65 N = N + 1
70   PRINT
80   PRINT "ENTER THE COEFFICIENTS"
90   PRINT
100  FOR I = 1  TO  N
110  PRINT "A";I;"= ";
120  INPUT  A(I)
124 B$(I) = "-"
126  IF   ABS (A(I)) = A(I)  THEN  B$(I) = "+"
130  NEXT  I
133  PRINT
135  INPUT "WHAT IS THE VALUE OF X: ";X
140  G = A(1)
150  FOR  I = 2  TO  N
160  G = G * X + A(I)
```

```
170   NEXT  I
180   PRINT : PRINT : PRINT : PRINT
190   PRINT "THE POLYNOMIAL:"
200   PRINT
201   IF N = 1 THEN  PRINT X;" = ";X: GOTO 270
205   IF N = 2 THEN 234
210   FOR I = 1  TO  N - 2
220   PRINT  B$(I); ABS (A(I));"X↑";N - I;
230   NEXT  I
234   PRINT B$(N - 1); ABS (A(N - 1)); "X "; B$(N); ABS (A(N));""
      ;
240   PRINT " = ";G
250   PRINT
260   PRINT "FOR X = ";X
270   PRINT : PRINT : PRINT : PRINT
280   PRINT "DO YOU WANT TO TRY ANOTHER VALUE OF X";
290   INPUT Z$
295   PRINT
300   IF   LEFT$ (Z$,1) = "Y"  THEN  135
310   PRINT "DO YOU WANT TO TRY A NEW POLYNOMIAL";
320   INPUT Z$
330   IF   LEFT$ (Z$,1) = "Y"  THEN  55
340   END
```

```
                POLYNOMIAL EVALUATOR


     THIS PROGRAM EVALUATES POLYNOMIALS
     TO USE, YOU MUST ENTER THE COEFFICIENTS
     OF THE POLYNOMIAL, THE ORDER (HIGHEST
     POWER) OF THE POLYNOMIAL AND A VALUE
     FOR X TO BE EVALUATED.

     ENTER THE ORDER OF THE POLYNOMIAL: 4

     ENTER THE COEFFICIENTS

     A1= ?5
     A2= ?178
     A3= ?3
     A4= ?0
     A5= ?9

     WHAT IS THE VALUE OF X: 3



     THE POLYNOMIAL:

     +5X↑4+178X↑3+3X↑2+0X +9 = 5247

     FOR X = 3



     DO YOU WANT TO TRY ANOTHER VALUE OF X?YES
     WHAT IS THE VALUE OF X: 5



     THE POLYNOMIAL:

     +5X↑4+178X↑3+3X↑2+0X +9 = 25459

     FOR X = 5



     DO YOU WANT TO TRY ANOTHER VALUE OF X?NO
     DO YOU WANT TO TRY A NEW POLYNOMIAL?NO
```

2.3 QUADRATIC EQUATION SOLVER

One of the most familiar equations to engineers and scientists is the quadratic equation. This program solves quadratic equations for all three special cases: real roots, real repeating roots, and complex roots. It solves equations of the form

$$A X \uparrow 2 + B X + C = \emptyset$$

and simply requires that the coefficients of the equation A, B, and C be entered.

```
0   CALL  - 936
1   PRINT : PRINT : PRINT : PRINT "WRITTEN BY JULES H. GILDER"
2   PRINT : PRINT "COPYRIGHT (C) HAYDEN BOOK CO. 1978"
3   FOR X = 1 TO 4000: NEXT X
4   PRINT : PRINT : PRINT : PRINT
5   PRINT  TAB( 7)"QUADRATIC EQUATION SOLVER"
6   PRINT : PRINT : PRINT : PRINT
40   PRINT "THIS PROGRAM SOLVES QUADRATIC EQUATIONS"
50   PRINT "OF THE FORM:"
60   PRINT "            AX↑2+BX+C=0"
70   PRINT
80   PRINT "FOR REAL, COMPLEX AND REPEATING ROOTS."
90   PRINT
100   INPUT "ENTER COEFFICIENTS A,B,C: ";A,B,C
110   PRINT
115   PRINT : PRINT
120  Z = B ↑ 2 - (4 * A * C)
125  Z =  INT (100 * Z + .5) / 100
130   IF  Z < 0  THEN  200
140   IF  Z = 0  THEN  180
150  X1 = ( - B +  SQR (Z)) / (2 * A)
155  X1 =  INT (100 * X1 + .5) / 100
160  X2 = ( - B -  SQR (Z)) / (2 * A)
165  X2 =  INT (100 * X2 + .5) / 100
170   PRINT : PRINT "THE ROOTS TO THE EQUATION ARE REAL."
172   PRINT
174   PRINT "ROOT 1 = ";X1;"   ROOT 2 = ";X2
175   END
180  X1 =  - B / (2 * A)
185  X1 =  INT (100 * X1 + .5) / 100
190  X2 = X1
192   PRINT
193   PRINT "THE ROOTS TO THE EQUATION ARE REAL AND"
194   PRINT "REPEATING."
195   GOTO  172
200  R1 =  - B / (2 * A)
205  R1 =  INT (100 * R1 + .5) / 100
210  R2 = R1
220  I1 =  SQR ( ABS (Z)) / (2 * A)
225  I1 =  INT (100 * I1 + .5) / 100
230  I2 =  - I1
240   PRINT
250   PRINT "THE ROOTS TO THE EQUATION ARE COMPLEX"
260   PRINT
270   PRINT "ROOT 1 = ";R1;" + J "; ABS (I1)
280   PRINT "ROOT 2 = ";R2;" - J "; ABS (I2)
290   END
```

THIS PROGRAM SOLVES QUADRATIC EQUATIONS
OF THE FORM:
                AX↑2+BX+C=0
FOR REAL, COMPLEX AND REPEATING ROOTS.
ENTER COEFFICIENTS A,B,C: 7,23,-6

THE ROOTS TO THE EQUATION ARE REAL
ROOT 1 = .24 ROOT 2 = -3.53

2.4 NEWTON-RAPHSON ROOTS

In the solution of equations, knowing one of the equation's roots often makes it much easier to find the others. An approximation technique, known as the Newton-Raphson Method, can be used to find the first positive real root of an equation. The approximation is calculated according to the following formula:

$$X(N + 1) = X(N) - F(X(N))/F'(X(N))$$

where $F(X)$ is the function, $F'(X)$ is its derivative, and N is the iteration.

By repeating this calculation, it is possible to get successively finer estimates of the root of the equation. The accuracy of the process is determined by the value of 1E − 6 in line 17Ø, which should be small enough for any requirements.

The iteration formula itself is evaluated in lines 15Ø to 2ØØ. The FOR . . . NEXT loop here has been introduced to limit the number of iterations to 3Ø. It should be understood that this will affect accuracy in cases where the 1E − 6 value is not reached in 3Ø iterations. The only reason it was included was to speed things up, at the expense of accuracy, of course. If the full accuracy is desired, line 15Ø can be eliminated and line 2ØØ replaced with a GO TO 16Ø statement. This will permit calculation to continue until the condition in line 17Ø is met.

It is important to note that when the computer's instructions are followed and the function is defined in line 1ØØ, the automatic switch that causes the operating instructions to be printed is eliminated. To get it back, line 1ØØ should have a GO TO 2Ø statement in it.

```
0    CALL  - 936
1    PRINT : PRINT : PRINT : PRINT : PRINT "WRITTEN BY JULES H. GIL
     DER"
2    PRINT : PRINT "COPYRIGHT (C) HAYDEN BOOK CO. 1978"
3    FOR X = 1 TO 4000: NEXT X
4    PRINT : PRINT : PRINT : PRINT
6    PRINT  TAB( 10 )"NEWTON RAPHSON ROOTS"
7    PRINT : PRINT : PRINT : PRINT
10   GOTO 100
20   PRINT "THIS PROGRAM FINDS THE FIRST POSITIVE"
30   PRINT "REAL ROOT OF AN EQUATION WHICH YOU MUST"
40   PRINT "DEFINE IN LINE 100. THE DERIVATIVE"
50   PRINT "MUST BE DEFINED IN LINE 110. E.G.:"
60   PRINT : PRINT "    100 DEF FNF(X)=X↑2-25"
78   PRINT "    110 DEF FND(X)=2*X"
80   PRINT "    RUN"
85   PRINT
90   PRINT "THIS MUST BE DONE BEFORE RUNNING THE"
95   PRINT "PROGRAM": PRINT
96   GOTO 215
100   GOTO 20
140  X = .5
150   FOR  N = 1  TO  30
160  XN = X - ( FN F(X) /  FN D(X))
170   IF   ABS (X - XN) < 1E - 6  THEN   210
190  X = XN
200   NEXT  N
210   PRINT : PRINT : PRINT "THE ROOT IS ";X
215   END
```

THIS PROGRAM FINDS THE FIRST POSITIVE
REAL ROOT OF AN EQUATION WHICH YOU MUST
DEFINE IN LINE 100. THE DERIVATIVE
MUST BE DEFINED IN LINE 110. E.G.:

```
    100 DEF FNF(X)=X↑2-25
    110 DEF FND(X)=2*X
    RUN
```

THIS MUST BE DONE BEFORE RUNNING THE
PROGRAM

]100 DEF FNF(X)=X↑2-25

]110 DEF FND(X)=2*X

]RUN

        NEWTON RAPHSON ROOTS

THE ROOT IS 5

2.5 DERIVATIVE OF A FUNCTION

The derivative (or tangent) of a curve at a particular point can be approximated by moving a small distance along the curve to another point and comparing the change in the Y-coordinate to the change in the X-coordinate. This method of determining the derivative is known as the First Forward Difference Method, and it is very easy to implement on a computer.

This program contains a switching statement in line 100. The statement is eliminated when the computer's operating instructions are followed, so that once the function is entered into the program, the instructions do not get printed out. Instead, the program branches to the instructions that evaluate the function's derivative. To get the instructions back, put a GO TO 20 statement on line 100.

In calculating the derivative, the program first evaluates the function at a given value of X (line 130). It is then evaluated again (line 140) for X equal to the original value of X plus a small difference, or delta X. The value used for delta X is determined in line 120.

Finally, the value of the function at X is subtracted from the value of the function at X plus delta X, and that difference is divided by delta X, producing the derivative (line 150). The answer is then rounded off to two places in line 156.

```
0    CALL   - 936
1    PRINT : PRINT : PRINT : PRINT "WRITTEN BY JULES H. GILDER"
2    PRINT : PRINT "COPYRIGHT (C) HAYDEN BOOK CO. 1978"
3    FOR X = 1 TO 4000: NEXT X
10   PRINT : PRINT : PRINT : PRINT
15   PRINT  TAB( 8)"DERIVATIVE OF A FUNCTION"
16   PRINT : PRINT : PRINT : PRINT
17   GOTO 100
20   PRINT "THIS PROGRAM CALCULATES THE DERIVATIVE"
30   PRINT "OF A FUNCTION BY USING THE 'FIRST"
40   PRINT "FORWARD DIFFERENCE METHOD'. YOU MUST"
50   PRINT "DEFINE THE FUNCTION IN LINE 100 E.G.:"
55   PRINT
60   PRINT : PRINT "     100 DEF FNF(X)=X↑2+3*X-2"
65   PRINT "      RUN"
66   PRINT
70   PRINT : PRINT "AND ENTER THE POINT AT WHICH YOU WANT"
85   PRINT "WANT THE DERIVATIVE EVALUATED."
90   PRINT : PRINT
95   GOTO 200
100   GOTO 20
110   PRINT : INPUT "ENTER X TO BE EVALUATED: ";X
120  DX = .0001
130  Y1 =   FN F(X)
140  Y2 =   FN F(X + DX)
150  DY = (Y2 - Y1) / DX
155   PRINT : PRINT : PRINT : PRINT
156  DY =   INT (DY * 100 + .5) / 100
160   PRINT "DERIVATIVE AT X = ";X;" IS ";DY
170   PRINT : PRINT :
180   INPUT "EVALUATE IT AT ANOTHER POINT? ";A$
185   PRINT : PRINT
190   IF  LEFT$ (A$,1) = "Y" THEN 110
200   END
```

DERIVATIVE OF A FUNCTION

THIS PROGRAM CALCULATES THE DERIVATIVE
OF A FUNCTION BY USING THE 'FIRST
FORWARD DIFFERENCE METHOD'. YOU MUST
DEFINE THE FUNCTION IN LINE 100 E.G.:

```
    100 DEF FNF(X)=X↑2+3*X-2
    RUN
```

AND ENTER THE POINT AT WHICH YOU
WANT THE DERIVATIVE EVALUATED.

```
]100 DEF FNF(X)=X↑2+3*X-2

]RUN
```


        DERIVATIVE OF A FUNCTION

ENTER X TO BE EVALUATED: 5

DERIVATIVE AT X = 5 IS 13

EVALUATE IT AT ANOTHER POINT? NO

2.6 INTEGRATION BY SIMPSON'S RULE

The integral of a function or data is really the area underneath a curve formed by it. This program will calculate that area, or integral, by an approximation technique known as Simpson's Rule, which states:

$$\text{Area} = \Delta X(Y1 + 4\ Y2 + 2\ Y3 + 4\ Y4 + \ldots + 4\ Y24 + Y25)/3$$

The program is actually two programs in one; data integration and function integration are treated differently. Line 220 asks which type of integration is to be performed. If data integration is performed, the number of data points must be entered as well as the value for each point. The data points should be taken at equal intervals, and the program will ask for the interval width. The integral is then evaluated in lines 370 to 475.

If the function option is chosen, the program instructs the user to enter the function in line 200 and then stops the program. Entering the function at line 200 eliminates the switching statement SW = 1, which is used later to suppress the printing of the instructions. The program asks for the limits of integration of the function and then automatically divides the integration range into intervals. The function is then evaluated.

```
0    CALL  - 936
1    PRINT : PRINT : PRINT : PRINT "WRITTEN BY JULES H. GILDER"
2    PRINT : PRINT "COPYRIGHT (C) HAYDEN BOOK CO. 1978"
3    FOR X = 1 TO 4000: NEXT X
5    PRINT : PRINT : PRINT : PRINT
10   PRINT  TAB( 10 )"SIMPSON INTEGRATION"
20   PRINT : PRINT : PRINT : PRINT
22 SW = 0
25   GOTO 200
30   PRINT "THIS PROGRAM PERFORMS  INTEGRATION"
40   PRINT "ACCORDING TO SIMPSON'S RULE. YOU MAY"
50   PRINT "INTEGRATE EITHER A FUNCTION OR DATA. "
52   PRINT : PRINT
55   PRINT : PRINT "HIT ANY KEY TO CONTINUE";: GET AZ$: CALL  - 93
       6
57   PRINT : PRINT : PRINT
60   PRINT "   IF YOU ARE ENTERING DATA YOU MUST "
70   PRINT "ENTER THE NUMBER OF SPACES INTO WHICH"
80   PRINT "THE INTEGRATION INTERVAL HAS BEEN "
90   PRINT "DIVIDED. THIS MUST BE AN EVEN NUMBER.
100  PRINT "YOU MUST ALSO ENTER THE WIDTH OF EACH"
110  PRINT "SPACE. "
120  PRINT
130  PRINT "   IF YOU ARE INTEGRATING A FUNCTION,"
140  PRINT "THEN YOU MUST DEFINE IT AT LINE 200"
150  PRINT "AND THEN RUN THE PROGRAM. FOR EXAMPLE:"
160  PRINT : PRINT "    200 DEF FNF( X )=X↑2-25"
170  PRINT "     RUN"
180  GOTO 210
200 SW = 1
205  IF SW = 1 GOTO 30
210  PRINT : PRINT : PRINT
215  IF SW = 0 GOTO 235
220  PRINT : INPUT "WHICH INTEGRAL (1) FUNCTION OR (2) DATA ";R
222  IF R < 1 OR R > 2 THEN 220
225  IF SW = 1 AND R = 1 THEN 680
```

```
230   IF R = 2 THEN 260
235   PRINT : PRINT
240   INPUT "ENTER LIMITS (LOWER, UPPER): ";A,B
250   GOTO 515
260   PRINT : PRINT
270   INPUT "HOW MANY INTERVALS: ";K
280   PRINT
290   INPUT "WHAT IS THE INTERVAL WIDTH: ";D
300   PRINT
305 P = K + 1
310   DIM Y(P)
320   FOR H = 1 TO P
330   PRINT "Y(";H;") = ";
340   INPUT Y(H)
350   NEXT H
360 X = 0
370   FOR G = 2 TO K STEP 2
380 X = X + Y(G)
390   NEXT G
400 Z = 0
410 M = K - 1
420   FOR I = 3 TO M STEP 2
430 Z = Z + Y(I)
440   NEXT I
450 J = Y(1) + Y(P)
460 H = J + 4 * X + 2 * Z
470 G = D / 3 * H
475 G =   INT (1E4 * G + .5) / 1E4
480   PRINT : PRINT : PRINT : PRINT
490   PRINT "THE INTEGRAL IS    ";G
500   PRINT : PRINT
510   GOTO 680
515 KK = 25
517   DIM Y(KK)
520 D = (B - A) / (KK - 1)
530 X = A
540   FOR J = 1 TO KK
550 Y(J) =   FN F(X)
560 X = X + D
570   NEXT J
580 ODD = 0
590   FOR J = 3 TO KK - 2 STEP 2
600 ODD = ODD + 2 * Y(J)
610   NEXT J
620 EVEN = 0
630   FOR J = 2 TO KK - 1 STEP 2
640 EVEN = EVEN + 4 * Y(J)
650   NEXT J
660 G = D / 3 * (Y(1) + EVEN + ODD + Y(KK))
670   GOTO 475
680   END
```

SIMPSON INTEGRATION

THIS PROGRAM PERFORMS INTEGRATION
ACCORDING TO SIMPSON'S RULE. YOU MAY
INTEGRATE EITHER A FUNCTION OR DATA.

HIT ANY KEY TO CONTINUE

    IF YOU ARE ENTERING DATA YOU MUST
ENTER THE NUMBER OF SPACES INTO WHICH
THE INTEGRATION INTERVAL HAS BEEN
DIVIDED. THIS MUST BE AN EVEN NUMBER.
YOU MUST ALSO ENTER THE WIDTH OF EACH
SPACE.

```
     IF YOU ARE INTEGRATING A FUNCTION,
THEN YOU MUST DEFINE IT AT LINE 200
AND THEN RUN THE PROGRAM. FOR EXAMPLE:

     200 DEF FNF(X)=X↑2-25
     RUN



WHICH INTEGRAL (1) FUNCTION OR (2) DATA 2

HOW MANY INTERVALS: 4

WHAT IS THE INTERVAL WIDTH: 2

Y(1) = ?0
Y(2) = ?2
Y(3) = ?4
Y(4) = ?16
Y(5) = ?32



THE INTEGRAL IS   74.6667




          SIMPSON INTEGRATION



THIS PROGRAM PERFORMS  INTEGRATION
ACCORDING TO SIMPSON'S RULE. YOU MAY
INTEGRATE EITHER A FUNCTION OR DATA.


HIT ANY KEY TO CONTINUE

     IF YOU ARE ENTERING DATA YOU MUST
ENTER THE NUMBER OF SPACES INTO WHICH
THE INTEGRATION INTERVAL HAS BEEN
DIVIDED. THIS MUST BE AN EVEN NUMBER.
YOU MUST ALSO ENTER THE WIDTH OF EACH
SPACE.

     IF YOU ARE INTEGRATING A FUNCTION,
THEN YOU MUST DEFINE IT AT LINE 200
AND THEN RUN THE PROGRAM. FOR EXAMPLE:

     200 DEF FNF(X)=X↑2-25
     RUN



WHICH INTEGRAL (1) FUNCTION OR (2) DATA 1

]200 DEF FNF(X)=X↑2-25

]RUN




          SIMPSON INTEGRATION



ENTER LIMITS (LOWER, UPPER): 0,10



THE INTEGRAL IS   83.3333
```

3 Complex Mathematics

Complex numbers frequently crop up in engineering calculations, and it is convenient to be able to perform calculations with them on the computer. Unfortunately, this is another area where BASIC is not up to par with FORTRAN. Because of the unique properties of complex numbers, they cannot be handled in the same way as conventional or real numbers. A complex number is really a pair of numbers A and B and is expressed as

$$A + JB \quad \text{or} \quad A + BI$$

where J and I have the property that I^2 or J^2 is equal to -1. The part of the number that is preceded by the J or followed by the I is called the imaginary part (in the example above, B is the imaginary part). The other part (A) is called the real part.

The series of programs that follow were designed to overcome the lack of complex capability in BASIC and to improve the ability to perform complex computations provided by FORTRAN. This is done by including evaluations not offered as standard functions in FORTRAN.

3.1 COMPLEX ADDITION

The addition of complex numbers can be performed by following the general rule:

$$(A + JB) + (C + JD) = (A + C) + J(B + D)$$

The program is very general and lets you add any amount of complex numbers desired. The addition of the real and imaginary parts is done separately in lines 130 and 140. Line 142 determines which sign will be placed in front of the J in the final printout. A minus sign is stored in B$ in line 115. If the absolute value of the imaginary part is the same as the real value of the imaginary part, then the number must be positive and B$ is reassigned as a plus. If the imaginary part is negative, B$ stays as a minus sign. The addition and final printout are accomplished through line 150. The remainder of the program is used to convert the complex number to polar notation, where it is expressed as a magnitude and a direction (angle). Lines 360 to 415 determine the angle in degrees.

```
0    CALL  - 936
1    PRINT : PRINT : PRINT : PRINT "WRITTEN BY JULES H. GILDER"
2    PRINT : PRINT "COPYRIGHT (C) HAYDEN BOOK CO. 1978"
3    FOR X = 1 TO 4000: NEXT X
5    PRINT : PRINT : PRINT : PRINT
6    PRINT  TAB( 12 )"COMPLEX ADDITION"
7    PRINT : PRINT : PRINT : PRINT
10   PRINT "THIS PROGRAM PERFORMS COMPLEX MATH"
20   PRINT "IT WILL ADD ANY NUMBER OF COMPLEX"
30   PRINT "NUMBERS."
40   PRINT
85   PRINT
90   INPUT "HOW MANY NUMBERS ARE YOU ADDING? ";N
95   PRINT
100  PRINT "ENTER THE REAL AND IMAGINARY PARTS"
102  PRINT
105 RT = 0
107 AM = 0
110   FOR  I = 1  TO  N
115 B$ = "-"
120   PRINT "NUMBER ";I;"        ";
122   INPUT  R( I ),IM( I )
130 RT = RT + R( I )
140 AM  = AM  + IM( I )
142   IF    ABS ( AM ) = AM   THEN   B$ = "+"
145   NEXT  I
147   PRINT : PRINT
150   PRINT "THE SUM IS ";RT;"  ";B$;" J ";ABS ( AM )
300   PRINT  : PRINT "DO YOU WANT IT IN POLAR FORM";
320   INPUT Z$
330   PRINT : PRINT
340   IF  LEFT$ ( Z$,1 ) = "N" THEN 440
350 MAG =  INT ( 100 *  SQR ( RT ↑ 2 + AM ↑ 2 ) + .5 ) / 100
360   IF  RT = 0  AND  AM < 0  THEN  410
370   IF  RT = 0  AND  AM > 0  THEN  400
375   IF  RT < 0  AND  AM = 0  THEN  415
380 THETA =   INT ( ATN ( AM / RT ) * 57.2958 * 100 + .5 ) / 100
382   IF  RT < 0  AND  AM > 0  THEN  THETA = 180 + THETA
384   IF RT < 0 AND AM < 0 THEN THETA = 180 + THETA
```

52   BASIC Computer Programs in Science and Engineering

```
390  GOTO  420
400  THETA = 90
405  GOTO  420
410  THETA = 270
412  GOTO  420
415  THETA = 180
420  PRINT "MAGNITUDE = ";MAG
430  PRINT : PRINT "ANGLE = ";THETA;" DEGREES"
440  PRINT : PRINT
450  INPUT "DO YOU HAVE MORE DATA? ";Z$
460  PRINT : PRINT
470  IF  LEFT$ (Z$,1) = "Y" THEN 50
480  END
```

```
            COMPLEX ADDITION


THIS PROGRAM PERFORMS COMPLEX MATH
IT WILL ADD ANY NUMBER OF COMPLEX
NUMBERS.

HOW MANY NUMBERS ARE YOU ADDING? 4

ENTER THE REAL AND IMAGINARY PARTS

NUMBER 1        ?2,3
NUMBER 2        ?0,-5
NUMBER 3        ?23,12
NUMBER 4        ?-30,5


THE SUM IS -5 + J 15

DO YOU WANT IT IN POLAR FORM?YES


MAGNITUDE = 15.81

ANGLE = 108.43 DEGREES


DO YOU HAVE MORE DATA? NO
```

3.2 COMPLEX SUBTRACTION

The subtraction of complex numbers is very similar to the addition of complex numbers. The only difference is the signs. It is performed according to the following rule:

$$(A + JB) - (C + JD) = (A - C) + J(B - D)$$

Operation of this program is identical to the addition program in that B$ is used to determine the sign of the imaginary component of the answer. The polar format routine is also included.

```
0    CALL   - 936
1    PRINT : PRINT : PRINT "WRITTEN BY JULES H. GILDER"
2    PRINT : PRINT "COPYRIGHT (C) HAYDEN BOOK CO. 1978"
3    FOR X = 1 TO 4000: NEXT X
5    PRINT : PRINT : PRINT : PRINT
6    PRINT  TAB( 12)"COMPLEX SUBTRACTION"
7    PRINT : PRINT : PRINT : PRINT
10   PRINT "THIS PROGRAM PERFORMS COMPLEX MATH"
20   PRINT "IT WILL SUBTRACT COMPLEX NUMBERS."
40   PRINT
50 B$ = "-"
100  PRINT "WHAT ARE THE NUMBERS YOU ARE SUBTRACTING"
110  PRINT "ENTER THE REAL AND IMAGINARY PARTS"
120  PRINT
130  INPUT R1,A1
140  INPUT R2,A2
150 RT = R1 - R2
160 AM = A1 - A2
162  PRINT
165  IF  ABS (AM) = AM THEN B$ = "+"
170  PRINT "THE DIFFERENCE IS ";RT;" ";B$;" J"; ABS (AM)
200  PRINT : PRINT "DO YOU WANT IT IN POLAR FORM";
210  INPUT Z$
220  PRINT : PRINT
230  IF  LEFT$ (Z$,1) = "N" THEN 440
350 MAG =  INT (100 *  SQR (RT ↑ 2 + AM ↑ 2) + .5) / 100
360  IF  RT = 0  AND  AM < 0   THEN  410
370  IF  RT = 0  AND  AM > 0   THEN  400
375  IF  RT < 0  AND  AM = 0   THEN  415
380 THETA =  INT ( ATN (AM / RT) * 57.2958 * 100 + .5) / 100
382  IF  RT < 0  AND  AM > 0   THEN  THETA = 180 + THETA
384  IF  RT < 0 AND AM < 0 THEN THETA = 180 + THETA
390  GOTO  420
400 THETA = 90
405  GOTO  420
410 THETA = 270
412  GOTO  420
415 THETA = 180
420  PRINT "MAGNITUDE = ";MAG
430  PRINT : PRINT "ANGLE = ";THETA;" DEGREES"
440  PRINT : PRINT
450  INPUT "DO YOU HAVE MORE DATA? ";Z$
460  PRINT : PRINT
470  IF  LEFT$ (Z$,1) = "Y" THEN 50
480  END
```

COMPLEX SUBTRACTION

THIS PROGRAM PERFORMS COMPLEX MATH
IT WILL SUBTRACT COMPLEX NUMBERS.

WHAT ARE THE NUMBERS YOU ARE SUBTRACTING
ENTER THE REAL AND IMAGINARY PARTS

?23,-12
?14,89

THE DIFFERENCE IS 9 - J101

DO YOU WANT IT IN POLAR FORM?YES

MAGNITUDE = 101.4

ANGLE = -84.91 DEGREES

DO YOU HAVE MORE DATA? NO

3.3 COMPLEX MULTIPLICATION

Multiplication of complex numbers is somewhat different from the multiplication of ordinary numbers. The real part of the final answer is found by subtracting the product of the imaginary parts of the two numbers from the product of the real parts of the two numbers.

The imaginary part of the answer is found by multiplying the real part of the first number by the imaginary part of the second number and adding it to the product of the real part of the second number and the imaginary part of the first number. More clearly stated,

$$(1) \qquad (A + JB)(C + JD) = (AC - BD) + J(BC + AD)$$

This result can be obtained by treating the two parts of one complex number as two separate numbers. So multiplying C + JD first by A and then by JB gives

$$(2) \qquad A(C + JD) = AC + JAD$$

$$(3) \qquad JB(C + JD) = JCB + J^2 BD$$

But since $J^2 = -1$, adding equations (2) and (3) gives the result in equation 1.

In this program, as in the previous ones, the real and imaginary parts of the final answer are evaluated separately (lines 11Ø and 12Ø). The ability to get results in polar form is included.

```
0   CALL  - 936
1   PRINT : PRINT : PRINT : PRINT "WRITTEN BY JULES H. GILDER"
2   PRINT : PRINT "COPYRIGHT (C) HAYDEN BOOK CO. 1978"
3   FOR X = 1 TO 4000: NEXT X
5   PRINT : PRINT : PRINT : PRINT
7   PRINT  TAB( 11)"COMPLEX MULTIPLICATION"
10   PRINT : PRINT : PRINT : PRINT
20   PRINT "THIS PROGRAM PERFORMS MULTIPLICATION OF"
30   PRINT "COMPLEX NUMBERS."
40   PRINT
50  B$ = "-"
60   PRINT "WHAT ARE THE NUMBERS YOU ARE MULTIPLYING"
70   PRINT "ENTER THE REAL AND IMAGINARY PARTS.".
80   PRINT
90   INPUT  R1,A1
100    INPUT  R2,A2
110 RT = R1 * R2 - (A1 * A2 )
120 AM = A1 * R2 + R1 * A2
130   IF   ABS (AM) = AM   THEN   B$ = "+"
140   PRINT
150   PRINT "THE PRODUCT IS ";RT;" ";B$;" J "; ABS (AM)
160   PRINT  : PRINT "DO YOU WANT IT IN POLAR FORM";
180   INPUT Z$
190   PRINT : PRINT
200   IF  LEFT$ (Z$,1) = "N" THEN 320
210 MAG =  INT (100 *  SQR (RT ↑ 2 + AM ↑ 2) + .5) / 100
220   IF  RT = 0  AND  AM < 0  THEN  270
230   IF  RT = 0  AND  AM > 0  THEN  260
235   IF  RT < 0  AND  AM = 0  THEN  280
240 THETA  =  INT ( ATN (AM / RT) * 57.2958 * 100 + .5) / 100
```

```
242   IF  RT < 0   AND  AM > 0  THEN  THETA = 180 + THETA
245   IF RT < 0 AND AM < 0 THEN THETA = 180 + THETA
250   GOTO  300
260 THETA = 90
265   GOTO  300
270 THETA = 270
275   GOTO  300
280 THETA  = 180
285   GOTO  300
300   PRINT "MAGNITUDE = ";MAG
310   PRINT : PRINT "ANGLE = ";THETA;" DEGREES"
320   PRINT : PRINT
330   INPUT "DO YOU HAVE MORE DATA? ";Z$
340   PRINT : PRINT
350   IF  LEFT$ (Z$,1) = "Y" THEN 50
360   END
```

COMPLEX MULTIPLICATION

THIS PROGRAM PERFORMS MULTIPLICATION OF
COMPLEX NUMBERS.

WHAT ARE THE NUMBERS YOU ARE MULTIPLYING
ENTER THE REAL AND IMAGINARY PARTS.

?15,18
?-6,-2

THE PRODUCT IS -54 - J 138

DO YOU WANT IT IN POLAR FORM?YES

MAGNITUDE = 148.19

ANGLE = 248.63 DEGREES

DO YOU HAVE MORE DATA? NO

3.4 COMPLEX DIVISION

Division of complex numbers is performed according to the following rule:

$$(A + JB)/(C + JD) = \frac{(AC + BD)^2 + J(BD - AC)^2}{C^2 + D^2}$$

This is accomplished separately for the real and imaginary parts on lines 12$\emptyset$ and 13$\emptyset$.

```
0   CALL  - 936
1   PRINT : PRINT : PRINT : PRINT "WRITTEN BY JULES H. GILDER"
2   PRINT : PRINT "COPYRIGHT (C) HAYDEN BOOK CO. 1978"
3   FOR X = 1 TO 4000: NEXT X
5   PRINT : PRINT : PRINT : PRINT
7   PRINT  TAB( 12)"COMPLEX DIVISION"
10  PRINT : PRINT : PRINT : PRINT
20  PRINT "THIS PROGRAM PERFORMS DIVISION OF"
30  PRINT "COMPLEX NUMBERS."
40  PRINT
50  B$ = "-"
60  PRINT "WHAT NUMBER (FIRST) ARE YOU DIVIDING"
70  PRINT "BY THE OTHER (SECOND)"
75  PRINT : PRINT
80  PRINT "ENTER REAL AND IMAGINARY PARTS"
90  PRINT
100  INPUT  R1,A1
110  INPUT  R2,A2
120 RT = (R1 * R2 + A1 * A2) / (R2 ↑ 2 + A2 ↑ 2)
130 AM = (A1 * R2 - R1 * A2) / (R2 ↑ 2 + A2 ↑ 2)
140  PRINT
150  IF   ABS (AM) = AM   THEN  B$ = "+"
160  PRINT "THE ANSWER IS ";RT;" ";B$;" J "; ABS (AM)
170  PRINT  : PRINT "DO YOU WANT IT IN POLAR FORM";
190  INPUT Z$
200  PRINT : PRINT
210  IF  LEFT$ (Z$,1) = "N" THEN 310
220 MAG =  INT (100 *  SQR (RT ↑ 2 + AM ↑ 2) + .5) / 100
230  IF  RT = 0  AND  AM < 0  THEN  280
240  IF  RT = 0  AND  AM > 0  THEN  270
245  IF  RT < 0  AND  AM = 0  THEN  285
250 THETA  =  INT ( ATN (AM / RT) * 57.2958 * 100 + .5) / 100
252  IF RT < 0 AND AM < 0 THEN THETA = 180 + THETA
255  IF  RT < 0  AND  AM > 0  THEN  THETA = THETA + 180
260  GOTO  290
270 THETA = 90: GOTO  290
280 THETA = 270
283  GOTO 290
285 THETA = 180
290  PRINT "MAGNITUDE = ";MAG
300  PRINT : PRINT "ANGLE = ";THETA;" DEGREES"
310  PRINT : PRINT
320  INPUT "DO YOU HAVE MORE DATA? ";Z$
330  PRINT : PRINT
340  IF  LEFT$ (Z$,1) = "Y" THEN 40
350  END
```

COMPLEX DIVISION

THIS PROGRAM PERFORMS DIVISION OF
COMPLEX NUMBERS.

WHAT NUMBER (FIRST) ARE YOU DIVIDING
BY THE OTHER (SECOND)

ENTER REAL AND IMAGINARY PARTS

?2,7
?3,4

THE ANSWER IS 46.24 + J 6.76

DO YOU WANT IT IN POLAR FORM?YES

MAGNITUDE = 46.73

ANGLE = 8.32 DEGREES

DO YOU HAVE MORE DATA? YES

WHAT NUMBER (FIRST) ARE YOU DIVIDING
BY THE OTHER (SECOND)

ENTER REAL AND IMAGINARY PARTS

?23,5
?-6,0

THE ANSWER IS 529 + J 25

DO YOU WANT IT IN POLAR FORM?YES

MAGNITUDE = 529.59

ANGLE = 2.71 DEGREES

DO YOU HAVE MORE DATA? NO

3.5 ABSOLUTE VALUE

Another function provided in the FORTRAN complex math package is the absolute value function. This essentially is the subroutine that does the polar conversion in the previous programs. Unlike the CABS function in FORTRAN, this program will also return the angle as well as the magnitude of the complex number. The magnitude is found by taking the square root of the sum of the squares of the real part and the imaginary part:

$$\text{Magnitude} = (\text{Real}^2 + \text{Imag}^2)^{1/2}$$

The angle is determined by calculating the inverse tangent of the imaginary part divided by the real part:

$$\text{Angle} = \text{Arctan (Imag/Real)}$$

This is a tricky calculation to make in BASIC since the result of the inverse tangent function in BASIC is a value in radians in the range of $\pi/2$ to $-\pi/2$. As a result, it is necessary to convert the answer to degrees and then determine which quadrant the angle is in to get the final result. The conversion to degrees is done in line 250, and the determination of the quadrant, and thus the true angle, is done in lines 252 to 285.

```
0    CALL  - 936
1    PRINT : PRINT : PRINT : PRINT "WRITTEN BY JULES H. GILDER"
2    PRINT : PRINT "COPYRIGHT (C) HAYDEN BOOK CO. 1978"
3    FOR X = 1 TO 4000: NEXT X
5    PRINT : PRINT : PRINT : PRINT
7    PRINT  TAB( 13 )"ABSOLUTE VALUE"
10   PRINT : PRINT : PRINT : PRINT
20   PRINT "THIS PROGRAM CALCULATES THE ABSOLUTE"
30   PRINT "VALUE OF A COMPLEX NUMBER AND ITS ANGLE"
40   PRINT
70   PRINT : PRINT
100  PRINT "ENTER REAL AND IMAGINARY PARTS ";
200  INPUT RT,AM
210  PRINT : PRINT : PRINT : PRINT
220  MAG =  INT (100 *  SQR (RT ↑ 2 + AM ↑ 2) + .5) / 100
230  IF  RT = 0  AND  AM < 0  THEN  280
240  IF  RT = 0  AND  AM > 0  THEN  270
245  IF  RT < 0  AND  AM = 0  THEN  285
250  THETA  =  INT ( ATN (AM / RT) * 57.2958 * 100 + .5) / 100
252  IF RT < 0 AND AM < 0 THEN THETA = 180 + THETA
255  IF  RT < 0  AND  AM > 0  THEN  THETA = THETA + 180
260  GOTO  290
270  THETA = 90: GOTO  290
280  THETA = 270
283  GOTO 290
285  THETA = 180
290  PRINT "MAGNITUDE = ";MAG
300  PRINT : PRINT "ANGLE = ";THETA;" DEGREES"
310  PRINT : PRINT
320  INPUT "DO YOU HAVE MORE DATA? ";Z$
330  PRINT : PRINT
340  IF  LEFT$ (Z$,1) = "Y" THEN 40
350  END
```

```
                ABSOLUTE VALUE


THIS PROGRAM CALCULATES THE ABSOLUTE
VALUE OF A COMPLEX NUMBER AND ITS ANGLE

ENTER REAL AND IMAGINARY PARTS ?3,4


MAGNITUDE = 5
ANGLE = 53.13 DEGREES

DO YOU HAVE MORE DATA? YES



ENTER REAL AND IMAGINARY PARTS ?5,6


MAGNITUDE = 7.81
ANGLE = 50.19 DEGREES

DO YOU HAVE MORE DATA? NO
```

3.6 COMPLEX NUMBER TO A REAL POWER

This is one of the programs that provides more capability than the FORTRAN complex functions. With it, BASIC can be used to raise a complex number to a real power. The calculation is based on De Moivre's theorem that states:

$$Z{\uparrow}N = R{\uparrow}N (COS\ N*THETA + J\ SIN\ N*THETA)$$

where N is the number of roots.

In order to implement this equation, it is necessary to call the polar conversion routine twice, once to calculate the results and a second time to display the results in polar notation.

In order to suppress the printing of the conversion results on the first pass through, variable SW has been added. In line 29Ø, SW is tested. If it is equal to 1, the first pass is indicated and printing should be skipped. After the results are calculated, SW is set to zero. The next time through the subroutine, the results are printed in polar format.

De Moivre's equation is evaluated in lines 36Ø to 39Ø.

```
0    CALL  - 936
1    PRINT : PRINT : PRINT : PRINT "WRITTEN BY JULES H. GILDER"
2    PRINT : PRINT "COPYRIGHT (C) HAYDEN BOOK CO. 1978"
3    FOR X = 1 TO 4000: NEXT X
5    PRINT : PRINT : PRINT : PRINT
7    PRINT  TAB(15)"COMPLEX NUMBER TO A REAL POWER"
10   PRINT : PRINT : PRINT : PRINT
20     PRINT "THIS PROGRAM WILL CALCULATE THE VALUE"
30     PRINT "OF A COMPLEX NUMBER RAISED TO A REAL"
40     PRINT "POWER.": PRINT : PRINT
50     PRINT : INPUT "ENTER EXPONENT: ";R
70     PRINT : PRINT
100    PRINT "ENTER COMPLEX NUMBER (REAL, IMAGINARY) ";
200    INPUT RT,AM
205  SW = 1
210    PRINT : PRINT : PRINT : PRINT
220  MAG =  INT (100 *  SQR (RT ↑ 2 + AM ↑ 2) + .5) / 100
230    IF  RT = 0  AND  AM < 0   THEN  280
240    IF  RT = 0  AND  AM > 0   THEN  270
245    IF  RT < 0  AND  AM = 0   THEN  285
250  THETA  =  INT ( ATN (AM / RT) * 57.2958 * 100 + .5) / 100
252    IF  RT < 0 AND AM < 0 THEN THETA = 180 + THETA
255    IF  RT < 0  AND  AM > 0  THEN  THETA = THETA + 180
260    GOTO  290
270  THETA = 90: GOTO  290
280  THETA = 270
283    GOTO 290
285  THETA = 180
290    IF SW = 1 THEN 350
292    PRINT : PRINT
295    PRINT "MAGNITUDE = ";MAG
296    PRINT
300    PRINT "ANGLE = ";THETA;" DEGREES"
310    PRINT : PRINT : PRINT
320    RETURN
345    END
```

```
350 THETA = THETA / 57.2958
360 R1 = MAG ↑ R *  COS (R * THETA)
370 I1 = MAG ↑ R *  SIN (R * THETA)
380 R1 =  INT (100 * R1 + .5) / 100
390 I1 =  INT (100 * I1 + .5) / 100
392 B$ = " -":C$ = " -"
394  IF  ABS (AM) = AM THEN C$ = " +"
396  IF  ABS (I1) = I1 THEN B$ = " +"
400  PRINT : PRINT : PRINT : PRINT
405  PRINT "("RT;C$;" J "; ABS (AM);")↑";R;" = ";R1;B$;" J "; ABS
     (I1)
410  PRINT : PRINT : PRINT : PRINT
420 RT = R1
430 AM = I1
460  INPUT "DO YOU WANT IT IN POLAR FORM? ";Z$
470  IF  LEFT$ (Z$,1) = "N" THEN 345
480 SW = 0
490  PRINT : PRINT
500  GOSUB 220
510  INPUT "DO YOU HAVE MORE DATA? ";Z$
515  PRINT : PRINT
520  IF  LEFT$ (Z$,1) = "Y" THEN 50
```

COMPLEX NUMBER TO A REAL POWER

THIS PROGRAM WILL CALCULATE THE VALUE
OF A COMPLEX NUMBER RAISED TO A REAL
POWER.

ENTER EXPONENT: 3

ENTER COMPLEX NUMBER (REAL, IMAGINARY) ?0,8

(0 + J 8)↑3 = 0,- J 512

DO YOU WANT IT IN POLAR FORM? YES

MAGNITUDE = 512

ANGLE = 270 DEGREES

DO YOU HAVE MORE DATA? NO

3.7 COMPLEX ROOTS

By substituting the inverse power into De Moivre's equation and expanding, it becomes possible to calculate the N Nth roots of a complex number. The resulting equation is

$$Z\uparrow(1/N) = R\uparrow(1/N) (COS((THETA + 2K)/N) + J \ SIN ((THETA + 2K)/N)$$

where

$$K = 0, 1, 2, 3, \ldots\ldots\ldots, N - 1$$

N = the desired root

To implement this equation, the polar conversion routine is called into action twice, and the variable SW is used to suppress printing on the first pass through. The above equation is evaluated on lines 360 to 390.

```
0    CALL  - 936
1    PRINT : PRINT : PRINT : PRINT "WRITTEN BY JULES H. GILDER"
2    PRINT : PRINT "COPYRIGHT (C) HAYDEN BOOK CO. 1978"
3    FOR X = 1 TO 4000: NEXT X
5    PRINT : PRINT : PRINT : PRINT
7    PRINT  TAB( 6)"NTH ROOTS OF A COMPLEX NUMBER"
10   PRINT : PRINT : PRINT : PRINT
20   PRINT "THIS PROGRAM WILL CALCULATE THE 'N'"
30   PRINT "NTH ROOTS OF A COMPLEX NUMBER."
40   PRINT : PRINT
50   INPUT "ENTER ROOT DESIRED: ";R
70   PRINT : PRINT
100   PRINT "ENTER REAL AND IMAGINARY PARTS ";
200   INPUT RT,AM
205  SW = 1
210   PRINT : PRINT : PRINT : PRINT
220  MAG =  INT (100 *  SQR (RT ↑ 2 + AM ↑ 2) + .5) / 100
230   IF  RT = 0  AND  AM < 0   THEN  280
240   IF  RT = 0  AND  AM > 0   THEN  270
245   IF  RT < 0  AND  AM = 0   THEN  285
250  THETA  =  INT ( ATN (AM / RT) * 57.2958 * 100 + .5) / 100
252   IF  RT < 0  AND  AM < 0  THEN  THETA = 180 + THETA
255   IF  RT < 0  AND  AM > 0   THEN  THETA = THETA + 180
260   GOTO  290
270  THETA = 90: GOTO  290
280  THETA = 270
283  GOTO 290
285  THETA = 180
290   IF SW = 1 THEN 350
295   PRINT "MAGNITUDE = ";MAG
300   PRINT "ANGLE = ";THETA;" DEGREES"
310   PRINT : PRINT
320   RETURN
345  END
350  THETA = THETA / 57.2958
355   DIM R1(R),I1(R)
360   FOR L = 1 TO R
362  RR = 1 / R:T = THETA + 2 * L * 3.14159
364  T = T / R
370  R1(L) = MAG ↑ RR *  COS (T)
375  R1(L) =  INT ( 1E3 * R1(L) + .5) / 1E3
380  I1(L) = MAG ↑ RR *  SIN (T)
385  I1(L) =  INT ( 1E3 * I1(L) + .5) / 1E3
```

```
390   NEXT L
395   REM
400   PRINT : PRINT : PRINT "THE ROOTS ARE:"
410   PRINT : PRINT
411   FOR KK = 1 TO R
412 B$ = "-"
415   IF  ABS (I1(KK)) =  I1(KK) THEN B$ = "+"
430   PRINT R1(KK);" ";B$;" J ";  ABS (I1(KK))
440   NEXT KK
450   PRINT : PRINT
460   INPUT "DO YOU WANT IT IN POLAR FORM? ";Z$
470   IF  LEFT$ (Z$,1) = "N" THEN 345
480 SW = 0
490   PRINT : PRINT
500   FOR KK = 1 TO R
510 RT = R1(KK)
520 AM = I1(KK)
530   GOSUB 220
535   NEXT KK
540   GOTO 345
```

NTH ROOTS OF A COMPLEX NUMBER

THIS PROGRAM WILL CALCULATE THE 'N'
NTH ROOTS OF A COMPLEX NUMBER.

ENTER ROOT DESIRED: 5

ENTER REAL AND IMAGINARY PARTS ?8,-3

THE ROOTS ARE:

.578 + J 1.423
-1.174 + J .989
-1.304 - J .811
.369 - J 1.491
1.532 - J .11

DO YOU WANT IT IN POLAR FORM? YES

MAGNITUDE = 1.54
ANGLE = 67.89 DEGREES

MAGNITUDE = 1.54
ANGLE = 139.89 DEGREES

MAGNITUDE = 1.54
ANGLE = 211.88 DEGREES

MAGNITUDE = 1.54
ANGLE = -76.1 DEGREES

MAGNITUDE = 1.54
ANGLE = -4.11 DEGREES

3.8 COMPLEX EXPONENTIAL

Calculus often requires the evaluation of the exponential function,

$$EXP \uparrow Z$$

where $Z = A + JB$.

The exponential raised to a complex power can be calculated by using the following formula:

$$EXP \uparrow Z = EXP \uparrow X (COS\ Y + J\ SIN\ Y)$$

where $Z = X + JY$.

Evaluation of this formula is done for separate parts in lines 120 and 130. Rounding off to three decimal places is done in lines 135 and 137. Once again, polar output capability is provided.

```
0    CALL  - 936
1    PRINT : PRINT : PRINT : PRINT "WRITTEN BY JULES H. GILDER"
2    PRINT : PRINT "COPYRIGHT (C) HAYDEN BOOK CO. 1978"
3    FOR X = 1 TO 4000: NEXT X
5    PRINT : PRINT : PRINT : PRINT
6    PRINT  TAB( 10 )"COMPLEX EXPONENTIAL"
7    PRINT : PRINT : PRINT : PRINT
10   PRINT "THIS PROGRAM CALCULATES THE VALUE OF "
20   PRINT "THE EXPONENTIAL (E) RAISED TO A COMPLEX"
30   PRINT "POWER."
40   PRINT
50   B$ = "-"
60   C$ = "-"
85   PRINT
90   PRINT "WHAT IS THE COMPLEX POWER TO WHICH YOU"
95   PRINT "WANT THE EXPONENTIAL RAISED? "
100   PRINT : PRINT : INPUT "ENTER THE REAL AND IMAGINARY PARTS: "
      ;RT,AM
120  ER =  EXP (RT) * ( COS (AM))
130  EI =  EXP (RT) * ( SIN (AM))
135  ER =  INT (1E3 * ER + .5) / 1E3
137  EI =  INT (1E3 * EI + .5) / 1E3
140   IF  ABS (EI) = EI THEN B$ = "+"
145   IF  ABS (AM) = AM THEN C$ = "+"
147  PRINT : PRINT
150   PRINT : PRINT : PRINT "EXP↑("¡RT¡" "¡C$¡" J "¡ ABS (AM)¡") =
      "¡ER¡" "¡B$¡" J "¡ ABS (EI)
200  RT = ER
210  AM = EI
290  PRINT : PRINT
300  PRINT  : PRINT "DO YOU WANT IT IN POLAR FORM"¡
320   INPUT Z$
330  PRINT : PRINT
340   IF  LEFT$ (Z$,1) = "N" THEN 440
350  MAG =  INT (1E3 *  SQR (RT ↑ 2 + AM ↑ 2) + .5) / 1E3
360   IF  RT = 0  AND  AM < 0  THEN  410
370   IF  RT = 0  AND  AM > 0  THEN  400
375   IF  RT < 0  AND  AM = 0  THEN  415
380  THETA =  INT ( ATN (AM / RT) * 57.2958 * 100 + .5) / 100
382   IF  RT < 0  AND  AM > 0  THEN  THETA = 180 + THETA
```

```
384   IF RT < 0 AND AM < 0 THEN THETA = 180 + THETA
390   GOTO  420
400  THETA = 90
405   GOTO  420
410  THETA = 270
412   GOTO  420
415  THETA = 180
420   PRINT : PRINT "MAGNITUDE = ";MAG
430   PRINT : PRINT "ANGLE = ";THETA;" DEGREES"
440   PRINT : PRINT
450   INPUT "DO YOU HAVE MORE DATA? ";Z$
460   PRINT : PRINT
470   IF  LEFT$ (Z$,1) = "Y" THEN 50
480   END
```

COMPLEX EXPONENTIAL

THIS PROGRAM CALCULATES THE VALUE OF
THE EXPONENTIAL (E) RAISED TO A COMPLEX
POWER.

WHAT IS THE COMPLEX POWER TO WHICH YOU
WANT THE EXPONENTIAL RAISED?

ENTER THE REAL AND IMAGINARY PARTS: 2,6

EXP↑(2 + J 6) = 7.095 - J 2.065

DO YOU WANT IT IN POLAR FORM?YES

MAGNITUDE = 7.389

ANGLE = -16.23 DEGREES

DO YOU HAVE MORE DATA? YES

WHAT IS THE COMPLEX POWER TO WHICH YOU
WANT THE EXPONENTIAL RAISED?

ENTER THE REAL AND IMAGINARY PARTS: 3,0

EXP↑(3 + J 0) = 20.086 + J 0

DO YOU WANT IT IN POLAR FORM?NO

DO YOU HAVE MORE DATA? NO

4 Matrix Mathematics

If you've ever worked with a BASIC compiler on a time-sharing system, you're probably envious of the matrix functions it includes. Most home computer systems do not have the capability of performing any matrix math. However, with the programs in chapter 4, this disadvantage can be overcome.

The first five programs perform operations on two-dimensional matrices, which are standard in the more advanced BASICs. The remaining three programs extend the computer's capabilities to a third dimension. When working with three-dimensional matrices, you should be aware that memory space gets used up very quickly.

The output of these programs has been arranged so that the results are printed in straight columns. You can see how this is done and apply the technique to other programs where straight columns of numbers are needed. Also, be aware that all answers are rounded off to the same number of decimal places, a process that can affect accuracy. In most applications, however, the effect should be negligible.

4.1 ADDITION AND SUBTRACTION OF TWO-DIMENSIONAL SQUARE MATRICES

To add or subtract two matrices, it is simply necessary to perform the operation with the corresponding elements in each of the arrays. When this program is run, it asks for the size of the array. It is only necessary to answer with one number, since the matrix is assumed to be square.

If you wish to add arrays that are not square, this is done by simply entering zero as elements in those rows or columns not used.

After the size of the array is entered, the program uses this value to dimension three arrays (set aside space to store variables that will be needed by the program). The program then asks which operation, addition or subtraction, is to be performed. Although the program indicates that you must answer addition or subtraction, it only checks the first letter of your answer (line 274). An A or S will suffice. In fact, for any answer that does not start with an A, the computer will assume subtraction.

If the answer is addition, the program branches to line 280. If not, the operation on line 275 is performed.

```
0   CALL  - 936
1   PRINT : PRINT : PRINT : PRINT "WRITTEN BY JULES H. GILDER"
2   PRINT : PRINT "COPYRIGHT (C) HAYDEN BOOK CO. 1978"
3   FOR X = 1 TO 4000: NEXT X
4   PRINT : PRINT : PRINT : PRINT
5   PRINT  TAB( 3)"2D MATRIX ADDITION AND SUBTRACTION"
6   PRINT : PRINT : PRINT : PRINT
10   PRINT "THIS PROGRAM ADDS AND SUBTRACTS"
20   PRINT "TWO 2-DIMENSIONAL SQUARE MATRICES."
30   PRINT
40   INPUT "ENTER SIZE OF MATRICES: ";N
45   IF N = 0 THEN 330
50   PRINT
55   DIM A(N,N),B(N,N),C(N,N)
65   INPUT "ADDITION OR SUBTRACTION? ";Z$
69   PRINT
70   PRINT "ENTER THE ELEMENTS OF ARRAY 'A'"
80   PRINT
90   FOR I = 1 TO N
100   FOR J = 1 TO N
110   PRINT "A(";I;",";J;") = ";
120   INPUT A(I,J)
130   NEXT J
135   PRINT
140   NEXT I
150   PRINT
160   PRINT "ENTER THE ELEMENTS OF ARRAY 'B'"
170   PRINT
180   FOR I = 1 TO N
190   FOR J = 1 TO N
200   PRINT "B(";I;",";J;") = ";
210   INPUT B(I,J)
220   C(I,J) = 0
230   NEXT J
```

```
235   PRINT
240   NEXT  I
245   PRINT : PRINT : PRINT : PRINT "THE ANSWER IS:"
247   PRINT : PRINT : PRINT : PRINT
250   FOR  I = 1  TO  N
260   FOR  J = 1  TO  N
274   IF   LEFT$ (Z$,1) = "A"  THEN  280
275 C(I,J) = C(I,J) + A(I,J) - B(I,J)
278   GOTO  285
280 C(I,J) = C(I,J) + A(I,J) + B(I,J)
285 C(I,J) =  INT (100 * C(I,J) + .5) / 100
290 Z =  LEN ( STR$ (C(I,J)))
300   PRINT  TAB( 8 * J - Z);C(I,J);
310   NEXT  J
315   PRINT : PRINT
320   NEXT I
330   END
```

```
      2D MATRIX ADDITION AND SUBTRACTION


THIS PROGRAM ADDS AND SUBTRACTS
TWO 2-DIMENSIONAL SQUARE MATRICES.

ENTER SIZE OF MATRICES: 2

ADDITION OR SUBTRACTION? ADDITION

ENTER THE ELEMENTS OF ARRAY 'A'

A(1,1) = ?2
A(1,2) = ?12

A(2,1) = ?18
A(2,2) = ?9

ENTER THE ELEMENTS OF ARRAY 'B'

B(1,1) = ?0
B(1,2) = ?3

B(2,1) = ?4
B(2,2) = ?12


THE ANSWER IS:


      2       15
     22       21
```

4.2 TWO-DIMENSIONAL MATRIX MULTIPLICATION

Matrix multiplication can be performed only when the number of columns of one matrix is equal to the number of rows of the other. In this program, the matrices are assumed to be square, so this is not a problem. However, as with the former program, nonsquare matrices can be accommodated by entering zero as the value for unused rows or columns

The product of two matrices is defined by the following equation:

$$C_{ij} = (A_{ik})(B_{ki}) + C_{ij}$$

The program prints out the results of the multiplication rounded off for convenience to two decimal places. If this is not desired, simply omit line 285.

```
0   CALL - 936
1   PRINT : PRINT : PRINT : PRINT "WRITTEN BY JULES H. GILDER"
2   PRINT : PRINT "COPYRIGHT (C) HAYDEN BOOK CO. 1978"
3   FOR X = 1 TO 4000: NEXT X
4   PRINT : PRINT : PRINT : PRINT
5   PRINT "  2-DIMENSIONAL MATRIX MULTIPLICATION"
6   PRINT : PRINT : PRINT : PRINT
10  PRINT "THIS PROGRAM MULTIPLIES TWO SQUARE"
20  PRINT "MATRICES."
30  PRINT
35  INPUT " ENTER SIZE OF MATRICES: ";N
40  DIM A(N,N),B(N,N),C(N,N)
45  IF N = 0 THEN 330
50  PRINT
60  PRINT
70  PRINT "ENTER THE ELEMENTS OF ARRAY 'A'"
80  PRINT
90  FOR I = 1 TO N
100 FOR J = 1 TO N
110 PRINT "A(";I;",";J;") = ";
120 INPUT A(I,J)
130 NEXT J
135 PRINT
140 NEXT I
150 PRINT
160 PRINT "ENTER THE ELEMENTS OF ARRAY 'B'"
170 PRINT
180 FOR I = 1 TO N
190 FOR J = 1 TO N
200 PRINT "B(";I;",";J;") = ";
210 INPUT B(I,J)
220 C(I,J) = 0
230 NEXT J
235 PRINT
240 NEXT I
245 PRINT : PRINT : PRINT : PRINT : PRINT "THE ANSWER IS:"
247 PRINT : PRINT : PRINT : PRINT
250 FOR I = 1 TO N
260 FOR J = 1 TO N
270 FOR K = 1 TO N
280 C(I,J) = C(I,J) + A(I,K) * B(K,J)
285 C(I,J) = INT (100 * C(I,J) + .5) / 100
```

```
290  NEXT  K
295  Z =  LEN ( STR$ (C(I,J)))
300  PRINT  TAB( 8 * J - Z);C(I,J);
310  NEXT  J
315  PRINT : PRINT
320  NEXT I
330  END
```

        2-DIMENSIONAL MATRIX MULTIPLICATION

THIS PROGRAM MULTIPLIES TWO SQUARE
MATRICES.
 ENTER SIZE OF MATRICES: 3

ENTER THE ELEMENTS OF ARRAY 'A'

A(1,1) = ?3.1
A(1,2) = ?4
A(1,3) = ?1

A(2,1) = ?8.3
A(2,2) = ?6.6
A(2,3) = ?0

A(3,1) = ?3
A(3,2) = ?12
A(3,3) = ?9

ENTER THE ELEMENTS OF ARRAY 'B'

B(1,1) = ?0
B(1,2) = ?0
B(1,3) = ?0

B(2,1) = ?2
B(2,2) = ?5
B(2,3) = ?8

B(3,1) = ?15
B(3,2) = ?21
B(3,3) = ?6

THE ANSWER IS:

     23   41   38
   13.2   33   52.8
    159   249   150
```
```

4.3 TRANSPOSITION OF TWO-DIMENSIONAL MATRICES

Sometimes it is necessary to exchange the rows and the columns of a matrix. This operation is known as *transposition*.

To perform the transposition, the program sets the elements of the original array A(I,J) equal to B(J,I), which is the transposed array. This is done in line 18Ø.

```
0    CALL  - 936
1    PRINT : PRINT : PRINT "WRITTEN BY JULES H. GILDER"
2    PRINT : PRINT "COPYRIGHT (C)  HAYDEN BOOK COMPANY 1978"
3    FOR X = 1 TO 4000: NEXT X
5    PRINT : PRINT : PRINT : PRINT
6    PRINT  TAB( 9)"2-D MATRIX TRANSPOSITION"
7    PRINT : PRINT : PRINT
10   PRINT "THIS PROGRAM TRANSPOSES A 2-DIMENSIONAL"
20   PRINT "MATRIX."
30   PRINT
40   INPUT "ENTER SIZE OF MATRIX: ";N
45   DIM A(N,N),B(N,N)
50   PRINT : PRINT
55   IF N = 0 THEN 330
70   PRINT "ENTER MATRIX ELEMENTS"
80   PRINT
90   FOR  I = 1  TO  N
100   FOR  J = 1  TO  N
110   PRINT "A(";I;",";J;") = ";
120   INPUT  A(I,J)
130   NEXT  J
135   PRINT
140   NEXT  I
150   PRINT
160   FOR  I = 1  TO  N
170   FOR  J = 1  TO  N
180  B(J,I) = A(I,J)
190   NEXT  J
200   NEXT  I
210   PRINT : PRINT : PRINT : PRINT
220   PRINT "THE TRANSPOSED MATRIX IS:"
230   PRINT : PRINT : PRINT : PRINT
250   FOR  I = 1  TO  N
260   FOR  J = 1  TO  N
270  Z =  LEN ( STR$ (B(I,J)))
290   PRINT  TAB( 8 * J - Z);B(I,J);
300   NEXT J
310   PRINT : PRINT
320   NEXT I
330   END
```

2-D MATRIX TRANSPOSITION

THIS PROGRAM TRANSPOSES A 2-DIMENSIONAL
MATRIX.

ENTER SIZE OF MATRIX: 4

ENTER MATRIX ELEMENTS

A(1,1) = ?1
A(1,2) = ?2.3
A(1,3) = ?6
A(1,4) = ?3

A(2,1) = ?1.1
A(2,2) = ?3.3
A(2,3) = ?6
A(2,4) = ?12

A(3,1) = ?3
A(3,2) = ?3
A(3,3) = ?2
A(3,4) = ?1

A(4,1) = ?0
A(4,2) = ?6
A(4,3) = ?4
A(4,4) = ?1

THE TRANSPOSED MATRIX IS:

1	1.1	3	0
2.3	3.3	3	6
6	6	2	4
3	12	1	1

4.4 SCALAR MULTIPLICATION OF A TWO-DIMENSIONAL MATRIX

The multiplication of a matrix by an ordinary number (not another matrix) is called *scalar multiplication*.

Scalar multiplication is accomplished by multiplying each element of the matrix by the scalar number.

```
0   CALL  - 936
1   PRINT : PRINT : PRINT : PRINT "WRITTEN BY JULES H. GILDER"
2   PRINT : PRINT "COPYRIGHT (C) HAYDEN BOOK CO. 1978"
3   FOR X = 1 TO 4000: NEXT X
4   PRINT : PRINT : PRINT : PRINT
5   PRINT  TAB( 4)"2D MATRIX SCALAR MULTIPLICATION"
6   PRINT : PRINT : PRINT : PRINT
10   PRINT "THIS PROGRAM MULTIPLIES A MATRIX BY A"
20   PRINT "SCALAR VALUE."
30   PRINT : INPUT "ENTER THE SIZE OF THE MATRIX: ";N
35   IF N = 0 THEN 330
40   DIM A(N,N),B(N,N)
45   PRINT : INPUT "ENTER THE SCALAR VALUE: ";X
50   PRINT
60   PRINT
70   PRINT "ENTER THE MATRIX ELEMENTS:"
80   PRINT
90   FOR  I = 1  TO  N
100   FOR  J = 1  TO  N
110   PRINT "A(";I;",";J;") = ";
120   INPUT  A(I,J)
130   NEXT  J
135   PRINT
140   NEXT  I
150   PRINT
245   PRINT : PRINT : PRINT : PRINT : PRINT "THE ANSWER IS:"
247   PRINT : PRINT : PRINT : PRINT
250   FOR  I = 1  TO  N
260   FOR  J = 1  TO  N
280  B(I,J) = A(I,J) * X
285  B(I,J) =  INT (100 * B(I,J) + .5) / 100
295  Z =  LEN ( STR$ (B(I,J)))
300   PRINT  TAB( 8 * J - Z);B(I,J);
310   NEXT  J
315   PRINT : PRINT
320   NEXT I
330   END
```

2D MATRIX SCALAR MULTIPLICATION

THIS PROGRAM MULTIPLIES A MATRIX BY A
SCALAR VALUE.

ENTER THE SIZE OF THE MATRIX: 3

ENTER THE SCALAR VALUE: 3

ENTER THE MATRIX ELEMENTS:

A(1,1) = ?0
A(1,2) = ?1
A(1,3) = ?1

A(2,1) = ?3
A(2,2) = ?12
A(2,3) = ?34

A(3,1) = ?7
A(3,2) = ?17
A(3,3) = ?2

THE ANSWER IS:

0	3	3
9	36	102
21	51	6

4.5 MATRIX INVERSION

Division of matrices is not possible. Instead, another operation, which essentially accomplishes the same thing, is performed. To divide one matrix by another, one of the matrices is first inverted and then multiplied by the other. This is similar to the algebraic operation of taking the reciprocal of a number and multiplying it by another number to perform the equivalent of division.

Not all matrices can be inverted. Some of them have a determinant that is equal to zero. These matrices cannot be inverted and are known as singular matrices. If a matrix is multiplied by its inverse, it will result in a unit matrix, that is, a matrix in which all the elements of the diagonal are equal to one and all other elements are equal to zero.

```
0   CALL  - 936
10   PRINT : PRINT : PRINT : PRINT "WRITTEN BY JULES H. GILDER"
20   PRINT : PRINT "COPYRIGHT (C) HAYDEN BOOK CO. 1978"
30   FOR X = 1 TO 4000: NEXT X
40   PRINT : PRINT : PRINT : PRINT
50   PRINT  TAB( 12)"MATRIX INVERSION"
60   PRINT : PRINT : PRINT : PRINT
70   INPUT "ENTER MATRIX SIZE: ";X
80   DIM A(X,X),B(X,X)
90   PRINT : PRINT
100   PRINT "ENTER MATRIX ELEMENTS"
110   PRINT : PRINT
120   FOR I = 1 TO X
130   FOR J = 1 TO X
140   PRINT "A(";I;",";J;") = ";
150   INPUT "";A(I,J)
160   NEXT J
170   PRINT
180  B(I,I) = 1
190   NEXT I
200   FOR J = 1 TO X
210   FOR I = J TO X
220   IF A(I,J) < > 0 THEN 250
230   NEXT I
240   PRINT : PRINT "THE MATRIX IS SINGULAR": END
250   FOR H = 1 TO X
260  T = A(J,H)
270  A(J,H) = A(I,H)
280  A(I,H) = T
290  M = B(J,H)
300  B(J,H) = B(I,H)
310  B(I,H) = M
320   NEXT H
330  D = A(J,J)
340   FOR H = 1 TO X
350  A(J,H) = A(J,H) / D
360  B(J,H) = B(J,H) / D
370   NEXT H
380   FOR H = 1 TO X
390   IF J = H THEN 450
400  D = A(H,J)
410   FOR K = 1 TO X
```

```
420 A(H,K) = A(H,K) - A(J,K) * D
430 B(H,K) = B(H,K) - B(J,K) * D
440  NEXT K
450  NEXT H
460  NEXT J
470  PRINT : PRINT : PRINT
480  PRINT "THE INVERTED MATRIX IS:"
490  PRINT : PRINT : PRINT
500  FOR I = 1 TO X
510  FOR J = 1 TO X
520 B(I,J) =   INT (B(I,J) * 100 + .5) / 100
525 Z =  LEN ( STR$ (B(I,J)))
530  PRINT  TAB( 8 * J - Z);B(I,J);
540  NEXT J
550  PRINT : PRINT
560  NEXT I
570  END
```

```
          MATRIX INVERSION


ENTER MATRIX SIZE: 3

ENTER MATRIX ELEMENTS

A(1,1) = 0
A(1,2) = .2
A(1,3) = -1

A(2,1) = 4
A(2,2) = -.125
A(2,3) = 3

A(3,1) = 0
A(3,2) = 10
A(3,3) = 2


THE INVERTED MATRIX IS:

   .73      .25     -.01

   .19        0      .1

  -.96        0      .02
```

4.6 ADDITION AND SUBTRACTION OF THREE-DIMENSIONAL MATRICES

BASICS that do permit matrix mathematics to be performed are limited to two-dimensional matrices. This program offers the capability of adding or subtracting two three-dimensional matrices.

Aside from the fact that an extra FOR ... NEXT loop is used, the program is quite similar to the two-dimensional addition/subtraction program.

When working with three-dimensional matrices, be aware that the matrix size is much more limited than with two-dimensional matrices. This is because more memory is needed for a three-dimensional matrix. A 10-by-10 matrix requires only 100 places set aside for numbers; a 10-by-10-by-10 matrix needs 1000 places. If large three-dimensional matrices are used, therefore, a memory problem may be encountered.

```
0    CALL  - 936
1    PRINT : PRINT : PRINT : PRINT "WRITTEN BY JULES H. GILDER"
2    PRINT : PRINT "COPYRIGHT (C)  HAYDEN BOOK CO. 1978"
3    FOR X = 1 TO 4000: NEXT X
5    PRINT : PRINT : PRINT : PRINT
6    PRINT  TAB( 3)"3D MATRIX ADDITION AND SUBTRACTION"
7    PRINT : PRINT : PRINT : PRINT
10   PRINT "THIS PROGRAM ADDS AND SUBTRACTS TWO"
20   PRINT "3-DIMENSIONAL MATRICES."
30   PRINT
40   INPUT " ENTER SIZE OF MATRICES: ";N
45   DIM  A(N,N,N),B(N,N,N),C(N,N,N)
50   PRINT : INPUT "ADDITION OR SUBTRACTION? ";Z$
60   PRINT
70   PRINT "ENTER THE ELEMENTS OF ARRAY 'A'"
80   PRINT
85 S = 1
90   FOR  I = 1  TO  N
100  FOR  J = 1  TO  N
105  FOR  K = 1  TO  N
110  PRINT "A(";I;",";J;",";K;") = ";
120  INPUT  A(I,J,K)
125  NEXT  K
127  PRINT
130  NEXT  J
135  PRINT
140  NEXT  I
150  PRINT
160  PRINT "ENTER THE ELEMENTS OF ARRAY 'B'"
170  PRINT
180  FOR  I = 1  TO  N
185  FOR  J = 1  TO  N
190  FOR  K = 1  TO  N
200  PRINT "B(";I;",";J;",";K;") = ";
210  INPUT  B(I,J,K)
220 C(I,J,K) = 0
225  NEXT  K
227  PRINT
230  NEXT  J
235  PRINT
240  NEXT  I
```

```
242  PRINT : PRINT : PRINT : PRINT
245  PRINT "THE ANSWER IS:"
246  PRINT : PRINT : PRINT : PRINT
248  IF  LEFT$ (Z$,1) = "S" THEN S =  - 1
250  FOR  I = 1  TO  N
260  FOR  J = 1  TO  N
270  FOR  K = 1  TO  N
275  C(I,J,K) =  INT (100 * (A(I,J,K) + S * B(I,J,K)) + .5) / 100
280  Z =  LEN ( STR$ (C(I,J,K)))
290  PRINT  TAB( 8 * K - Z);C(I,J,K);
300  NEXT  K
305  PRINT : PRINT
310  NEXT  J
315  PRINT : PRINT : PRINT
320  NEXT I
325  PRINT
350  END
```

3D MATRIX ADDITION AND SUBTRACTION

THIS PROGRAM ADDS AND SUBTRACTS TWO
3-DIMENSIONAL MATRICES.

 ENTER SIZE OF MATRICES: 2

ADDITION OR SUBTRACTION? SUBTRACTION

ENTER THE ELEMENTS OF ARRAY 'A'

A(1,1,1) = ?34
A(1,1,2) = ?65

A(1,2,1) = ?12
A(1,2,2) = ?38

A(2,1,1) = ?72
A(2,1,2) = ?42

A(2,2,1) = ?10
A(2,2,2) = ?91

ENTER THE ELEMENTS OF ARRAY 'B'

B(1,1,1) = ?18
B(1,1,2) = ?33

B(1,2,1) = ?54
B(1,2,2) = ?58

B(2,1,1) = ?90
B(2,1,2) = ?7

B(2,2,1) = ?15
B(2,2,2) = ?23

THE ANSWER IS:

     16   32
    -42   -20

    -18   35
     -5   68
```
```

4.7 MULTIPLICATION OF THREE-DIMENSIONAL MATRICES

This program is very similar to its two-dimensional counterpart. The major difference between the two is the addition of an extra FOR . . . NEXT loop in the input and output statements. Again, rounding off to two decimal places is performed.

```
0    CALL  - 936
1    PRINT : PRINT : PRINT : PRINT "WRITTEN BY JULES H. GILDER"
2    PRINT : PRINT "COPYRIGHT (C)  HAYDEN BOOK CO. 1978"
3    FOR X = 1 TO 4000: NEXT X
5    PRINT : PRINT : PRINT : PRINT
6.   PRINT  TAB( 8)"3-D MATRIX MULITPLICATION"
7    PRINT : PRINT : PRINT : PRINT
10   PRINT "THIS PROGRAM MULTIPLIES TWO 3-DIMEN-"
20   PRINT "SIONAL MATRICES ELEMENT-BY-ELEMENT."
30   PRINT
40   INPUT "ENTER SIZE OF MATRICES: ";N
45   DIM  A(N,N,N),B(N,N,N),C(N,N,N)
50   PRINT
60   PRINT
70   PRINT "ENTER THE ELEMENTS OF ARRAY 'A'"
80   PRINT
90   FOR  I = 1  TO  N
100  FOR  J = 1  TO  N
105  FOR  K = 1  TO  N
110  PRINT "A(";I;",";J;",";K;") = ";
120  INPUT  A(I,J,K)
125  NEXT  K
127  PRINT
130  NEXT  J
135  PRINT
140  NEXT  I
150  PRINT
160  PRINT "ENTER THE ELEMENTS OF ARRAY 'B'"
170  PRINT
180  FOR  I = 1  TO  N
185  FOR  J = 1  TO  N
190  FOR  K = 1  TO  N
200  PRINT "B(";I;",";J;",";K;") = ";
210  INPUT  B(I,J,K)
220  C(I,J,K) = 0
225  NEXT  K
227  PRINT
230  NEXT  J
235  PRINT
240  NEXT  I
242  PRINT : PRINT : PRINT : PRINT
244  PRINT "THE ANSWER IS:"
245  PRINT : PRINT
246  PRINT : PRINT : PRINT : PRINT
250  FOR  I = 1  TO  N
260  FOR  J = 1  TO  N
270  FOR  K = 1  TO  N
280  C(I,J,K) =  INT (100 * A(I,J,K) * B(I,J,K) + .5) / 100
```

```
290    PRINT  TAB( 8 * K - Z);C(I,J,K);
300    NEXT  K
305    PRINT : PRINT
310    NEXT  J
315    PRINT : PRINT : PRINT
320    NEXT  I
325    PRINT
350    END
```

             3-D MATRIX MULITPLICATION

THIS PROGRAM MULTIPLIES TWO 3-DIMEN-
SIONAL MATRICES ELEMENT-BY-ELEMENT.

ENTER SIZE OF MATRICES: 3

ENTER THE ELEMENTS OF ARRAY 'A'

A(1,1,1) = ?1
A(1,1,2) = ?2
A(1,1,3) = ?3

A(1,2,1) = ?4
A(1,2,2) = ?5
A(1,2,3) = ?6

A(1,3,1) = ?7
A(1,3,2) = ?8
A(1,3,3) = ?9

A(2,1,1) = ?0
A(2,1,2) = ?12
A(2,1,3) = ?13

A(2,2,1) = ?14
A(2,2,2) = ?115
A(2,2,3) = ?213

A(2,3,1) = ?312
A(2,3,2) = ?56
A(2,3,3) = ?78

A(3,1,1) = ?21
A(3,1,2) = ?43
A(3,1,3) = ?55

A(3,2,1) = ?6
A(3,2,2) = ?4
A(3,2,3) = ?3

A(3,3,1) = ?7
A(3,3,2) = ?0
A(3,3,3) = ?0

ENTER THE ELEMENTS OF ARRAY 'B'

B(1,1,1) = ?0
B(1,1,2) = ?0
B(1,1,3) = ?0

B(1,2,1) = ?3
B(1,2,2) = ?1
B(1,2,3) = ?5

B(1,3,1) = ?7
B(1,3,2) = ?8
B(1,3,3) = ?3

B(2,1,1) = ?5
B(2,1,2) = ?1
B(2,1,3) = ?1

B(2,2,1) = ?2
B(2,2,2) = ?8
B(2,2,3) = ?0

```
B(2,3,1) = ?3
B(2,3,2) = ?6
B(2,3,3) = ?8

B(3,1,1) = ?3
B(3,1,2) = ?1
B(3,1,3) = ?1

B(3,2,1) = ?0
B(3,2,2) = ?5
B(3,2,3) = ?3

B(3,3,1) = ?2
B(3,3,2) = ?4
B(3,3,3) = ?8
```

THE ANSWER IS:

```
 0        0        0
 12       5        30
 49       64       27


 0        12       13
 28       920      0
 936      336      624


 63       43       55
 0        20       9
 14       0        0
```

4.8 SCALAR MULTIPLICATION OF THREE-DIMENSIONAL MATRICES

With this program, a three-dimensional matrix can be multiplied by a scalar value. The program, like the other programs performing three-dimensional mathematics, is very similar to its two-dimensional counterpart.

```
0    CALL  - 936
1    PRINT : PRINT : PRINT : PRINT "WRITTEN BY JULES H. GILDER"
2    PRINT : PRINT "COPYRIGHT (C)  HAYDEN BOOK CO. 1978"
3    FOR X = 1 TO 4000: NEXT X
5    PRINT : PRINT : PRINT : PRINT
6    PRINT  TAB( 6)"3-D MATRIX SCALAR MULTIPLICATION"
7    PRINT : PRINT : PRINT : PRINT
10   PRINT "THIS PROGRAM MULTIPLIES A 3-DIMENSIONAL"
20   PRINT "MATRIX BY A SCALING FACTOR."
30   PRINT
40   INPUT "ENTER SIZE OF MATRIX: ";N
42   IF N = 0 THEN 310
45   DIM A(N,N,N),B(N,N,N)
50   PRINT : PRINT
55   INPUT "ENTER SCALING FACTOR ";X
60   PRINT : PRINT
70   PRINT "ENTER THE ELEMENTS OF ARRAY 'A' "
80   PRINT
90   FOR  I = 1  TO  N
100  FOR  J = 1  TO  N
105  FOR  K = 1  TO  N
110  PRINT "A(";I;",";J;",";K;") = ";
120  INPUT  A(I,J,K)
125  NEXT  K
127  PRINT
130  NEXT  J
135  PRINT
140  NEXT  I
150  PRINT
160  PRINT : PRINT : PRINT : PRINT
170  PRINT "THE ANSWER IS:"
180  PRINT : PRINT : PRINT : PRINT
190  FOR I = 1 TO N
200  FOR J = 1 TO N
210  FOR K = 1 TO N
220 B(I,J,K) = A(I,J,K) * X
230 B(I,J,K) =  INT (100 * B(I,J,K) + .5) / 100
240 Z =  LEN ( STR$ (B(I,J,K)))
250  PRINT  TAB( 8 * K - Z);B(I,J,K);
260  NEXT K
270  PRINT : PRINT
280  NEXT J
290  PRINT : PRINT : PRINT
300  NEXT I
310  END
```

THIS PROGRAM MULTIPLIES A 3-DIMENSIONAL
MATRIX BY A SCALING FACTOR.

ENTER SIZE OF MATRIX: 2

ENTER SCALING FACTOR 3.3

ENTER THE ELEMENTS OF ARRAY 'A'
A(1,1,1) = ?10
A(1,1,2) = ?32

A(1,2,1) = ?4
A(1,2,2) = ?19

A(2,1,1) = ?73
A(2,1,2) = ?0

A(2,2,1) = ?1
A(2,2,2) = ?37

THE ANSWER IS:

```
      33    105.6
    13.2     62.7


   240.9        0
     3.3    122.1
```

5 Data Analysis

The programs in this chapter are designed to make the interpretation of experimental data easy. The first three programs require the input of a set of data, which then results in the calculation of either the geometric mean, average and median, or variance and standard deviation.

The next two programs allow you to enter several data points and interpolate for a value between them. They do this by forming the second or third order La Grange polynomial that represents the given data.

The last four programs in this section are curve-fitting programs. From the input, the programs try to form the equation that best fits the data. The four programs try to fit four different types of equations. Once the equation is formed, it is printed. Then the program permits interpolation of data. In addition to printing the equation, the program also prints the sum of the deviations squared. This value is a measure of how well the equations fit. The smaller its value, the better the fit. A value of zero indicates a very good fit, but not necessarily perfect. The value in the output is rounded off to three decimal places.

5.1 GEOMETRIC MEAN

Mathematically, the geometric mean is the Nth root of the product of N numbers. In other words, the geometric mean is the second term of three consecutive terms in a geometric progression. Thus, for the progression 2, 4, 8, the geometric mean is 4 because it is the middle term; and 2*4*8 = 64, whose third root is also 4.

In order to set up a loop to read the input numbers, the user must first specify the quantity of numbers to be entered. The mean is calculated in lines 120 and 140. Rounding off to two places is done in line 145.

```
0   CALL  - 936
1   PRINT : PRINT : PRINT : PRINT "WRITTEN BY JULES H. GILDER"
2   PRINT : PRINT "COPYRIGHT (C)  HAYDEN BOOK CO. 1978"
3   FOR X = 1 TO 4000: NEXT X
10   PRINT : PRINT : PRINT : PRINT
20   PRINT "              GEOMETRIC MEAN"
30   PRINT : PRINT : PRINT : PRINT
40   PRINT "THIS PROGRAM WILL COMPUTE THE GEOMETRIC"
50   PRINT "MEAN OF A SET OF DATA.  YOU MUST ENTER"
60   PRINT "THE NUMBER OF POINTS AND THEIR VALUE"
70   PRINT : PRINT : PRINT
80   INPUT "HOW MANY DATA POINTS? ";N
82   PRINT
84   DIM P(N)
85 M = 1
90   FOR  X = 1  TO  N
100   PRINT "ENTER POINT ";X;" ";
110   INPUT  P(X)
120 M = M * P(X)
130   NEXT  X
140 MM = M ↑ ( 1 / N )
145 MM =  INT ( 100 * MM + .5) / 100
150   PRINT : PRINT : PRINT
160   PRINT "THE DATA ARE:"
170   PRINT
180   FOR  X = 1  TO  N
190   PRINT P(X)
200   NEXT  X
210   PRINT : PRINT
220   PRINT "THE GEOMETRIC MEAN IS ";MM
230   END
```

GEOMETRIC MEAN

THIS PROGRAM WILL COMPUTE THE GEOMETRIC
MEAN OF A SET OF DATA.   YOU MUST ENTER
THE NUMBER OF POINTS AND THEIR VALUE

HOW MANY DATA POINTS? 5

ENTER POINT 1 ?75
ENTER POINT 2 ?68
ENTER POINT 3 ?97
ENTER POINT 4 ?55
ENTER POINT 5 ?30

THE DATA ARE:

75
68
97
55
30

THE GEOMETRIC MEAN IS 60.59

5.2 AVERAGE AND MEDIAN CALCULATOR

In the analysis of data, two of the most elementary operations performed are averaging and determination of the median. Averaging is a simple operation. It entails the summing of all data points and the division of this sum by the number of points.

Finding the median is a little more difficult. By definition, the median is the value of the data point, in an ordered set of data, below and above which there is an equal number of data points. If there is no middle number, which occurs when there is an even number of data points, the median is calculated as the arithmetic mean of the two middle values.

In order to find the median, it is first necessary to order (or sort) the data. The sorting function has a long history, and there are countless subroutines for it. The one used here is fairly fast and memory efficient. The sorting takes place from lines 170 to 270. After the data is sorted, a test is made in lines 300 to 310 to determine if the number of data points is even. If it is, the program branches to line 350, where the average of the two middle data points is calculated as the median. If not, the middle data point is chosen.

An advantage of the program, resulting from the median calculation, is the outputting of data in ordered form, highest value first.

```
0    CALL  - 936
1    PRINT : PRINT : PRINT : PRINT "WRITTEN BY JULES H. GILDER"
2    PRINT : PRINT "COPYRIGHT (C) HAYDEN BOOK CO. 1978"
3    FOR X = 1 TO 4000: NEXT X
4    PRINT : PRINT : PRINT : PRINT
5    PRINT  TAB( 5)"AVERAGE AND MEDIAN CALCULATOR"
10   PRINT : PRINT : PRINT : PRINT
40   PRINT "THIS PROGRAM CALCULATES THE AVERAGE"
50   PRINT "AND MEDIAN OF A SET OF DATA."
60   PRINT : PRINT
70   INPUT "HOW MANY DATA POINTS? ";N
80   PRINT
90   DIM  A(N)
100  NM = N - 1
110   PRINT "ENTER DATA:"
120   PRINT
130   FOR  I = 1  TO  N
140   PRINT "A";I;" = ";
150   INPUT  A(I)
160   NEXT  I
170   FOR  I = 1  TO  NM
180  IP = I + 1
190  M = I
200   FOR  J = IP  TO  N
210   IF  A(M) = > A(J)  THEN  230
220  M = J
230   NEXT  J
240  T = A(I)
250  A(I) = A(M)
260  A(M) = T
270   NEXT  I
```

```
280 D = N / 2
290 ID =  INT (D)
300  IF  D = ID  THEN  350
310  IF  D < ID  THEN  340
320 MED = A(ID + 1)
330  GOTO  360
340 MED = A(ID)
345  GOTO  360
350 MED = (A(ID) + A(ID + 1)) / 2
360 SUM = 0
370  FOR  I = 1  TO  N
380 SUM = SUM + A(I)
390  NEXT  I
400 AVG = SUM / N
410  PRINT
420  PRINT "AVERAGE = ";AVG;"    MEDIAN = ";MED
430  PRINT
440  PRINT "THE DATA IN DESCENDING ORDER ARE:"
450  PRINT
460  FOR  I = 1  TO  N
470  PRINT A(I)
480  NEXT  I
490  END
```

```
     AVERAGE AND MEDIAN CALCULATOR


THIS PROGRAM CALCULATES THE AVERAGE
AND MEDIAN OF A SET OF DATA.

HOW MANY DATA POINTS? 5

ENTER DATA:

A1 = ?75
A2 = ?68
A3 = ?97
A4 = ?55
A5 = ?30

AVERAGE = 65     MEDIAN = 68

THE DATA IN DESCENDING ORDER ARE:

97
75
68
55
30
```

5.3 VARIANCE AND STANDARD DEVIATION CALCULATION

The standard deviation is a measure of dispersion of a set of data. Mathematically, it is the square root of the arithmetic mean of the squares of the deviation of each data point from the average of the data set.

The variance of a set of data is simply the standard deviation squared. If all data points are close to the mean, the variance (and standard deviation) will be small. If the values are distributed far from the mean, the variance will be large.

Since the average (mean) must be calculated to find the variance and standard deviation, its value is also printed.

```
0   CALL  - 936
1   PRINT : PRINT : PRINT : PRINT "WRITTEN BY JULES H. GILDER"
2   PRINT : PRINT "COPYRIGHT (C) HAYDEN BOOK CO. 1978"
3   FOR X = 1 TO 4000: NEXT X
4   PRINT : PRINT : PRINT : PRINT
5   PRINT  TAB( 4)"VARIANCE AND STANDARD DEVIATION"
10  PRINT : PRINT : PRINT
40  PRINT "THIS PROGRAM CALCULATES THE VARIANCE"
50  PRINT "AND STANDARD DEVIATION OF A SET OF DATA"
60  PRINT
70  INPUT "HOW MANY DATA POINTS? ";N
80  PRINT : PRINT
90  DIM  A(N)
110  PRINT "ENTER DATA:"
120  PRINT
125 SUM = 0
130  FOR  I = 1  TO  N
140  PRINT "A";I;" = ";
150  INPUT  A(I)
160 SUM = SUM + A(I)
170  NEXT  I
180 AVG = SUM / N
190 SQ = 0
200  FOR  I = 1  TO  N
210 D = A(I) - AVG
220 SQ = SQ + D ↑ 2
230  NEXT  I
240 VAR = SQ / (N - 1)
245 VAR =  INT (100 * VAR + .5) / 100
250 STD =  SQR (VAR)
255 STD =  INT (STD * 100 + .5) / 100
260  PRINT : PRINT : PRINT : PRINT
265  PRINT "AVERAGE = ";AVG
266  PRINT
270  PRINT "VARIANCE = ";VAR
275  PRINT
280  PRINT "STANDARD DEVIATION = ";STD
290  END
```

```
VARIANCE AND STANDARD DEVIATION


THIS PROGRAM CALCULATES THE VARIANCE
AND STANDARD DEVIATION OF A SET OF DATA

HOW MANY DATA POINTS? 5

ENTER DATA:

A1 = ?75
A2 = ?68
A3 = ?97
A4 = ?55
A5 = ?30



AVERAGE = 65

VARIANCE = 614.5

STANDARD DEVIATION = 24.79
```

5.4   THREE-POINT INTERPOLATION

Very often after experimental data is taken, it is necessary to extrapolate to a point not included in the original set. One way of doing this is to use three of the known data points to form a La Grange polynomial. This polynomial represents the second order equation defined by the three points. The technique is also known as quadratic interpolation.

The coefficients of the equation are calculated in lines 120 to 170. The actual interpolation of values takes place in line 190. Line 195 rounds off the answer to two decimal places.

```
0   CALL  - 936
1   PRINT : PRINT : PRINT : PRINT "WRITTEN BY JULES H. GILDER"
2   PRINT : PRINT "COPYRIGHT (C)  HAYDEN BOOK CO. 1978"
3   FOR X = 1 TO 4000: NEXT X
10   PRINT : PRINT : PRINT : PRINT
20   PRINT "       THREE-POINT INTERPOLATION"
30   PRINT : PRINT : PRINT : PRINT
40   PRINT "THIS PROGRAM FORMS A LA GRANGE POLYNO-"
50   PRINT "MIAL WHICH REPRESENTS THE 2 ND ORDER"
60   PRINT "EQUATION DEFINED BY THREE POINTS."
65   PRINT "IT IS USED TO INTERPOLATE VALUES OF Y "
66   PRINT "FOR GIVEN VALUES OF X."
70   PRINT : PRINT
80   INPUT "ENTER FIRST POINT (X,Y)  ";X0,Y0
90   PRINT : INPUT "ENTER SECOND POINT (X,Y)   ";X1,Y1
100   PRINT : INPUT "ENTER THIRD POINT (X,Y)  ";X2,Y2
110   PRINT : PRINT : PRINT
120   R0 = Y0 / ((X0 - X1) * (X0 - X2))
130   R1 = Y1 / ((X1 - X0) * (X1 - X2))
140   R2 = Y2 / ((X2 - X0) * (X2 - X1))
150   C0 = R0 * X1 * X2 + R1 * X0 * X2 + R2 * X0 * X1
160   C1 =  - R0 * (X1 + X2) - R1 * (X0 + X2) - R2 * (X0 + X1)
170   C2 = R0 + R1 + R2
180   INPUT "ENTER X  ";X
190   Y = C0 + C1 * X + C2 * X ↑ 2
195   Y =  INT (100 * Y + .5) / 100
200   PRINT : PRINT : PRINT
210   PRINT "AT X = ";X;"    Y = ";Y
220   PRINT : INPUT "ANOTHER POINT (Y/N)?  ";AA$
225   PRINT
230   IF AA$ = "Y" THEN 180
240   END
```

THREE-POINT INTERPOLATION

THIS PROGRAM FORMS A LA GRANGE POLYNO-
MIAL WHICH REPRESENTS THE 2 ND ORDER
EQUATION DEFINED BY THREE POINTS.
IT IS USED TO INTERPOLATE VALUES OF Y
FOR GIVEN VALUES OF X.

ENTER FIRST POINT (X,Y)   1,8

ENTER SECOND POINT (X,Y)   4,38

ENTER THIRD POINT (X,Y)   2,16

ENTER X   3

AT X = 3   Y = 26

ANOTHER POINT (Y/N)?   Y

ENTER X   7

AT X = 7   Y = 86

ANOTHER POINT (Y/N)?   N

5.5 FOUR-POINT INTERPOLATION

While the three-point interpolation technique in the previous program will suffice for most applications, for greater accuracy it is possible to use four points and form a polynomial of the third degree.

The coefficients for the third-degree equation are calculated in lines 12Ø to 175. Interpolation of values takes place on line 19Ø.

```
0    CALL  - 936
1    PRINT : PRINT : PRINT : PRINT "WRITTEN BY JULES H. GILDER"
2    PRINT : PRINT "COPYRIGHT (C)  HAYDEN BOOK CO. 1978"
3    FOR X = 1 TO 4000: NEXT X
10   PRINT : PRINT : PRINT : PRINT
20   PRINT "          FOUR-POINT INTERPOLATION"
30   PRINT : PRINT : PRINT : PRINT
40   PRINT "THIS PROGRAM FORMS A LA GRANGE POLYNO-"
50   PRINT "MIAL WHICH REPRESENTS THE 3 RD ORDER"
60   PRINT "EQUATION DEFINED BY FOUR POINTS."
65   PRINT "IT IS USED TO INTERPOLATE VALUES OF Y "
66   PRINT "FOR GIVEN VALUES OF X."
70   PRINT : PRINT
80   INPUT "ENTER FIRST POINT (X,Y)  ";X0,Y0
90   PRINT : INPUT "ENTER SECOND POINT (X,Y)  ";X1,Y1
100  PRINT : INPUT "ENTER THIRD POINT (X,Y)  ";X2,Y2
105  PRINT : INPUT "ENTER FOURTH POINT (X,Y)  ";X3,Y3
110  PRINT : PRINT : PRINT
120  R0 = Y0 / ((X0 - X1) * (X0 - X2) * (X0 - X3))
130  R1 = Y1 / ((X1 - X0) * (X1 - X2) * (X1 - X3))
140  R2 = Y2 / ((X2 - X0) * (X2 - X1) * (X2 - X3))
145  R3 = Y3 / ((X3 - X0) * (X3 - X1) * (X3 - X2))
150  C0 =  - R0 * X1 * X2 * X3 - R1 * X0 * X2 * X3
155  C0 = C0 - R2 * X0 * X1 * X3 - R3 * X0 * X1 * X2
160  C1 = R0 * (X1 * X2 + X1 * X3 + X2 * X3) + R1 * (X0 * X2 + X2 *
     X3 + X0 * X3)
165  CA = R2 * (X0 * X1 + X1 * X3 + X0 * X3)
167  CB = R3 * (X0 * X1 + X1 * X2 + X0 * X2)
168  C1 = C1 + CA + CB
170  C2 =  - R0 * (X1 + X2 + X3) - R1 * (X0 + X2 + X3)
172  C2 = C2 - R2 * (X0 + X1 + X3)
173  C2 = C2 - R3 * (X0 + X1 + X2)
175  C3 = R0 + R1 + R2 + R3
180  INPUT "ENTER X ";X
190  Y = C0 + C1 * X + C2 * X ↑ 2 + C3 * X ↑ 3
195  Y =  INT (100 * Y + .5) / 100
200  PRINT : PRINT : PRINT
210  PRINT "AT X = ";X;"   Y = ";Y
215  PRINT
220  INPUT "ANOTHER POINT (Y/N)?  ";AA$
230  PRINT
240  IF AA$ = "Y" THEN 180
250  END
```

FOUR-POINT INTERPOLATION

THIS PROGRAM FORMS A LA GRANGE POLYNO-
MIAL WHICH REPRESENTS THE 3 RD ORDER
EQUATION DEFINED BY FOUR POINTS.
IT IS USED TO INTERPOLATE VALUES OF Y
FOR GIVEN VALUES OF X.

ENTER FIRST POINT (X,Y)   3,47

ENTER SECOND POINT (X,Y)   0,5

ENTER THIRD POINT (X,Y)   2,19

ENTER FOURTH POINT (X,Y)   1,7

ENTER X 4

AT X = 4   Y = 97

ANOTHER POINT (Y/N)?   Y

ENTER X 10

AT X = 10   Y = 1195

ANOTHER POINT (Y/N)?   N

5.6 LINEAR LEAST SQUARES FIT

After collecting data points from an experiment, it is often desirable to try and find a relationship to define that set of data.

This program uses the least squares technique to fit data points to a linear line whose equation is

$$Y = MX + B$$

Constants M and B are both calculated by the program.

Although the program tries to find an equation to approximate closely the data described, it doesn't always do a good job. An indication of this is a parameter called the "sum of the deviations squared." The smaller this number is, the better the fit is, and vice versa.

If no equation can be found, the program prints out a message to that effect.

```
0   CALL  - 936
1   PRINT : PRINT : PRINT : PRINT "WRITTEN BY JULES H. GILDER"
2   PRINT : PRINT "COPYRIGHT (C) HAYDEN BOOK CO. 1978"
3   FOR X = 1 TO 4000: NEXT X
4   PRINT : PRINT : PRINT : PRINT
5   PRINT  TAB( 8)"LEAST SQUARES LINEAR FIT"
10   PRINT : PRINT : PRINT : PRINT
20   PRINT "THIS PROGRAM PERFORMS A LEAST-SQUARES"
30   PRINT "APPROXIMATION OF A LINEAR LINE. IT "
40   PRINT "ACCEPTS THE X & Y COORDINATES OF GIVEN"
50   PRINT "DATA POINTS AND TRIES TO PRODUCE A BEST"
60   PRINT "FIT LINE THAT REPRESENTS THE DATA. "
70   PRINT "THE EQUATION OF THE LINE IS:"
80   PRINT : PRINT "   Y = MX + B"
85   PRINT
90   PRINT "WHERE M AND B ARE CALCULATED BY THE"
100   PRINT "PROGRAM."
110   PRINT
120   INPUT "HOW MANY DATA POINTS? ";N
125   DIM  X(N),Y(N)
130   PRINT
140   PRINT "ENTER DATA"
145   PRINT
150   FOR  I = 1  TO  N
160   PRINT "X"; I" Y"; I;" ";
170   INPUT  X(I),Y(I)
180   NEXT  I
182 B$ = "-"
185   GOTO 230
190 X1 = 0
200 Y1 = 0
210 XY = 0
220 X2 = 0
230   FOR  I = 1  TO  N
240 X1 = X1 + X(I)
250 Y1 = Y1 + Y(I)
260 XY = XY + X(I) * Y(I)
270 X2 = X2 + X(I) * X(I)
275   NEXT  I
280 J = N * X2 - X1 * X1
290   IF  J < > 0  THEN  310
300   PRINT : PRINT "NO SOLUTION FOUND": END
310 M = (N * XY - X1 * Y1) / J
```

```
315 M =   INT (1E3 * M + .5) / 1E3
320 B = (Y1 * X2 - X1 * XY) / J
325  IF   ABS (B) = B  THEN  B$ = "+"
330 D = 0
335 B =   INT (1E3 * B + .5) / 1E3
340 D2 = 0
350  FOR  I = 1  TO  N
355 D = D + Y(I) - M * X(I) - B
360 D2 = D2 + (Y(I) - M * X(I) - B) ↑ 2
365 D2 =   INT (1E3 * D2 + .5) / 1E3
370  NEXT I
380  PRINT
390  PRINT "THE LINEAR EQUATION THAT BEST FITS THE"
400  PRINT "GIVEN DATA IS:"
410  PRINT : PRINT "     Y = ";M;" X "B$; ABS (B)
420  PRINT : PRINT "FOR THIS EQUATION THE SUM OF DEVIATIONS"
430  PRINT "SQUARED IS ";D2
440  PRINT : PRINT
450  INPUT "DO YOU WANT TO INTERPOLATE DATA? ";A$
460  IF   LEFT$ (A$,1) = "N"  THEN  510
470  PRINT : INPUT "ENTER X: ";X
475  PRINT : PRINT
480 Y = M * X + B
490  PRINT "Y = ";Y
500  GOTO  440
510  END
```

LEAST SQUARES LINEAR FIT

THIS PROGRAM PERFORMS A LEAST-SQUARES
APPROXIMATION OF A LINEAR LINE. IT
ACCEPTS THE X & Y COORDINATES OF GIVEN
DATA POINTS AND TRIES TO PRODUCE A BEST
FIT LINE THAT REPRESENTS THE DATA.
THE EQUATION OF THE LINE IS:

     Y = MX + B

WHERE M AND B ARE CALCULATED BY THE
PROGRAM.

HOW MANY DATA POINTS? 3

ENTER DATA

X1 Y1 ?0,3
X2 Y2 ?10,53
X3 Y3 ?3,18

THE LINEAR EQUATION THAT BEST FITS THE
GIVEN DATA IS:

     Y = 5 X +3

FOR THIS EQUATION THE SUM OF DEVIATIONS
SQUARED IS 0

DO YOU WANT TO INTERPOLATE DATA? Y

ENTER X: 2

Y = 13

DO YOU WANT TO INTERPOLATE DATA? N

5.7 LEAST SQUARES FIT—LOGARITHMIC ORDINATE

Like the previous program, this one tries to fit data to an equation. The equation used, however, is not linear. It is semilogarithmic. The abscissa is linear, but the ordinate is logarithmic. The equation used here is

$$Y = B*(10\uparrow M)\uparrow X$$

where once again B and M are calculated by the program.

Once the equation has been found, the program asks if data interpolation is desired and evaluates Y for any value of X if the answer is yes. If no solution is found, the program will tell you.

```
0    CALL  - 936
1    PRINT : PRINT : PRINT : PRINT "WRITTEN BY JULES H. GILDER"
2    PRINT : PRINT "COPYRIGHT (C) HAYDEN BOOK CO. 1978"
3    FOR X = 1 TO 4000: NEXT X
4    PRINT : PRINT : PRINT : PRINT
5    PRINT  TAB( 5)"LEAST SQUARES FIT LOG ORDINATE"
10   PRINT : PRINT : PRINT : PRINT
20   PRINT "THIS PROGRAM PERFORMS A LEAST-SQUARES"
30   PRINT "APROXIMATION OF A SEMI-LOGARITHMIC LINE"
32   PRINT "THE ABSCISSA IS LINEAR AND THE ORDINATE"
34   PRINT "IS LOGARITHMIC. THIS PROGRAM"
40   PRINT "ACCEPTS THE X & Y COORDINATES OF GIVEN"
50   PRINT "DATA POINTS AND TRIES TO PRODUCE A BEST"
60   PRINT "FIT LINE THAT REPRESENTS THE DATA. "
70   PRINT "THE EQUATION OF THE LINE IS:"
80   PRINT : PRINT "    Y=B*(10↑M)↑X"
85   PRINT
90   PRINT "WHERE M AND B ARE CALCULATED BY THE"
100   PRINT "PROGRAM."
110   PRINT
120   INPUT "HOW MANY DATA POINTS? ";N
125   DIM  X(N),Y(N)
130   PRINT
140   PRINT "ENTER DATA"
145   PRINT
150   FOR  I = 1  TO  N
160   PRINT "X";I" Y";I;" ";
170   INPUT  X(I),Y(I)
180   NEXT  I
182 B$ = "-"
190 X1 = 0
200 Y1 = 0
210 XY = 0
220 X2 = 0
230   FOR  I = 1  TO  N
240 LY =  LOG (Y(I)) /  LOG (10)
250 X1 = X1 + X(I)
260 Y1 = Y1 + LY
265 XY = XY + X(I) * LY
270 X2 = X2 + X(I) * X(I)
275  NEXT  I
280 J = N * X2 - X1 * X1
290   IF  J < > 0  THEN  310
```

```
300  PRINT : PRINT "NO SOLUTION FOUND": END
310  M = (N * XY - X1 * Y1) / J
315  M =  INT (1E3 * M + .5) / 1E3
320  LB = (Y1 * X2 - X1 * XY) / J
325  B = 10 ↑ LB
326  B =  INT (1E3 * B + .5) / 1E3
330  D = 0
340  D2 = 0
350  FOR I = 1 TO N
360  D2 = D2 +  LOG (Y(I)) / ( LOG (10) - M * X(I) - LB) ↑ 2
365  D2 =  INT (D2 * 1E3 + .5) / 1E3
370  NEXT I
380  PRINT
390  PRINT "THE EQUATION THAT BEST FITS THE"
400  PRINT "GIVEN DATA IS:"
410  PRINT : PRINT "Y = ";B;"*(10↑";M;")↑ X"
420  PRINT : PRINT "FOR THIS EQUATION THE SUM OF DEVIATIONS"
430  PRINT "SQUARED IS ";D2
440  PRINT : PRINT
450  INPUT "DO YOU WANT TO INTERPOLATE DATA? ";A$
460  IF  LEFT$ (A$,1) = "N"  THEN  510
470  PRINT : INPUT "ENTER X: ";X
475  PRINT : PRINT
480  Y = B * (10 ↑ M) ↑ X
485  Y =  INT (100 * Y + .5) / 100
490  PRINT "Y = ";Y
500  GOTO  440
510  END
```

LEAST SQUARES FIT LOG ORDINATE

THIS PROGRAM PERFORMS A LEAST-SQUARES
APROXIMATION OF A SEMI-LOGARITHMIC LINE
THE ABSCISSA IS LINEAR AND THE ORDINATE
IS LOGARITHMIC. THIS PROGRAM
ACCEPTS THE X & Y COORDINATES OF GIVEN
DATA POINTS AND TRIES TO PRODUCE A BEST
FIT LINE THAT REPRESENTS THE DATA.
THE EQUATION OF THE LINE IS:

     Y=B*(10↑M)↑X

WHERE M AND B ARE CALCULATED BY THE
PROGRAM.

HOW MANY DATA POINTS? 3

ENTER DATA

X1 Y1 ?3,95
X2 Y2 ?0,3
X3 Y3 ?2,30

THE EQUATION THAT BEST FITS THE
GIVEN DATA IS:

Y = 2.999*(10↑.5)↑ X

FOR THIS EQUATION THE SUM OF DEVIATIONS
SQUARED IS 48.289

DO YOU WANT TO INTERPOLATE DATA? Y

ENTER X: 1

Y = 9.48

DO YOU WANT TO INTERPOLATE DATA? N

5.8   LEAST SQUARES FIT—LOGARITHMIC ABSCISSA

This program also finds the least squares fit for a semilogarithmic plot, but this time the ordinate (Y) is linear and the abscissa (X) is logarithmic. The equation of the curve used here is:

$$Y = M*\log(X)/\log(1\emptyset) + B$$

As with the previous programs, if no fit for the data can be found, the program prints out a message to that effect.

```
0   CALL  - 936
1   PRINT : PRINT : PRINT : PRINT "WRITTEN BY JULES H. GILDER"
2   PRINT : PRINT "COPYRIGHT (C) HAYDEN BOOK CO. 1978"
3   FOR X = 1 TO 4000: NEXT X
4   PRINT : PRINT : PRINT : PRINT
5   PRINT  TAB( 5)"LEAST SQUARES FIT LOG ABSCISSA"
10   PRINT : PRINT : PRINT : PRINT
20   PRINT "THIS PROGRAM PERFORMS A LEAST-SQUARES"
30   PRINT "APROXIMATION OF A SEMI-LOGARITHMIC LINE"
32   PRINT "THE ORDINATE IS LINEAR AND THE ABSCISSA"
34   PRINT "IS LOGARITHMIC. THIS PROGRAM"
40   PRINT "ACCEPTS THE X & Y COORDINATES OF GIVEN"
50   PRINT "DATA POINTS AND TRIES TO PRODUCE A BEST"
60   PRINT "FIT LINE THAT REPRESENTS THE DATA. "
70   PRINT "THE EQUATION OF THE LINE IS:"
80   PRINT : PRINT "     Y=M*LOG(X)/LOG(10 )+B"
85   PRINT
90   PRINT "WHERE M AND B ARE CALCULATED BY THE"
100   PRINT "PROGRAM."
110   PRINT
120   INPUT "HOW MANY DATA POINTS? ";N
125   DIM  X( N),Y( N)
130   PRINT
140   PRINT "ENTER DATA"
145   PRINT
150   FOR  I = 1  TO  N
160   PRINT "X";I" Y";I;" ";
170   INPUT  X( I),Y( I)
180   NEXT  I
182 B$ = "-"
190 X1 = 0
200 Y1 = 0
210 XY = 0
220 X2 = 0
230   FOR  I = 1  TO  N
240 LX =  LOG (X( I)) /  LOG (10)
250 Y1 = Y1 + Y(I)
260 X1 = X1 + LX
265 XY = XY + Y(I) * LX
270 X2 = X2 + LX * LX
275   NEXT  I
280 J = N * X2 - X1 * X1
290   IF  J < > 0  THEN  310
300   PRINT : PRINT "NO SOLUTION FOUND": END
310 M = (N * XY - X1 * Y1) / J
315 M =   INT (M * 1E3 + .5) / 1E3
320 B = (Y1 * X2 - X1 * XY) / J
325   IF   ABS (B) = B  THEN  B$ = "+"
330 D = 0
335 B =   INT ( 1E3 * B + .5) / 1E3
340 D2 = 0
```

```
350  FOR  I = 1  TO  N
360  D2 = D2 + (Y(I) - M * LOG (X(I)) / LOG (10) - B) ↑ 2
365  D2 = INT (1E3 * D2 + .5) / 1E3
370  NEXT I
380  PRINT
390  PRINT "THE EQUATION THAT BEST FITS THE"
400  PRINT "GIVEN DATA IS:"
410  PRINT : PRINT "Y = ";M; "*LOG(X)/LOG(10) ";B$; ABS (B)
420  PRINT : PRINT "FOR THIS EQUATION THE SUM OF DEVIATIONS"
430  PRINT "SQUARED IS ";D2
440  PRINT : PRINT
450  INPUT "DO YOU WANT TO INTERPOLATE DATA? ";A$
460  IF   LEFT$ (A$,1) = "N"   THEN  510
470  PRINT : INPUT "ENTER X: ";X
475  PRINT : PRINT
480  Y = M * ( LOG (X) / LOG (10)) + B
490  PRINT "Y = ";Y
500  GOTO  440
510  END
```

        LEAST SQUARES FIT LOG ABSCISSA

THIS PROGRAM PERFORMS A LEAST-SQUARES
APROXIMATION OF A SEMI-LOGARITHMIC LINE
THE ORDINATE IS LINEAR AND THE ABSCISSA
IS LOGARITHMIC. THIS PROGRAM
ACCEPTS THE X & Y COORDINATES OF GIVEN
DATA POINTS AND TRIES TO PRODUCE A BEST
FIT LINE THAT REPRESENTS THE DATA.
THE EQUATION OF THE LINE IS:

    Y=M*LOG(X)/LOG(10)+B

WHERE M AND B ARE CALCULATED BY THE
PROGRAM.

HOW MANY DATA POINTS? 3

ENTER DATA

X1 Y1 ?2,6.72
X2 Y2 ?10,8.4
X3 Y3 ?75,10.5

THE EQUATION THAT BEST FITS THE
GIVEN DATA IS:

Y = 2.401*LOG(X)/LOG(10) +5.998

FOR THIS EQUATION THE SUM OF DEVIATIONS
SQUARED IS 0

DO YOU WANT TO INTERPOLATE DATA? YES

ENTER X: 1

Y = 5.998

DO YOU WANT TO INTERPOLATE DATA? YES

ENTER X: 25

Y = 9.35445396

DO YOU WANT TO INTERPOLATE DATA? NO

5.9 LEAST SQUARES FIT—FULL LOG

To complete the set of programs, this one calculates the least squares fit for data in a full log coordinate system (both the X and Y coordinates are logarithmic).

In this case, the equation of the curve is:

$$Y = B*X \uparrow M$$

Again, if no solution is found, this fact is indicated.

```
0    CALL  - 936
1    PRINT : PRINT : PRINT : PRINT "WRITTEN BY JULES H. GILDER"
2    PRINT : PRINT "COPYRIGHT (C) HAYDEN BOOK CO. 1978"
3    FOR X = 1 TO 4000: NEXT X
4    PRINT : PRINT : PRINT : PRINT
5    PRINT  TAB( 10 )"LEAST SQUARES FIT FULL LOG"
10   PRINT : PRINT : PRINT : PRINT
20   PRINT "THIS PROGRAM PERFORMS A LEAST-SQUARES"
30   PRINT "APPROXIMATION OF A LOGARITHMIC LINE. IT"
40   PRINT "ACCEPTS THE X & Y COORDINATES OF GIVEN"
50   PRINT "DATA POINTS AND TRIES TO PRODUCE A BEST"
60   PRINT "FIT LINE THAT REPRESENTS THE DATA. "
70   PRINT "THE EQUATION OF THE LINE IS:"
80   PRINT : PRINT "     Y=B*X↑M"
85   PRINT
90   PRINT "WHERE M AND B ARE CALCULATED BY THE"
100    PRINT "PROGRAM."
110    PRINT
120    INPUT "HOW MANY DATA POINTS? ";N
125    DIM  LX(N),LY(N),X(N),Y(N)
130    PRINT
140    PRINT "ENTER DATA"
145    PRINT
150    FOR I = 1  TO  N
160    PRINT "X";I" Y";I;" ";
170    INPUT  X( I ),Y( I )
180    NEXT  I
190  X1 = 0
200  Y1 = 0
210  XY = 0
220  X2 = 0
230    FOR I = 1  TO  N
240  LX( I ) =  LOG (X( I )) /  LOG (10)
245  LY( I ) =  LOG (Y( I )) /  LOG (10)
250  Y1 = Y1 + LY( I )
260  X1 = X1 + LX( I )
265  XY = XY + LX( I ) * LY( I )
270  X2 = X2 + LX( I ) * LX( I )
275  NEXT  I
280  J = N * X2 - X1 * X1
290    IF  J < > 0  THEN  310
300    PRINT : PRINT "NO SOLUTION FOUND"; END
310  M = ( N * XY - X1 * Y1 ) / J
315  M =  INT ( 1E3 * M + .5 ) / 1E3
320  LB = ( Y1 * X2 - X1 * XY ) / J
322  B = 10 ↑ LB
325  B =  INT ( 1E3 * B + .5 ) / 1E3
330  D = 0
```

```
340  D2 = 0
350  FOR  I = 1  TO  N
360  D2 = D2 + (LY(I) - M * LX(I) - LB) ↑ 2
365  D2 =  INT (1E3 * D2 + .5) / 1E3
370  NEXT I
380  PRINT
390  PRINT "THE EQUATION THAT BEST FITS THE"
400  PRINT "GIVEN DATA IS:"
410  PRINT : PRINT "Y = ";B; "*X↑";M
420  PRINT : PRINT "FOR THIS EQUATION THE SUM OF DEVIATIONS"
430  PRINT "SQUARED IS ";D2
440  PRINT : PRINT
450  INPUT "DO YOU WANT TO INTERPOLATE DATA? ";A$
460  IF  LEFT$ (A$,1) = "N"  THEN  510
470  PRINT : INPUT "ENTER X: ";X
475  PRINT : PRINT
480  Y = B * X ↑ M
485  Y =  INT (100 * Y + .5) / 100
490  PRINT "Y = ";Y
500  GOTO  440
510  END
```

LEAST SQUARES FIT FULL LOG

THIS PROGRAM PERFORMS A LEAST-SQUARES
APPROXIMATION OF A LOGARITHMIC LINE. IT
ACCEPTS THE X & Y COORDINATES OF GIVEN
DATA POINTS AND TRIES TO PRODUCE A BEST
FIT LINE THAT REPRESENTS THE DATA.
THE EQUATION OF THE LINE IS:

    Y=B*X↑M

WHERE M AND B ARE CALCULATED BY THE
PROGRAM.

HOW MANY DATA POINTS? 4

ENTER DATA

X1 Y1 ?1,.71
X2 Y2 ?2,3.5
X3 Y3 ?7,62.5
X4 Y4 ?10,142

THE EQUATION THAT BEST FITS THE
GIVEN DATA IS:

Y = .71*X↑2.301

FOR THIS EQUATION THE SUM OF DEVIATIONS
SQUARED IS 0

DO YOU WANT TO INTERPOLATE DATA? YES

ENTER X: 3

Y = 8.89

DO YOU WANT TO INTERPOLATE DATA? NO

Data Analysis   105

6 Basic Electricity

For those readers who are new to the field of electricity, the first program in this chapter will help to overcome the problem of interpreting the value of a resistor from its color coded bands. The information on the value of the resistor and its tolerance are coded in three or four different colored bands. By entering the color of each band in turn, the computer will calculate the value of the resistor and its tolerance.

The next program in this series calculates the value of any number of parallel resistors. Calculating the value of series resistors is easy—just add. For parallel resistors, however, the reciprocals of the values are added together, and this final value is converted to the total resistance by taking its reciprocal. This program can also be used for inductors since their values are calculated the same way. In addition, the program can be used to calculate the value of series capacitors.

When resistor values are calculated, they almost never turn out to be standard values that can be easily purchased. Program 6.3 converts calculated values to the nearest standard value. This program has been included as a subroutine in several programs in this book.

The next two programs (6.4 and 6.5) convert resistor circuits from one configuration to another. This comes in handy if the equivalent resistance of one of these configurations is desired.

Programs 6.6 through 6.8 come in handy when doing electrical wiring or designing power transformers. With these programs, the size of wire can be calculated from desired resistance and length or desired current carrying capacity. In addition, given a particular wire size and type of material, the resistance of the wire is calculated.

The final program calculates the ratio of turns of primary to secondary in a transformer, given the primary and secondary resistances.

6.1 RESISTOR COLOR CODE INTERPRETATION

This program is designed for the novice electronic hobbyist who is not yet familiar with the standard resistor color code. The colors for each of the three or four bands are entered into the computer (write out the whole word), and the program interprets the colors and calculates the resistance.

When the colors are entered, the string to which it is assigned is then compared with the colors listed in the data statements (lines 250 and 255). When a match is found, the position in the data list is noted, and this is used as a multiplier. Although there are ten values, it is essential that the variables be assigned from 0 to 9 and not from 1 to 10.

The list of colors is displayed with the program, and only these colors should be used. Nonetheless, many people have a tendency to use different forms of the word grey. To compensate, a check is made (lines 75 to 95) to see if the correct form is used. If not, the incorrect form is converted to the correct one.

The fourth band on the resistor is not always present. The first two color bands specify the most significant digits of the value. The third band is the decimal multiplier that is determined by raising 10 to the power of the value of the color. For example, since black = 0 and $10 \uparrow 0 = 1$, black has a multiplier value of 1.

The color values are as follows:

Black	0
Brown	1
Red	2
Orange	3
Yellow	4
Green	5
Blue	6
Purple	7
Grey	8
White	9

The fourth color band represents the tolerance of the resistor and is either gold for 5 percent, silver for 10 percent, or no color for 20 percent.

```
0   CALL  - 936
1   PRINT : PRINT : PRINT : PRINT "WRITTEN BY JULES H. GILDER"
2   PRINT : PRINT "COPYRIGHT (C) HAYDEN BOOK CO. 1978
3   FOR X = 1 TO 4000: NEXT X
4   PRINT : PRINT : PRINT
5   PRINT  TAB( 11 )"RESISTOR COLOR CODE"
10  PRINT : PRINT : PRINT
15  DIM E$( 10 )
20  PRINT "THIS PROGRAM INTERPRETS THE RESISTOR"
30  PRINT "COLOR CODE. YOU MUST ENTER THE COLOR"
40  PRINT "OF EACH BAND AND THE PROGRAM WILL TELL"
45  PRINT "YOU WHAT THE VALUE OF THE RESISTOR IS."
```

```
50    RESTORE
51    PRINT : PRINT "POSSIBLE COLORS ARE:": PRINT
52    FOR  X = 0  TO  9
53    READ  E$(X)
54    PRINT E$(X)
55    NEXT  X
60    PRINT : PRINT
70    INPUT "ENTER COLOR OF FIRST BAND: ";A$
75    IF  A$ = "GRAY"   THEN   A$ = "GREY"
80    PRINT : INPUT "ENTER COLOR OF SECOND BAND: ";B$
85    IF  B$ = "GRAY"   THEN   B$ = "GREY"
90    PRINT : INPUT "ENTER COLOR OF THIRD BAND: ";C$
95    IF  C$ = "GRAY"   THEN   C$ = "GREY"
100   PRINT : PRINT "ENTER COLOR OF FOURTH BAND (GOLD,SILVER"
110   INPUT "OR NONE): ";D$
115   RESTORE
120   FOR  X = 0  TO  9
130   READ  E$(X)
140   IF  A$ = E$(X)   THEN   Q = X
150   IF  B$ = E$(X)   THEN   R = X
155   IF  C$ = E$(X)   THEN   S = X
156   IF  C$ = "WHITE"  OR  C$ = "GOLD"  THEN  S = - 1
160   IF  C$  = "GREY"  OR  C$ = "SILVER"  THEN  S = - 2
170   IF  D$ = "GOLD"   THEN  T = 5
180   IF  D$ = "SILVER"   THEN  T = 10
190   IF  D$ = "NONE"   THEN  T = 20
195   NEXT  X
200   GOSUB  300
205   PRINT : PRINT : PRINT
210   PRINT "RESISTOR VALUE IS ";RE;" ";G$
215   PRINT
220   PRINT "IT HAS A TOLERANCE OF ";T;" PERCENT"
250   DATA   "BLACK","BROWN","RED","ORANGE","YELLOW","GREEN","BLUE
      ","PURPLE"
255   DATA "GREY","WHITE"
260   GOTO  355
300 RR = 10 * Q + R
320   IF  S < 2  THEN  G$ = "OHMS"
330   IF  S = > 2 AND  S < 5  THEN  G$ = "KILOHMS"
335   IF  S = > 2  AND  S < 5  THEN  S = S - 3
340   IF  S = > 5  THEN  G$ = "MEGOHMS"
345   IF  S = > 5  THEN  S = S - 6
347 RE =  INT (RR + .5) *  INT (10 ↑ S + .5 * S)
348 RE =  INT (10 * RR * 10 ↑ S + .5) / 10
350   RETURN
355   PRINT : PRINT : PRINT
360   INPUT "DO YOU HAVE ANOTHER RESISTOR (Y/N)? ";AN$
370   IF  AN$ = "Y"  THEN  50
380   END
```

RESISTOR COLOR CODE

THIS PROGRAM INTERPRETS THE RESISTOR
COLOR CODE. YOU MUST ENTER THE COLOR
OF EACH BAND AND THE PROGRAM WILL TELL
YOU WHAT THE VALUE OF THE RESISTOR IS.

POSSIBLE COLORS ARE:

BLACK
BROWN
RED
ORANGE
YELLOW
GREEN
BLUE
PURPLE
GREY
WHITE

```
ENTER COLOR OF FIRST BAND: ORANGE
ENTER COLOR OF SECOND BAND: WHITE
ENTER COLOR OF THIRD BAND: YELLOW
ENTER COLOR OF FOURTH BAND (GOLD,SILVER
OR NONE): GOLD

RESISTOR VALUE IS 390 KILOHMS
IT HAS A TOLERANCE OF 5 PERCENT

DO YOU HAVE ANOTHER RESISTOR (Y/N)? NO
```

6.2 PARALLEL RESISTORS

Calculating the equivalent value of several parallel resistors can be time-consuming and inconvenient, particularly if the resistors are not of equal value or multiples of each other.

This program takes the tedium out of such calculations and performs them much quicker than can be done manually. The total parallel resistance of any number of resistors is calculated by first converting the resistances to conductances (conductance is the reciprocal of resistance) and adding the conductances together. Once the total conductance is calculated, the program takes the reciprocal, which is the total parallel resistance.

To use the program, it is necessary only to enter the number of parallel resistors involved and the value of each in ohms. The program will return an answer that is rounded off to two decimal places.

```
0   CALL  - 936
1   PRINT : PRINT : PRINT : PRINT "WRITTEN BY JULES H. GILDER"
2   PRINT : PRINT "COPYRIGHT (C)  HAYDEN BOOK CO. 1978"
3   FOR X = 1 TO 4000: NEXT X
10   PRINT : PRINT : PRINT : PRINT
20   PRINT  TAB( 11 )"PARALLEL RESISTORS"
30   PRINT : PRINT : PRINT : PRINT
40   PRINT "THIS PROGRAM WILL CALCULATE THE RESIS-"
50   PRINT "TANCE OF ANY NUMBER OF PARALLEL RESIS-"
60   PRINT "TORS.  YOU MUST ENTER THE NUMBER OF"
70   PRINT "RESISTORS AND THE VALUE OF THE RESIS-"
80   PRINT "TORS IN OHMS."
90   PRINT : PRINT : PRINT
95 RT = 0
100   INPUT "ENTER THE NUMBER OF RESISTORS   ";N
110   FOR X = 1 TO N
115   PRINT
130   PRINT "ENTER R ";X;"   ";
140   INPUT R
150 RT = 1 / R + RT
160   NEXT X
165 RT =  INT (1 / RT * 100 + .5) / 100
170   PRINT : PRINT : PRINT : PRINT
180   PRINT "THE EQUIVALENT PARALLEL RESISTANCE"
190   PRINT : PRINT "IS ";RT;" OHMS."
```

```
        PARALLEL RESISTORS

THIS PROGRAM WILL CALCULATE THE RESIS-
TANCE OF ANY NUMBER OF PARALLEL RESIS-
TORS.  YOU MUST ENTER THE NUMBER OF
RESISTORS AND THE VALUE OF THE RESIS-
TORS IN OHMS.

ENTER THE NUMBER OF RESISTORS   4

ENTER R 1   ?1000

ENTER R 2   ?1000

ENTER R 3   ?500

ENTER R 4   ?250

THE EQUIVALENT PARALLEL RESISTANCE

IS 125 OHMS.
```

6.3 STANDARD RESISTOR VALUES [1]

Resistor calculations, as was seen with the previous program, seldom result in standard resistor values. This program will accept such nonstandard numbers and calculate the value of the closest standard resistor. The calculation is based on the fact that standard resistor values are almost equally spaced on a logarithmic scale.

The program actually calculates the values of two standard resistors, one larger than the given value and one smaller. It then compares the given value with the geometric mean of the two calculated values. If the given value is larger than the mean, the larger value is selected. Otherwise, the lower value is selected.

To use the program, a value for resistor tolerance (in percent), must be entered.

This program is short enough to be easily added to other circuit design programs so that standard value resistors can be specified directly. This has been done with some of the programs in this book.

```
0   CALL  - 936
1   PRINT : PRINT : PRINT : PRINT "WRITTEN BY JULES H. GILDER"
2   PRINT : PRINT "COPYRIGHT (C)  HAYDEN BOOK CO. 1978"
3   FOR X = 1 TO 4000: NEXT X
10   PRINT : PRINT : PRINT : PRINT
20   PRINT  TAB( 7)"STANDARD RESISTOR VALUES"
30   PRINT : PRINT : PRINT : PRINT
40   PRINT "THIS PROGRAM COMPUTES THE CLOSEST"
50   PRINT "STANDARD VALUE OF RESISTORS."
60   PRINT "YOU MUST ENTER THE NON-STANDARD VALUE"
70   PRINT "AND THE TOLERANCE DESIRED."
80   PRINT : PRINT : PRINT
90   INPUT "ENTER COMPONENT VALUE: ";X
95 Y = X
100   INPUT "ENTER TOLERANCE (%) ";A(6)
110   PRINT : PRINT : PRINT
120 A(4) = 1.19927E - 2 *  INT (1 + 1.5 * A(6) + .004 * A(6) ↑ 2)

130 A(3) =  INT ( LOG (X) / LOG (10) -  INT (2.2 - 3 * A(4)))
140 X = X / 10 ↑ A(3)
150  FOR K = 1  TO 2
160 A(K) =  INT ( EXP (A(4) * ( INT ( LOG (X) / A(4)) + K - 1)) +
      .5)
170 A(5) = 1.88E - 5 * A(K) ↑ 3 - .00335 * A(K) ↑ 2 + .164 * A(K)
      - 1.284
180 A(K) = A(K) +  INT (A(5) *  INT (3 * A(4) + .8))
190  NEXT K
200 X = 10 ↑ A(3) * A(X /  SQR (A(1) * A(2)) + 1)
205 X =  INT (X + .5)
210  PRINT : PRINT : PRINT
220  PRINT "THE CLOSEST STANDARD VALUE TO ";Y
230  PRINT : PRINT "IS ";X
```

---

[1]Adapted from J. K. Brown, "Short Subroutine Computes Standard Component Values from Nonstandard," *Electronic Design* 10 (May 10, 1974): p. 134.

```
STANDARD RESISTOR VALUES


THIS PROGRAM COMPUTES THE CLOSEST
STANDARD VALUE OF RESISTORS.
YOU MUST ENTER THE NON-STANDARD VALUE
AND THE TOLERANCE DESIRED.


ENTER COMPONENT VALUE: 523
ENTER TOLERANCE (%) 5



THE CLOSEST STANDARD VALUE TO 523

IS 510
```

6.4   DELTA TO WYE TRANSFORMATION

Very often in the analysis of electrical circuits, resistors are connected as shown in Fig. 6.1(a). An example of such an instance is a Wheatstone resistance bridge [Fig. 6.1(b)]. in which there are actually two such circuits. This form of connection is called a "delta" or, sometimes, "pi" connection.

Calculating the equivalent resistance of a delta circuit can be difficult. To make it easier, the delta circuit is generally converted to an equivalent Wye circuit [Fig. 6.1(c)]. As far as connections to the terminals are concerned, the two circuits are equivalent.

This program converts the delta resistors RA, RB, and RC to Wye resistors R1, R2, and R3. This is done in lines 14∅ to 28∅. The subroutine located at 36∅ selects the correct resistance descriptor string and also rounds off the answer to one decimal place.

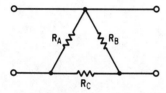

Fig. 6.1(a)   Original delta circuit

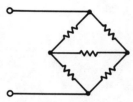

Fig. 6.1(b)   Wheatstone bridge contains delta circuit

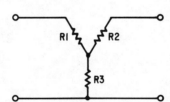

Fig. 6.1(c)   Equivalent Wye circuit

```
0   CALL  - 936
10    PRINT : PRINT : PRINT : PRINT "WRITTEN BY JULES H. GILDER"
20    PRINT : PRINT "COPYRIGHT (C) HAYDEN BOOK CO. 1978"
30    FOR X = 1 TO 4000: NEXT X
40    PRINT : PRINT : PRINT
50    PRINT  TAB( 8);"DELTA TO WYE CONVERSION"
60    PRINT : PRINT : PRINT : PRINT
70    PRINT "THIS PROGRAM CONVERTS RESISTOR NETWORKS"
80    PRINT "FROM A DELTA CONFIGURATION TO A WYE"
90    PRINT "CONFIGURATION."
```

```
100   PRINT
110   PRINT : PRINT : PRINT : PRINT
120   INPUT "ENTER R1, R2, R3 (OHMS): ";R1,R2,R3
130   PRINT : PRINT : PRINT
140 Z = R1 + R2 + R3
150 Z1 = R1 * R3 / Z
160 AA = Z1
170   GOSUB 360
180 Z1 = AA
190 R$ = A$
200 Z2 = R2 * R3 / Z
210 AA = Z2
220   GOSUB 360
230 Z2 = AA
240 S$ = A$
250 Z3 = R1 * R2 / Z
260 AA = Z3
270   GOSUB 360
280 Z3 = AA
290 T$ = A$
300   PRINT "FOR A DELTA TO WYE TRANSFORMATION THE"
310   PRINT "NEW RESISTOR VALUES ARE:"
320   PRINT : PRINT : PRINT "R1 = ";Z1;" ";R$
330   PRINT : PRINT "R2 = ";Z2;" ";S$
340   PRINT : PRINT "R3 = ";Z3;" ";T$
350   GOTO 470
360   IF AA < 1E6 THEN 400
370 A$ = "MEGOHMS"
380 AA =   INT (10 * AA / 1E6 + .5) / 10
390   GOTO  450
400   IF AA < 1E3 THEN 440
410 A$ = "KILOHMS"
420 AA =   INT (10 * AA / 1E3 + .5) / 10
430   GOTO 460
440 A$ = "OHMS"
450 AA =   INT (10 * AA + .5) / 10
460   RETURN
470   END
```

```
            DELTA TO WYE CONVERSION


THIS PROGRAM CONVERTS RESISTOR NETWORKS
FROM A DELTA CONFIGURATION TO A WYE
CONFIGURATION.



ENTER R1, R2, R3 (OHMS): 100,200,300


FOR A DELTA TO WYE TRANSFORMATION THE
NEW RESISTOR VALUES ARE:

R1 = 50 OHMS

R2 = 100 OHMS

R3 = 33.3 OHMS
```

6.5 WYE TO DELTA TRANSFORMATION

It is often desirable to convert Wye configurations to delta configurations. Calculations can be done with the Wye configuration. The resistors R1, R2, and R3 can then be converted to their delta circuit equivalents: RA, RB, and RC (Fig. 6.2).

The equations for the conversion are located in lines 140 to 260. As in the previous program, the subroutine located at 360 selects the correct resistance descriptor string and rounds off the answer to one decimal place.

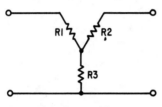

Fig. 6.2(a) Original Wye circuit

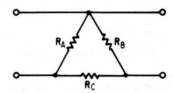

Fig. 6.2(b) Equivalent delta circuit

```
0   CALL  - 936
10   PRINT : PRINT : PRINT : PRINT "WRITTEN BY JULES H. GILDER"
20   PRINT : PRINT "COPYRIGHT (C) HAYDEN BOOK CO. 1978"
30   FOR X = 1 TO 4000: NEXT X
40   PRINT : PRINT : PRINT : PRINT
50   PRINT  TAB( 8)"WYE TO DELTA CONVERSION"
60   PRINT : PRINT : PRINT : PRINT
70   PRINT "THIS PROGRAM CONVERTS RESISTOR NETWORKS"
80   PRINT "FROM A WYE CONFIGURATION TO A DELTA"
90   PRINT "CONFIGURATION."
100   PRINT
110   PRINT : PRINT : PRINT : PRINT
120   INPUT "ENTER R1, R2, R3 (OHMS): ";R1,R2,R3
130   PRINT : PRINT : PRINT
140  ZA = R1 * R2 + R1 * R3 + R2 * R3
150  RA = ZA / R2
160  AA = RA
170   GOSUB 390
180  RA = AA
190  R$ = A$
200  RB = ZA / R1
210  AA = RB
220   GOSUB 390
230  RB = AA
240  S$ = A$
250  RC = ZA / R3
260  AA = RC
270   GOSUB 390
280  RC = AA
290  T$ = A$
300   PRINT "FOR A WYE TO DELTA TRANSFORMATION, THE"
310   PRINT "NEW RESISTOR VALUES ARE:"
320   PRINT : PRINT
330   PRINT "RA = ";RA;" ";R$
```

```
340   PRINT
350   PRINT "RB = ";RB;" ";S$
360   PRINT
370   PRINT "RC = ";RC;" ";T$
380   GOTO 500
390   IF AA < 1E6 THEN 430
400   A$ = "MEGOHMS"
410   AA =   INT ( 10 * AA / 1E6 + .5) / 10
420   GOTO 490
430   IF AA < 1E3 THEN 470
440   A$ = "KILOHMS"
450   AA =   INT ( 10 * AA / 1E3 + .5) / 10
460   GOTO 490
470   A$ = "OHMS"
480   AA =   INT ( 10 * AA + .5) / 10
490   RETURN
500   END
```

WYE TO DELTA CONVERSION

THIS PROGRAM CONVERTS RESISTOR NETWORKS
FROM A WYE CONFIGURATION TO A DELTA
CONFIGURATION.

ENTER R1, R2, R3 (OHMS): 100,200,300

FOR A WYE TO DELTA TRANSFORMATION, THE
NEW RESISTOR VALUES ARE:

RA = 550 OHMS

RB = 1.1 KILOHMS

RC = 366.7 OHMS

6.6　WIRE SIZE FROM RESISTANCE AND LENGTH

With this and the following two programs, it will never again be necessary to use wire gauge tables. Program 6.6 determines the American Wire Gauge (AWG) number to provide a given resistance for a given length of wire.

The program uses the two formulas listed below to perform its calculations. As it stands, the program will handle both copper and aluminum wires. If other materials are desired, line 8∅ should be changed, and the additional data should be entered between lines 11∅ and 12∅.

$$R = \rho \frac{L}{A}$$

$$AWG = \frac{\log (A/105532)}{\log .79304}$$

```
0   CALL  - 936
1   PRINT : PRINT : PRINT : PRINT "WRITTEN BY JULES H. GILDER"
2   PRINT : PRINT "COPYRIGHT (C) HAYDEN BOOK CO. 1978"
3   FOR X = 1 TO 4000: NEXT X
4   PRINT : PRINT : PRINT : PRINT
5   PRINT  TAB( 2)"WIRE SIZE FROM RESISTANCE AND LENGTH"
10   PRINT : PRINT : PRINT : PRINT
20   PRINT "THIS PROGRAM WILL FIND THE LARGEST"
30   PRINT "DIAMETER WIRE THAT WILL PRODUCE A GIVEN"
40   PRINT "RESISTANCE FOR A GIVEN LENGTH OF WIRE."
50   PRINT
55   PRINT : PRINT
60   INPUT "ENTER THE DESIRED RESISTANCE (OHMS): ";R
70   INPUT "ENTER THE LENGTH OF WIRE (FT): ";L
80   INPUT "COPPER (1)  OR ALUMINUM (2): ";T
90   PRINT
100  A$ = "COPPER"
110 RHO = 10.575
120   IF  T = 2  THEN  A$ = "ALUMINUM"
130   IF  T = 2  THEN  RHO = 17.34
140 A = RHO * L / R
150 AWG = ( LOG (A / 105532)) / LOG (.79304)
155 AWG =  INT (AWG + .5)
160   PRINT : PRINT
170   PRINT "A ";AWG;" AWG ";A$;" WIRE THAT IS ";L
180   PRINT    "FEET LONG WILL HAVE A RESISTANCE"
190   PRINT "OF ";R;" OHMS."
200   PRINT
210   INPUT "DO YOU WANT TO TRY AGAIN? ";B$
220   IF   LEFT$ (B$,1) = "Y"  THEN  50
230   END
```

WIRE SIZE FROM RESISTANCE AND LENGTH

THIS PROGRAM WILL FIND THE LARGEST
DIAMETER WIRE THAT WILL PRODUCE A GIVEN
RESISTANCE FOR A GIVEN LENGTH OF WIRE.

ENTER THE DESIRED RESISTANCE (OHMS): 8
ENTER THE LENGTH OF WIRE (FT): 100
COPPER (1)   OR ALUMINUM (2): 1

A 29 AWG COPPER WIRE THAT IS 100
FEET LONG WILL HAVE A RESISTANCE
OF 8 OHMS.

DO YOU WANT TO TRY AGAIN? YES

ENTER THE DESIRED RESISTANCE (OHMS): 8
ENTER THE LENGTH OF WIRE (FT): 100
COPPER (1)   OR ALUMINUM (2): 2

A 27 AWG ALUMINUM WIRE THAT IS 100
FEET LONG WILL HAVE A RESISTANCE
OF 8 OHMS.

DO YOU WANT TO TRY AGAIN? NO

6.7   WIRE SIZE FROM CURRENT CAPACITY

In the design of transformers, chokes, and electrical power circuits, one must determine what size wire can safely handle a particular current. This capability is also convenient for anyone repairing appliances or adding some additional wiring to his home.

This program will request an input for the desired current and ask if the application is for general use or for military requirements, where temperature ranges from -55 to 125°C. The military design is slightly more conservative and results in the need for larger wires (smaller AWG number).

```
0    CALL  - 936
1    PRINT : PRINT : PRINT : PRINT "WRITTEN BY JULES H. GILDER"
2    PRINT : PRINT "COPYRIGHT (C) HAYDEN BOOK CO. 1978
3    FOR X = 1 TO 4000: NEXT X
4    PRINT : PRINT : PRINT
5    PRINT  TAB( 5)"WIRE SIZE FROM CURRENT CAPACITY"
10   PRINT : PRINT : PRINT : PRINT
20   PRINT "THIS PROGRAM WILL FIND THE LARGEST DIA-"
30   PRINT "METER WIRE THAT CAN CARRY A DESIRED"
40   PRINT "AMOUNT OF CURRENT. YOU MUST INDICATE"
50   PRINT "IF IT IS FOR GENERAL USE OR MILITARY"
60   PRINT "ENVIRONMENT (-55 TO 125 C)"
70   PRINT : PRINT : PRINT
80   INPUT "ENTER CURRENT CAPACITY (AMPS): ";I
90   PRINT : INPUT "GENERAL USE (1) OR MILITARY (2): ";T
100  CMA = 400
110  A$ = "GENERAL"
120   IF  T = 2 THEN  CMA = 700
130   IF  T = 2  THEN  A$ = "MILITARY"
140  A = CMA * I
150  AWG = 10 * ( LOG (325 ↑ 2 / A)) / LOG (10)
160  AWG =   INT (AWG + .5)
170   PRINT : PRINT : PRINT : PRINT
180   PRINT "FOR ";A$;" APPLICATIONS:"
190   PRINT : PRINT : PRINT
200   PRINT "A ";AWG;" AWG WIRE IS REQUIRED TO CARRY"
205   PRINT
210   PRINT "A CURRENT OF ";I;" AMPERES."
220   END
```

```
WIRE SIZE FROM CURRENT CAPACITY


THIS PROGRAM WILL FIND THE LARGEST DIA-
METER WIRE THAT CAN CARRY A DESIRED
AMOUNT OF CURRENT.   YOU MUST INDICATE
IF IT IS FOR GENERAL USE OR MILITARY
ENVIRONMENT (-55 TO 125 C)


ENTER CURRENT CAPACITY (AMPS): 15

GENERAL USE (1) OR MILITARY (2): 1


FOR GENERAL APPLICATIONS:


A 12 AWG WIRE IS REQUIRED TO CARRY

A CURRENT OF 15 AMPERES.
```

6.8 WIRE RESISTANCE CALCULATOR

Long lengths of wire run between two points can often lead to the degradation of the signal because the resistance of the wire is too high. With this program, the resistance of a length of wire of a specific size and material can be quickly calculated.

The resistivity constants for aluminum and copper are already in the program, so either of these materials can be specified. If other materials are required, the rho for the material will have to be added, as will a material descriptor string such as that in line 120.

```
0    CALL - 936
1    PRINT : PRINT : PRINT : PRINT "WRITTEN BY JULES H. GILDER"
2    PRINT : PRINT "COPYRIGHT (C) HAYDEN BOOK CO. 1978"
3    FOR X = 1 TO 4000: NEXT X
4    PRINT : PRINT : PRINT : PRINT
5    PRINT TAB( 7)"WIRE RESISTANCE CALCULATOR"
10   PRINT : PRINT : PRINT : PRINT
20   PRINT "THIS PROGRAM WILL FIND THE RESISTANCE"
30   PRINT "OF A GIVEN AWG SIZE WIRE FOR A GIVEN"
40   PRINT "LENGTH OF WIRE."
50   PRINT
55   PRINT : PRINT
60   INPUT "ENTER AWG SIZE: ";AWG
70   INPUT "ENTER THE LENGTH OF WIRE: ";L
80   INPUT "COPPER (1)  OR ALUMINUM (2): ";T
90   PRINT
100  A$ = "COPPER"
110  RHO = 10.575
120  IF  T = 2  THEN  A$ = "ALUMINUM"
130  IF  T = 2  THEN  RHO = 17.34
140  A = 105532 * .79304 ↑ AWG
150  R = RHO * L / A
155  R = INT (R * 10 + .5) / 10
160  PRINT : PRINT
170  PRINT "A ";AWG;" AWG ";A$;" WIRE THAT IS ";L
180  PRINT    "FEET LONG WILL HAVE A RESISTANCE"
190  PRINT "OF ";R;" OHMS."
200  PRINT
210  INPUT "DO YOU WANT TO TRY AGAIN? ";B$
220  IF  LEFT$ (B$,1) = "Y"  THEN  50
230  END
```

```
         WIRE RESISTANCE CALCULATOR



THIS PROGRAM WILL FIND THE RESISTANCE
OF A GIVEN AWG SIZE WIRE FOR A GIVEN
LENGTH OF WIRE.


ENTER AWG SIZE: 29
ENTER THE LENGTH OF WIRE: 100
COPPER (1)  OR ALUMINUM (2): 1


A 29 AWG COPPER WIRE THAT IS 100
FEET LONG WILL HAVE A RESISTANCE
OF 8.3 OHMS.

DO YOU WANT TO TRY AGAIN? NO
```

6.9 TRANSFORMER TURNS RATIO

In addition to being used as voltage-changing devices in power supplies, transformers are also used as impedance-matching devices in audio equipment.

For those who like to "roll their own," this program will calculate the turns ratio required for a transformer given the primary and secondary impedances.

```
0    CALL - 936
1    PRINT : PRINT : PRINT : PRINT "WRITTEN BY JULES H. GILDER"
2    PRINT : PRINT "COPYRIGHT (C) HAYDEN BOOK CO. 1978"
3    FOR X = 1 TO 4000: NEXT X
10   PRINT : PRINT : PRINT : PRINT
20   PRINT  TAB( 8)"TRANSFORMER TURNS RATIO"
30   PRINT : PRINT : PRINT : PRINT
40   PRINT "THIS PROGRAM CALCULATES THE TURNS"
50   PRINT "RATIO REQUIRED FOR A TRANSFORMER GIVEN"
60   PRINT "THE DESIRED INPUT AND OUTPUT IMPEDANCE"
70   PRINT : PRINT : PRINT
80   INPUT "ENTER PRIMARY IMPEDANCE: ";Z1
90   INPUT "ENTER SECONDARY IMPEDANCE: ";Z2
100  PRINT : PRINT : PRINT
110  T =  SQR (Z1 / Z2)
115  T =  INT (10 * T + .5) / 10
120  PRINT : PRINT : PRINT
130  PRINT "THE TURNS RATIO FOR A TRANSFORMER WITH"
135  PRINT
140  PRINT "PRIMARY IMPEDANCE OF ";Z1;" OHMS"
145  PRINT
150  PRINT "AND A SECONDARY IMPEDANCE OF ";Z2;" OHMS"
155  PRINT
160  PRINT "IS ";T;"/ 1"
170  END
```

```
        TRANSFORMER TURNS RATIO



THIS PROGRAM CALCULATES THE TURNS
RATIO REQUIRED FOR A TRANSFORMER GIVEN
THE DESIRED INPUT AND OUTPUT IMPEDANCE


ENTER PRIMARY IMPEDANCE: 5000
ENTER SECONDARY IMPEDANCE: 8



THE TURNS RATIO FOR A TRANSFORMER WITH

PRIMARY IMPEDANCE OF 5000 OHMS

AND A SECONDARY IMPEDANCE OF 8 OHMS

IS 25/ 1
```

7 Basic Electronics

In the previous chapter, the programs dealt with some basic calculations in electricity. In this chapter, the programs deal with some basic calculations in electronics.

While electric circuits deal primarily with resistance, electronic circuits deal intimately with inductance and capacitance. The first three programs calculate the inductance of wires. This becomes an important factor when wire lengths are long and high frequencies or very fast logic circuits are used. The fourth program calculates the ac resistance of an inductor, known as inductive reactance.

Like an inductor, a capacitor has resistance to ac voltage. Program 7.5 calculates this capacitive reactance. In the design of electronic circuits, it is sometimes required to bypass a resistor with a capacitor to provide an alternate path for ac signals. Program 7.6 can be used to calculate the value of the capacitor required.

The final program performs resonant circuit calculations. It deals with frequency, capacitance, and inductance. Given any two of the above, the program will calculate the third.

7.1 INDUCTANCE OF A STRAIGHT WIRE

Circuit designs using high speed logic, such as ECL, can be seriously affected by the inductance of interconnecting leads. To overcome such potential problems, it is necessary to determine the inductance of these leads.

For a straight wire, the inductance increases as its length and permeability increases, and decreases as its diameter increases. These relationships are not linear, however, and cannot be determined without calculation.

This program performs these calculations. The user must enter the diameter and length of the wire, in centimeters, and the permeability.

```
0   CALL  - 936
1   PRINT : PRINT : PRINT : PRINT "WRITTEN BY JULES H. GILDER"
2   PRINT : PRINT "COPYRIGHT (C)  HAYDEN BOOK CO. 1978"
3   FOR X = 1 TO 4000: NEXT X
10    PRINT : PRINT : PRINT : PRINT
20    PRINT "     INDUCTANCE OF A STRAIGHT WIRE"
30    PRINT : PRINT : PRINT : PRINT
40    PRINT "THIS PROGRAM FINDS THE INDUCTANCE OF "
50    PRINT "A STRAIGHT WIRE.  YOU MUST ENTER THE "
60    PRINT "DIAMETER OF THE WIRE IN CENTIMETERS,"
70    PRINT "AND THE PERMEABILITY OF THE WIRE (MU)"
80    PRINT "THE WIRE LENGTH MUST ALSO BE ENTERED."
90    PRINT : PRINT : PRINT
100   INPUT "ENTER WIRE DIAMETER (CM): ";D
110   INPUT "ENTER PERMEABILITY: ";P
120   INPUT "ENTER WIRE LENGTH (CM): ";L1
130   PRINT : PRINT : PRINT
140 L = .002 * L1 * ( LOG (4 * L1 / D) - 1 + P / 4)
145 L =  INT (100 * L + .5) / 100
150   PRINT "FOR A WIRE WITH A:"
152   PRINT : PRINT : PRINT
155   PRINT "DIAMETER = ";D;" CENTIMETERS"
157   PRINT
160   PRINT "PERMEABILITY = ";P
161   PRINT
162   PRINT "LENGTH = ";L1;" CENTIMETERS"
165   PRINT : PRINT : PRINT
170   PRINT "INDUCTANCE = ";L;" MICROHENRIES"
```

INDUCTANCE OF A STRAIGHT WIRE

THIS PROGRAM FINDS THE INDUCTANCE OF
A STRAIGHT WIRE. YOU MUST ENTER THE
DIAMETER OF THE WIRE IN CENTIMETERS,
AND THE PERMEABILITY OF THE WIRE (MU)
THE WIRE LENGTH MUST ALSO BE ENTERED.

ENTER WIRE DIAMETER (CM): .016
ENTER PERMEABILITY: 1
ENTER WIRE LENGTH (CM): 200

FOR A WIRE WITH A:

DIAMETER = .016 CENTIMETERS

PERMEABILITY = 1

LENGTH = 200 CENTIMETERS

INDUCTANCE = 4.03 MICROHENRIES

7.2   INDUCTANCE OF A PARALLEL WIRE PAIR

The previous program found the inductance for a single straight wire. This one determines the inductance of two parallel wires viewed from one end (see Fig. 7.1).

As in the previous program, the diameter and length of the wires should be entered in centimeters. In addition, the distance between wires, also in centimeters, must be entered.

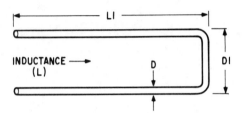

Fig. 7.1   Inductance of a parallel wire pair

```
0   CALL  - 936
1   PRINT : PRINT : PRINT : PRINT "WRITTEN BY JULES H. GILDER"
2   PRINT : PRINT "COPYRIGHT (C) HAYDEN BOOK CO. 1978"
3   FOR X = 1 TO 4000: NEXT X
10    PRINT : PRINT : PRINT : PRINT
20    PRINT "     INDUCTANCE OF A PARALLEL PAIR"
30    PRINT : PRINT : PRINT
40    PRINT "THIS PROGRAM FINDS THE INDUCTANCE OF "
50    PRINT "PARALLEL WIRES.  YOU MUST ENTER THE "
60    PRINT "DIAMETER OF THE WIRE IN CENTIMETERS,"
70    PRINT "AND THE PERMEABILITY OF THE WIRE (MU)"
80    PRINT "THE WIRE LENGTH MUST ALSO BE ENTERED."
90    PRINT : PRINT : PRINT
100   INPUT "ENTER WIRE DIAMETER (CM): ";D
110   INPUT "ENTER PERMEABILITY: ";P
120   INPUT "ENTER WIRE LENGTH (CM)  ";L1
124   INPUT "ENTER DISTANCE BETWEEN WIRES (CM): ";D1
130   PRINT : PRINT : PRINT
140 L = .004 * L1 * ( LOG (2 * D1 / D) + P / 4 - D1 / L1)
145 L =  INT (100 * L + .5) / 100
150   PRINT "FOR A WIRE PAIR WITH A:"
152   PRINT : PRINT : PRINT
155   PRINT "DIAMETER = ";D;" CENTIMETERS"
157   PRINT
160   PRINT "PERMEABILITY = ";P
161   PRINT
162   PRINT "LENGTH = ";L1;" CENTIMETERS"
163   PRINT : PRINT "PAIR DISTANCE = ";D1;" CENTIMETERS"
165   PRINT : PRINT : PRINT
170   PRINT "INDUCTANCE = ";L;" MICROHENRIES"
```

INDUCTANCE OF A PARALLEL PAIR

THIS PROGRAM FINDS THE INDUCTANCE OF
PARALLEL WIRES. YOU MUST ENTER THE
DIAMETER OF THE WIRE IN CENTIMETERS,
AND THE PERMEABILITY OF THE WIRE (MU)
THE WIRE LENGTH MUST ALSO BE ENTERED.

ENTER WIRE DIAMETER (CM): .016
ENTER PERMEABILITY: 1
ENTER WIRE LENGTH (CM) 200
ENTER DISTANCE BETWEEN WIRES (CM): 3

FOR A WIRE PAIR WITH A:

DIAMETER = .016 CENTIMETERS

PERMEABILITY = 1

LENGTH = 200 CENTIMETERS

PAIR DISTANCE = 3 CENTIMETERS

INDUCTANCE = 4.93 MICROHENRIES

7.3 INDUCTANCE OF A CIRCULARLY ARRANGED GROUP OF PARALLEL WIRES

Sometimes to reduce the inductance of the wiring, several wires are connected in parallel and arranged in a circle (Fig. 7.2). To calculate the inductance of wires with this arrangement, the diameter of the circle has to be taken into account.

When entering data for this configuration, the permeability should be entered as 1.

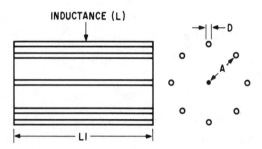

Fig. 7.2 Inductance of a circular group of wires

```
0   CALL  - 936
1   PRINT : PRINT : PRINT : PRINT "WRITTEN BY JULES H. GILDER"
2   PRINT : PRINT "COPYRIGHT (C)  HAYDEN BOOK CO. 1978"
3   FOR X = 1 TO 4000: NEXT X
10   PRINT : PRINT : PRINT : PRINT
20   PRINT "INDUCTANCE OF A GROUP OF PARALLEL WIRES"
30   PRINT : PRINT : PRINT
40   PRINT "THIS PROGRAM FINDS THE INDUCTANCE OF "
50   PRINT "A CIRCULARLY ARRANGED GROUP OF PARALLEL"
55   PRINT "WIRES.  TO USE YOU MUST ENTER THE"
60   PRINT "DIAMETER OF THE WIRE IN CENTIMETERS,"
70   PRINT "AND THE PERMEABILITY OF THE WIRE (MU)"
80   PRINT "THE WIRE LENGTH MUST ALSO BE ENTERED."
90   PRINT : PRINT : PRINT
100   INPUT "ENTER WIRE DIAMETER (CM): ";D
110   INPUT "ENTER PERMEABILITY: ";P
120   INPUT "ENTER WIRE LENGTH (CM): ";L1
124   INPUT "ENTER RADIUS OF WIRE CIRCLE (CM): ";A
126   INPUT "ENTER NUMBER OF WIRES: ";N
130   PRINT : PRINT : PRINT
135 R = (D / 2 * N * A ↑ (N - 1)) ↑ (1 / N)
140 L = .002 * L1 * ( LOG (2 * L1 / R) - 1)
145 L =   INT (100 * L + .5) / 100
150   PRINT "FOR ";N;" WIRES WITH A:"
152   PRINT : PRINT : PRINT
153   PRINT "CIRCLE RADIUS OF ";A;" CM"
154   PRINT
155   PRINT "WIRE DIAMETER OF ";D;" CM"
157   PRINT
160   PRINT "PERMEABILITY OF ";P
161   PRINT
162   PRINT "LENGTH OF ";L1;" CM"
165   PRINT : PRINT : PRINT
170   PRINT "INDUCTANCE = ";L;" MICROHENRIES"
180   END
1162   PRINT "LENGTH OF ";L1;" CM"
```

INDUCTANCE OF A GROUP OF PARALLEL WIRES

THIS PROGRAM FINDS THE INDUCTANCE OF
A CIRCULARLY ARRANGED GROUP OF PARALLEL
WIRES. TO USE YOU MUST ENTER THE
DIAMETER OF THE WIRE IN CENTIMETERS,
AND THE PERMEABILITY OF THE WIRE (MU)
THE WIRE LENGTH MUST ALSO BE ENTERED.

ENTER WIRE DIAMETER (CM): .016
ENTER PERMEABILITY: 1
ENTER WIRE LENGTH (CM): 200
ENTER RADIUS OF WIRE CIRCLE (CM): 3
ENTER NUMBER OF WIRES: 6

FOR 6 WIRES WITH A:

CIRCLE RADIUS OF 3 CM

WIRE DIAMETER OF .016 CM

PERMEABILITY OF 1

LENGTH OF 200 CM

INDUCTANCE = 1.83 MICROHENRIES

7.4 CAPACITIVE REACTANCE CALCULATOR

The resistance of the flow of ac current exhibited by a capacitor is called "capacitive reactance." The capacitive reactance, denoted by XC, is inversely proportional to the frequency of the ac voltage.

This program calculates the reactance of a capacitor at a given frequency according to the formula:

$$XC = 1/(2*\pi*F*C)$$

where π = 3.14159, F = frequency in hertz, and C equals the capacitance in farads.

When using the program, capacitance is entered in microfarads and not farads. The conversion to farads is done in line 96. The reactance returned by the program is in ohms.

```
0   CALL  - 936
1   PRINT : PRINT : PRINT : PRINT "WRITTEN BY JULES H. GILDER"
2   PRINT : PRINT "COPYRIGHT (C) HAYDEN BOOK CO. 1978"
3   FOR X = 1 TO 4000: NEXT X
10    PRINT : PRINT : PRINT : PRINT
20    PRINT  TAB( 10)"CAPACITIVE REACTANCE"
30    PRINT : PRINT : PRINT : PRINT
40    PRINT "THIS PROGRAM CALCULATES THE CAPACITIVE"
50    PRINT "REACTANCE OF A CAPACITOR. YOU MUST"
60    PRINT "ENTER THE VALUE OF CAPACITANCE IN"
70    PRINT "MICROFARADS AND THE FREQUENCY IN HERTZ"
80    PRINT : PRINT : PRINT
90    INPUT "ENTER CAPACITANCE (UF): ";C
95  CC = C
96  C = C * 1E - 6
100   PRINT : INPUT "ENTER FREQUENCY (HZ): ";F
105 XC = 1 / (2 * 3.14159 * F * C)
106 XC =  INT (100 * XC + .5) / 100
110   PRINT : PRINT : PRINT
120   PRINT "THE REACTANCE OF A ";CC
125   PRINT
130   PRINT "MICROFARAD CAPACITOR AT ";F;" HERTZ"
135   PRINT
140   PRINT "IS ";XC;" OHMS"
```

```
        CAPACITIVE REACTANCE


THIS PROGRAM CALCULATES THE CAPACITIVE
REACTANCE OF A CAPACITOR. YOU MUST
ENTER THE VALUE OF CAPACITANCE IN
MICROFARADS AND THE FREQUENCY IN HERTZ


ENTER CAPACITANCE (UF): .0033

ENTER FREQUENCY (HZ): 1E6


THE REACTANCE OF A 3.3E-03

MICROFARAD CAPACITOR AT 1000000 HERTZ

IS 48.23 OHMS
```

7.5 INDUCTIVE REACTANCE CALCULATOR

Just as a capacitor can act as an ac reactance, so can an inductor. However, unlike the capacitor whose reactance increased with a decrease in frequency, the reactance of an inductor increases with an increase in frequency.

The inductive reactance, denoted by XL, is calculated according to the following formula:

$$XL = 2*\pi*F*L$$

where again $\pi = 3.14159$, F is the frequency in hertz, and L is the inductance in henries.

When using the program, the inductance must be entered in henries and the frequency, in hertz. The inductive reactance is returned in ohms.

```
0   CALL  - 936
1   PRINT : PRINT : PRINT : PRINT "WRITTEN BY JULES H. GILDER"
2   PRINT : PRINT "COPYRIGHT (C)  HAYDEN BOOK CO. 1978"
3   FOR X = 1 TO 4000: NEXT X
10   PRINT : PRINT : PRINT : PRINT
20   PRINT  TAB( 10 )"INDUCTIVE REACTANCE"
30   PRINT : PRINT : PRINT : PRINT
40   PRINT "THIS PROGRAM CALCULATES THE INDUCTIVE"
50   PRINT "REACTANCE OF AN INDUCTOR. YOU MUST"
60   PRINT "ENTER THE VALUE OF INDUCTANCE IN"
70   PRINT "HENRIES AND THE FREQUENCY IN HERTZ"
80   PRINT : PRINT : PRINT
90   INPUT "ENTER INDUCTANCE (H): ";L
100   PRINT : INPUT "ENTER FREQUENCY (HZ): ";F
105 XL =  INT (100 * (2 * 3.14159 * F * L) + .5) / 100
110   PRINT : PRINT : PRINT
120   PRINT "THE REACTANCE OF A ";L
125   PRINT
130   PRINT "HENRY INDUCTOR AT ";F;" HERTZ"
135   PRINT
140   PRINT "IS ";XL;" OHMS."
```

```
            INDUCTIVE REACTANCE


THIS PROGRAM CALCULATES THE INDUCTIVE
REACTANCE OF AN INDUCTOR. YOU MUST
ENTER THE VALUE OF INDUCTANCE IN
HENRIES AND THE FREQUENCY IN HERTZ


ENTER INDUCTANCE (H): 3

ENTER FREQUENCY (HZ): 60


THE REACTANCE OF A 3

HENRY INDUCTOR AT 60 HERTZ

IS 1130.97 OHMS.
```

7.6 BYPASS CAPACITOR CALCULATION

In the design of amplifiers, it is frequently necessary to bypass the resistor in the emitter leg of the circuit. The value of the capacitor can be easily determined by using a variation of the relationship between frequency, resistance, and capacitance shown below (this variation is listed in line 150 of the program):

$$f = \frac{1}{2\pi RC}$$

In this program, the frequency (F) is the lowest frequency that is attenuated 3 dB. To calculate the value of the bypass capacitor, the value of the resistor to be bypassed and the frequency must be entered. The answer is given in microfarads.

```
0   CALL  - 936
1   PRINT : PRINT : PRINT : PRINT "WRITTEN BY JULES H. GILDER"
2   PRINT : PRINT "COPYRIGHT (C)  HAYDEN BOOK CO. 1978"
3   FOR X = 1 TO 4000: NEXT X
10    PRINT : PRINT : PRINT : PRINT
20    PRINT  TAB( 12)"BYPASS CAPACITOR"
30    PRINT : PRINT : PRINT : PRINT
40    PRINT "THIS PROGRAM CALCULATES THE VALUE OF"
50    PRINT "A BYPASS CAPACITOR FOR A CATHODE OR"
60    PRINT "EMITTER RESISTOR IN AN AMPLIFIER CIR-"
70    PRINT "CUIT. YOU MUST ENTER THE LOWEST FRE-"
80    PRINT "QUENCY TO BE BYPASSED AND THE VALUE OF"
90    PRINT "THE RESISTOR IT IS BYPASSING."
100   PRINT : PRINT : PRINT
110   INPUT "ENTER BYPASS FREQUENCY (HERTZ): ";F
120   INPUT "ENTER BYPASS RESISTOR (OHMS): ";R
130   PRINT : PRINT : PRINT
140 PI = 3.14159
150 C = 1E7 / (2 * PI * F * R)
155 C =  INT (100 * C + .5) / 100
160   PRINT "BYPASS CAPACITOR IS ";C;" MICROFARADS"
170   PRINT : PRINT
180   END
```

```
        BYPASS CAPACITOR


THIS PROGRAM CALCULATES THE VALUE OF
A BYPASS CAPACITOR FOR A CATHODE OR
EMITTER RESISTOR IN AN AMPLIFIER CIR-
CUIT. YOU MUST ENTER THE LOWEST FRE-
QUENCY TO BE BYPASSED AND THE VALUE OF
THE RESISTOR IT IS BYPASSING.


ENTER BYPASS FREQUENCY (HERTZ): 60
ENTER BYPASS RESISTOR (OHMS): 200


BYPASS CAPACITOR IS 132.63 MICROFARADS
```

7.7 RESONANT CIRCUIT CALCULATIONS

Anyone involved in the design of electronic circuits will sooner or later have to perform resonant circuit calculations. With this program, it is a simple matter to determine the resonant frequency of an L-C circuit or, given the frequency, to determine the capacitance or inductance when one of the two is known.

When run, the program displays a menu that will determine which of the possible calculations will be performed. The determination of the resonant frequency is done in lines 170 to 195. Capacitance is determined in lines 200 to 240. Finally, the inductance is determined in lines 164 to 166.

The formulas used in these calculations are variations of the basic relationship between frequency, inductance and capacitance for resonant circuits. This relationship is:

$$f = \frac{1}{2\pi\sqrt{LC}}$$

```
0   CALL  - 936
1   PRINT : PRINT : PRINT : PRINT "WRITTEN BY JULES H. GILDER"
2   PRINT : PRINT "COPYRIGHT (C)  HAYDEN BOOK CO. 1978"
3   FOR X = 1 TO 4000: NEXT X
10  PRINT : PRINT : PRINT : PRINT
30  PRINT  TAB( 11)"RESONANT CIRCUITS"
35  PRINT : PRINT : PRINT : PRINT
40  PRINT "THIS PROGRAM WILL CALCULATE THE RESO-"
50  PRINT "NANT FREQUENCY OF AN L-C CIRCUIT. IF"
60  PRINT "L OR C IS UNKNOWN AND THE FREQUENCY IS"
70  PRINT "GIVEN, IT WILL CALCULATE THE UNKNOWN."
80  PRINT : PRINT : PRINT
90  PRINT " WHAT DO YOU WANT TO CALCULATE:"
100  PRINT : PRINT "1.FREQUENCY"
110  PRINT "2.CAPACITANCE"
120  PRINT "3.INDUCTANCE"
130  PRINT : INPUT "ENTER CHOICE: ";N
135  PRINT : PRINT : PRINT
140  IF  N = 1  THEN  170
150  IF  N = 2  THEN  200
160  INPUT "ENTER CAPACITANCE (UF) ";C
162  INPUT "ENTER FREQUENCY (HZ) ";F
163  PRINT : PRINT : PRINT
164 L = 1 / (39.4783553 * F ↑ 2 * C * 1E - 6)
165 L =  INT (1000 * L + .5) / 1000
166  PRINT "L = ";L;" HENRIES"
168  GOTO 250
170  INPUT "ENTER CAPACITANCE (UF) ";C
175  INPUT "ENTER INDUCTANCE (HENRIES) ";L
180  PRINT : PRINT : PRINT
182 C = C * 1E - 6
185 F = 1 / (2 * 3.14159 *  SQR (L * C))
190 F =  INT (F + .5)
195  PRINT "F = ";F;" HERTZ"
196  GOTO 250
200  INPUT "ENTER FREQUENCY (HZ) ";F
210  INPUT "ENTER INDUCTANCE (HENRIES) ";L
```

```
220   PRINT : PRINT : PRINT
230   C = 1 / (39.4783553 * F ↑ 2 * L)
235   C =   INT (1E12 * C + .5) / 1E6
240   PRINT "C = ";C;" MICROFARADS"
250   END
```

RESONANT CIRCUITS

THIS PROGRAM WILL CALCULATE THE RESO-
NANT FREQUENCY OF AN L-C CIRCUIT. IF
L OR C IS UNKNOWN AND THE FREQUENCY IS
GIVEN, IT WILL CALCULATE THE UNKNOWN.

 WHAT DO YOU WANT TO CALCULATE:

1.FREQUENCY
2.CAPACITANCE
3.INDUCTANCE

ENTER CHOICE: 3

ENTER CAPACITANCE (UF) 2.2
ENTER FREQUENCY (HZ) 1000

L = .012 HENRIES

8 Computer-Aided Circuit Design

One area where computers have traditionally been used is computer-aided design. Computers are a great design aid because they make it easy to change the design to accommodate a particular parameter. In addition, changes can be made in the original design without the need for building a prototype to see how the change will affect the final results.

The seven programs in this chapter will help you design a particular circuit or tell you how it will react to a particular set of conditions. The first program solves the equations for a class A amplifier and permits the use of either germanium or silicon transistors.

The second program designs a discrete transistor Schmitt Trigger, which converts any inputted waveform to a square wave signal. Triggering levels are selectable. The third program in this chapter is not really a design program. It calculates how long a given power supply will continue to provide current to a load after the ac voltage has ceased. It is design related, however, in that various parameters of the power supply can be altered until the desired time is reached.

The last four programs deal with the design of various types of power supplies. The first of these (8.4) is unusual in that it does not use any power transformer to drop the ac voltage to the required level. Instead, it uses the reactance of a capacitor, saving much weight and expense. This type of supply, however, is limited to low currents and must be used carefully because it is not isolated from the ac line.

The other three supplies are variations on the same theme and similar in makeup. These are full-capability supplies that should give trouble-free service.

8.1   CLASS A TRANSISTOR AMPLIFIER DESIGN [1]

Computer-aided circuit design is very popular among engineers because it enables the designer to change the value of one or more components and lets him see what the effect will be on the rest of the design. It does this quickly, without the need for actually building the circuit.

This program solves the circuit equations for a stabilized, self-biased transistor operating as a class A amplifier under small signal conditions. The method used in the program involves simultaneously solving the circuit equation at both extremes. An assumption is made that ICBO = $\emptyset$ at the low temperature extreme.

This program contains a subroutine starting at line 400 that converts the calculated resistor values to standard value resistors whose tolerance is equal to that designated by the input. The resistor values returned by the program are in ohms. The diagram of the circuit is given in Fig. 8-1.

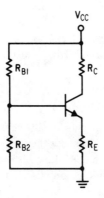

Fig. 8.1   Class A transistor amplifier

```
0    CALL  - 936
1    PRINT : PRINT : PRINT : PRINT "WRITTEN BY JULES H. GILDER"
2    PRINT : PRINT "COPYRIGHT (C) HAYDEN BOOK CO. 1978"
3    FOR X = 1 TO 4000: NEXT X
4    PRINT : PRINT : PRINT : PRINT
5    PRINT  TAB( 9)"CLASS A TRANSISTOR AMP"
6    PRINT : PRINT : PRINT : PRINT
10   PRINT "THIS PROGRAM SOLVES THE CIRCUIT"
20   PRINT "EQUATIONS FOR A STABILIZED, SELF-BIASED"
30   PRINT "TRANSISTOR OPERATING AS A CLASS A AMP-"
40   PRINT "LIFIER UNDER SMALL SIGNAL CONDITIONS."
50   PRINT : PRINT
55   INPUT "ENTER TOLERANCE OF RESISTORS (%): ";A(6)
56   PRINT
60   PRINT "IS THIS FOR SILICON(1) OR GERMANIUM(0)"
70   PRINT "TRANSISTORS: ";: INPUT "";S
80   PRINT : INPUT "ENTER MIN. AND MAX. TEMPERATURES: ";T1,T2
95   PRINT : INPUT "ENTER MIN. AND MAX. BETA: ";B1,B2
```

[1] Adapted from C. P. Popenoe, "Basic Program Designs Bias Circuits," *Electronic Design* 13 (June 21, 1970): p. 93.

```
100   PRINT : INPUT "WHAT IS THE SUPPLY VOLTAGE: ";VS
110   PRINT : PRINT "ENTER A VALUE FOR  THE EMITTER"
120   INPUT "RESISTOR AND PERCENT  TOLERANCE: ";R4,T
130   PRINT : INPUT "ENTER V(CE) AND I(CBO) IN MA: ";VCE,ICBO
140   PRINT : INPUT "ENTER I(E) MAX,MIN IN MA: ";I1,I2
150   I1 = I1 * (1 - .03 * T)
160   I2 = I2 * (1 + .03 * T)
170   B1 = B1 * .865 *  EXP (.00575 * T1)
180   T3 = T2 - 25
185   BZ = (.00895 - .00565 * T3 + .00048 * T3 ↑ 2)
190   B2 = B2 * (.865 *  EXP (.00575 * T2) - (S - 1) * BZ)
200   IF  S = 1  THEN  220
210   ICBO = ICBO *  EXP (.075 * T3)
220   R3 = 2000 * (VS - VCE) / (I1 + I2) - R4
225   X = R3: GOSUB 400:R3 = X
227   BX = B2 + 1
230   R6 = ((I1 - I2) * R4 + 2.5 * (T2 - T1)) / (ICBO + I2 / (B1 +
      1) - I1 / BX)
240   IF  R6 > 0  THEN  270
250   PRINT : PRINT  "THE RANGE OF I(E) IS TOO NARROW"
260   GOTO 370
270   V6 = I2 * .001 * (R6 / (B1 + 1) + R4) + .2 + .5 * S - .0025 *
      (T1 - 25)
275   R1 = VS * R6 / V6:X = R1
276   GOSUB  400
277   R1 = X
280   R2 = VS * R6 / (VS - V6):X = R2: GOSUB 400
282   R2 = X
285   PRINT : PRINT : PRINT
287   V6 =  INT (100 * V6 + .5) / 100
310   PRINT : PRINT : PRINT : PRINT
320   PRINT "FOR A STABILIZED BIAS CIRCUIT:"
325   PRINT : PRINT
330   PRINT : PRINT "R(B1) = ";R1;" OHMS"
340   PRINT "R(B2) = ";R2;" OHMS"
350   PRINT "R(C) = ";R3;" OHMS"
360   PRINT "R(E) = ";R4;" OHMS"
362   PRINT : PRINT
365   PRINT : PRINT "BIAS VOLTAGE = ";V6;" VOLTS"
366   PRINT : PRINT : PRINT
370   END
400   A(4) = 1.19927E - 2 *  INT (1 + 1.5 * A(6) + .004 * A(6) ↑ 2)

410   A(3) =  INT ( LOG (X) /  LOG (10) -  INT (2.2 - 3 * A(4)))
420   X = X / 10 ↑ A(3)
430   FOR  K = 1  TO 2
440   A(K) =  INT ( EXP (A(4) * ( INT ( LOG (X) / A(4)) + K - 1)) +
      .5)
450   A(5) = 1.88E - 5 * A(K) ↑ 3 - .00335 * A(K) ↑ 2 + .164 * A(K)
      - 1.284
460   A(K) = A(K) +  INT (A(5) *  INT (3 * A(4) + .8))
470   NEXT  K
480   X = 10 ↑ A(3) * A(X /  SQR (A(1) * A(2)) + 1)
490   X =  INT (X + .5)
500   RETURN
```

CLASS A TRANSISTOR AMP

THIS PROGRAM SOLVES THE CIRCUIT
EQUATIONS FOR A STABILIZED, SELF-BIASED
TRANSISTOR OPERATING AS A CLASS A AMP-
LIFIER UNDER SMALL SIGNAL CONDITIONS.

ENTER TOLERANCE OF RESISTORS (%): 10

IS THIS FOR SILICON(1) OR GERMANIUM(0)
TRANSISTORS: 0

ENTER MIN. AND MAX. TEMPERATURES: -25,75

ENTER MIN. AND MAX. BETA: 50,150

WHAT IS THE SUPPLY VOLTAGE: 12

ENTER A VALUE FOR THE EMITTER
RESISTOR AND PERCENT TOLERANCE: 2000,5

ENTER V(CE) AND I(CBO) IN MA: 5,.002

ENTER I(E) MAX,MIN IN MA: .8,1.2

FOR A STABILIZED BIAS CIRCUIT:

R(B1) = 47000 OHMS
R(B2) = 18000 OHMS
R(C) = 4700 OHMS
R(E) = 2000 OHMS

BIAS VOLTAGE = 3.58 VOLTS

8.2 SCHMITT TRIGGER CIRCUIT DESIGN [1]

Schmitt Trigger circuits are commonly used in digital designs (see Fig. 8.2). They come in handy to convert various shaped signals (sine wave and so forth) into square wave pulses. The Schmitt Trigger has an upper and lower threshold voltage. The incoming signal is compared to these threshold voltages, and a square wave output is produced with the same frequency as the input waveform.

Like the previous program, this one also contains the standard value resistor subroutine. The routine starts at line 500.

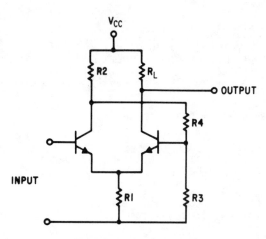

Fig. 8.2 Schmitt trigger

```
0   CALL  - 936
1   PRINT : PRINT : PRINT : PRINT "WRITTEN BY JULES H. GILDER"
2   PRINT : PRINT "COPYRIGHT (C) HAYDEN BOOK CO. 1978"
3   FOR X = 1 TO 4000: NEXT X
4   PRINT : PRINT : PRINT : PRINT
5   PRINT  TAB( 9)"SCHMITT TRIGGER DESIGN"
10  PRINT : PRINT : PRINT : PRINT
20  PRINT "THIS PROGRAM DESIGNS A 2-TRANSISTOR"
30  PRINT "SCHMITT TRIGGER CIRCUIT.  TO USE IT"
40  PRINT "YOU MUST ENTER THE UPPER AND LOWER"
50  PRINT "VOLTAGE TRIP POINTS, THE VALUE OF THE"
60  PRINT "SUPPLY VOLTAGE BEING USED, THE BASE-"
70  PRINT "TO-EMITTER VOLTAGE DROP OF THE TRAN-"
80  PRINT "SISTOR, AND THE RESISTANCE OF THE LOAD."
90  PRINT : PRINT "THE PROGRAM WILL ALSO ASK FOR THE"
100 PRINT "TOLERANCE OF THE RESISTORS USED AND"
110 PRINT "THEN CALCULATE THE NEAREST STANDARD"
120 PRINT "VALUE.  ENTER ALL VOLTAGES IN VOLTS."
130 PRINT : PRINT
140 INPUT "ENTER UPPER THRESHOLD VOLTAGE: ";VU
150 INPUT "ENTER LOWER THRESHOLD VOLTAGE: ";VL
```

---

[1] Adapted from A. C. Caggiano, "Schmitt Trigger Program Uses Standard Resistor Values," *Electronic Design* 12 (June 7, 1970): p. 100.

```
160  PRINT : INPUT "ENTER SUPPLY VOLTAGE: ";VCC
170  INPUT "ENTER EMITTER-BASE VOLTAGE: ";VBE
180  PRINT : INPUT "ENTER LOAD IMPEDANCE (OHMS): ";RL
185  INPUT "ENTER RESISTOR TOLERANCE (%): ";A(6)
190  PRINT : PRINT : PRINT
200 R(1) = RL * (VU - VBE) / (VCC - VU + VBE)
210 X = R(1)
220  GOSUB 500
230 R(1) = X
240 R(2) = R(1) * (VCC - VL + VBE) / (VL - VBE)
250 X = R(2)
260  GOSUB 500
270 R(2) = X
280 R(3) = 10 * R(1)
290 R(4) = R(3) * VCC / VU - R(3) - R(2)
300 X = R(4)
310  GOSUB 500
320 R(4) = X
330 I = (VU - VBE) / R(1)
340 P =  INT (1E4 * I ↑ 2 * RL + .5) / 10
350  PRINT "FOR A SCHMITT TRIGGER WITH AN UPPER"
360  PRINT "THRESHOLD OF ";VU;" VOLTS AND A LOWER"
370  PRINT "THRESHOLD OF ";VL;" VOLTS THE CLOSEST"
380  PRINT "STANDARD VALUES OF ";A(6);" % RESISTORS ARE:"
385  PRINT : PRINT
390  FOR J = 1 TO 4
400  PRINT "R(";J;") = ";R(J);" OHMS"
410  NEXT J
415  PRINT
420  PRINT : PRINT "THE POWER DISSIPATED BY THE LOAD IS"
430  PRINT P;" MILLIWATTS. THE ACTUAL THRESHOLD"
440  PRINT "VOLTAGES ARE:"
450 U = R(3) * VCC / (R(2) + R(3) + R(4))
455 U =  INT (100 * U + .5) / 100
460 L = VBE + R(1) * VCC / (R(1) + R(2))
465 L =  INT (100 * L + .5) / 100
470  PRINT : PRINT "UPPER THRESHOLD = ";U;" VOLTS"
480  PRINT "LOWER THRESHOLD = ";L;" VOLTS"
482  PRINT : PRINT
485  INPUT "WANT TO TRY ANOTHER DESIGN? ";Z$
490  IF  LEFT$ (Z$,1) = "Y" THEN 130
495  END
500 A(4) = 1.19927E - 2 *  INT (1 + 1.5 * A(6) + .004 * A(6) ↑ 2)
510 A(3) =  INT ( LOG (X) /  LOG (10) -  INT (2.2 - 3 * A(4)))
520 X = X / 10 ↑ A(3)
530  FOR K = 1 TO 2
540 A(K) =  INT ( EXP (A(4) * ( INT ( LOG (X) / A(4)) + K - 1)) +
     .5)
550 A(5) = 1.88E - 5 * A(K) ↑ 3 - .00335 * A(K) ↑ 2 + .164 * A(K)
     - 1.284
560 A(K) = A(K) +  INT (A(5) *  INT (3 * A(4) + .8))
570  NEXT K
580 X = 10 ↑ A(3) * A(X /  SQR (A(1) * A(2)) + 1)
590 X =  INT (X + .5)
600  RETURN
```

SCHMITT TRIGGER DESIGN

THIS PROGRAM DESIGNS A 2-TRANSISTOR
SCHMITT TRIGGER CIRCUIT. TO USE IT
YOU MUST ENTER THE UPPER AND LOWER
VOLTAGE TRIP POINTS, THE VALUE OF THE
SUPPLY VOLTAGE BEING USED, THE BASE-
TO-EMITTER VOLTAGE DROP OF THE TRAN-
SISTOR, AND THE RESISTANCE OF THE LOAD.

THE PROGRAM WILL ALSO ASK FOR THE
TOLERANCE OF THE RESISTORS USED AND
THEN CALCULATE THE NEAREST STANDARD
VALUE. ENTER ALL VOLTAGES IN VOLTS.

ENTER UPPER THRESHOLD VOLTAGE: 9
ENTER LOWER THRESHOLD VOLTAGE: 5

ENTER SUPPLY VOLTAGE: 12
ENTER EMITTER-BASE VOLTAGE: .6

ENTER LOAD IMPEDANCE (OHMS): 300
ENTER RESISTOR TOLERANCE (%): 5

FOR A SCHMITT TRIGGER WITH AN UPPER
THRESHOLD OF 9 VOLTS AND A LOWER
THRESHOLD OF 5 VOLTS THE CLOSEST
STANDARD VALUES OF 5 % RESISTORS ARE:

R(1) = 680 OHMS
R(2) = 1200 OHMS
R(3) = 6800 OHMS
R(4) = 1100 OHMS

THE POWER DISSIPATED BY THE LOAD IS
45.8 MILLIWATTS. THE ACTUAL THRESHOLD
VOLTAGES ARE:

UPPER THRESHOLD = 8.97 VOLTS
LOWER THRESHOLD = 4.94 VOLTS

WANT TO TRY ANOTHER DESIGN? NO

8.3 POWER SUPPLY INTERRUPT TIME

With the increased use of computers in home and industry, the loss of data due to an interruption of the power supply is of ever increasing importance. In applications where the loss of data is intolerable, backup power supplies are integrated into the system. Unfortunately, it takes a certain amount of time for the backup supply to be switched in. This program will calculate how long the main power supply will continue to produce a regulated voltage to the load even after the power has been cut. It can then be determined if the period is long enough to cover the time required to switch in the backup. If it's not, the storage capacitor in the main supply can be increased until the desired time is reached.

Another way of increasing the time is to increase the unregulated voltage fed into the voltage regulator. However, the regulator will have to be able to withstand the higher voltage during light loads.

To use this program, values for five variables must be entered: the unregulated voltage, minimum voltage drop across the regulator, the load voltage, the load current in amperes, and the value of the storage capacitor in microfarads.

The program will then calculate the amount of time regulated voltage can be supplied to the load in milliseconds.

```
0    CALL  - 936
1    PRINT : PRINT : PRINT : PRINT "WRITTEN BY JULES H. GILDER"
2    PRINT : PRINT "COPYRIGHT (C) HAYDEN BOOK CO. 1978"
3    FOR X = 1 TO 4000: NEXT X
4    PRINT : PRINT : PRINT : PRINT
5    PRINT  TAB( 6)"POWER SUPPLY INTERRUPT TIME"
6    PRINT : PRINT : PRINT : PRINT
10    PRINT "THIS PROGRAM WILL CALCULATE THE AMOUNT"
20    PRINT "OF TIME A REGULATED POWER SUPPLY WILL"
30    PRINT "CONTINUE TO PROVIDE A REGULATED OUTPUT"
40    PRINT "AFTER THE LINE VOLTAGE HAS BEEN "
50    PRINT "INTERRUPTED. YOU MUST ENTER THE POWER"
60    PRINT "SUPPLY PARAMETERS AS FOLLOWS:"
70    PRINT
100    INPUT "UNREGULATED VOLTAGE (VOLTS): ";VIN
120    INPUT "MINIMUM REGULATOR DROP (VOLTS): ";VR
130    INPUT "LOAD VOLTAGE (VOLTS): ";VL
140    INPUT "LOAD CURRENT (AMPERES): ";IL
150    INPUT "STORAGE CAPACITOR (MICROFARADS): ";C
160    PRINT
165    PRINT : PRINT
170    C = C * 1E - 6
180    T = ((VIN - VR - VL) * C) / IL * 1000
185    T =   INT (T + .5)
190    PRINT "THIS POWER SUPPLY WILL CONTINUE TO"
200    PRINT "SUPPLY THE LOAD WITH REGULATED VOLTAGE"
210    PRINT "FOR ";T;" MILLISECONDS AFTER THE "
220    PRINT "LINE VOLTAGE HAS BEEN INTERRUPTED."
230    PRINT
240    INPUT "DO YOU HAVE MORE DATA? ";Z$
245    PRINT
250    IF   LEFT$ (Z$,1) = "Y"  THEN  100
260    END
```

POWER SUPPLY INTERRUPT TIME

THIS PROGRAM WILL CALCULATE THE AMOUNT
OF TIME A REGULATED POWER SUPPLY WILL
CONTINUE TO PROVIDE A REGULATED OUTPUT
AFTER THE LINE VOLTAGE HAS BEEN
INTERRUPTED. YOU MUST ENTER THE POWER
SUPPLY PARAMETERS AS FOLLOWS:

UNREGULATED VOLTAGE (VOLTS): 16
MINIMUM REGULATOR DROP (VOLTS): 3
LOAD VOLTAGE (VOLTS): 12
LOAD CURRENT (AMPERES): 2
STORAGE CAPACITOR (MICROFARADS): 5000

THIS POWER SUPPLY WILL CONTINUE TO
SUPPLY THE LOAD WITH REGULATED VOLTAGE
FOR 3 MILLISECONDS AFTER THE
LINE VOLTAGE HAS BEEN INTERRUPTED.

DO YOU HAVE MORE DATA? YES

UNREGULATED VOLTAGE (VOLTS): 16
MINIMUM REGULATOR DROP (VOLTS): 3
LOAD VOLTAGE (VOLTS): 12
LOAD CURRENT (AMPERES): 2
STORAGE CAPACITOR (MICROFARADS): 20000

THIS POWER SUPPLY WILL CONTINUE TO
SUPPLY THE LOAD WITH REGULATED VOLTAGE
FOR 10 MILLISECONDS AFTER THE
LINE VOLTAGE HAS BEEN INTERRUPTED.

DO YOU HAVE MORE DATA? NO

8.4 TRANSFORMERLESS POWER SUPPLY

Most low-current dc-operated devices such as radios, tape recorders, and so forth, use small power packs that plug into a wall socket to adapt the device for ac use (see Fig. 8.3). Most of the time, these power packs use a transformer to step the line voltage down to a value that is close to the dc voltage value. That's why these little supplies are so heavy. In addition to its weight, the transformer is probably the most expensive part of the power supply. If left plugged in for any length of time, it heats up due to losses in the transformer core.

An alternate way to drop the voltage to the desired value without the cost, weight, or heat generation of the transformer is to use a capacitor. While the capacitor represents an open circuit for dc applications, in ac circuits it presents a resistance to the flow of electricity. This resistance to current flow varies with the frequency of the "ac" voltage. It is known as capacitive reactance and is generally denoted by XC. The formula for capacitive reactance is

$$XC = 1/(2*\pi*F*C)$$

where π = 3.14159, F is the frequency in hertz, and C is the capacitance in farads. The formula gives a value for XC in ohms.

Using this property of the capacitor, it is possible to design a small light-weight power supply. The key design formula is

$$C = 1/(2*\pi*F*RL*(VL\uparrow2/VO\uparrow2-1)\uparrow.5)$$

where RL is the load resistance, VO is the desired output voltage, and VL is the RMS value of the line voltage (most of the time 11Ø to 117 volts). This equation is implemented in line 11Ø of the program with an extra factor of 1E6 to yield an answer in microfarads. Line 115 rounds off the answer to two decimal places.

Since the value calculated by the program will most likely be a nonstandard value, the program allows the user to enter the closest standard value (line 16Ø). The output voltage is then calculated.

Since this is an unregulated supply, the range of output current is rather limited. It can be increased considerably by adding a zener diode to the circuit.

When using a power supply of this type, there are a few important things to remember. First, the output voltage is inversely proportional to the frequency. Therefore, if the frequency goes down (6Ø to 5Ø Hz), the output voltage will go up. Another important point is that this power supply is not isolated from the line. If the case of the device being powered is not nonconductive or grounded, the possibility of electrical shock exists.

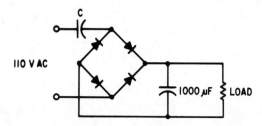

Fig. 8.3 Transformerless power supply

```
0    CALL  - 936
1    PRINT : PRINT : PRINT : PRINT "WRITTEN BY JULES H. GILDER"
2    PRINT : PRINT "COPYRIGHT (C) HAYDEN BOOK CO. 1978
3    FOR X = 1 TO 4000: NEXT X
4    PRINT : PRINT : PRINT : PRINT
5    PRINT  TAB( 6)"TRANSFORMERLESS POWER SUPPLY"
6    PRINT : PRINT : PRINT : PRINT
10   PRINT "THIS PROGRAM DESIGNS A LOW COST, TRANS-"
20   PRINT "FORMERLESS DC POWER SUPPLY. YOU MUST"
30   PRINT "ENTER THE AC LINE VOLTAGE (110/220) AND"
40   PRINT "THE FREQUENCY (50/60 HZ). ALSO REQUIRED"
50   PRINT "ARE THE LOAD RESISTANCE AND•DESIRED"
60   PRINT "VOLTAGE.
65   PRINT : PRINT : PRINT
70   INPUT "ENTER AC VOLTAGE: ";VL
75   PRINT : INPUT "ENTER FREQUENCY (HZ): ";F
80   PRINT
90   INPUT "ENTER DC OUTPUT VOLTAGE: ";VO
94   PRINT : INPUT "ENTER LOAD RESISTANCE (OHMS): ";RL
95   PRINT : PRINT : PRINT
100  W = 6.2831854 * F
110  C = 1 / (W * RL    * (VL ↑ 2 / VO ↑ 2 - 1) ↑ .5) * 1E6
115  C =  INT (100 * C + .5) / 100
120  PRINT "THE VALUE FOR 'C' SHOULD BE CLOSE TO"
130  PRINT C;" MICROFARADS. SELECT"
140  PRINT "THE NEAREST STANDARD VALUE"
150  PRINT
160  INPUT "ENTER C (MICROFARADS): ";C
165  C = C * 1E - 6
170  PRINT : PRINT : PRINT
180  VC = VL * RL /  SQR (RL ↑ 2 + (1 / (W * C) ↑ 2))
185  C =  INT (C * 1E6 * 100 + .5) / 100
187  VC =  INT (VC * 100 + .5) / 100
190  PRINT "WITH A CAPACITOR OF ";C;" MICROFARADS"
200  PRINT "THE OUTPUT VOLTAGE WILL BE ";VC;" VOLTS"
210  PRINT : PRINT
220  PRINT "DO YOU WANT TO TRY ANOTHER DESIGN? ";
230  INPUT "";A$
235  PRINT : PRINT
240  IF  LEFT$ (A$,1) = "Y" THEN 70
250  END
```

```
        TRANSFORMERLESS POWER SUPPLY


THIS PROGRAM DESIGNS A LOW COST, TRANS-
FORMERLESS DC POWER SUPPLY. YOU MUST
ENTER THE AC LINE VOLTAGE (110/220) AND
THE FREQUENCY (50/60 HZ). ALSO REQUIRED
ARE THE LOAD RESISTANCE AND DESIRED
VOLTAGE.

ENTER AC VOLTAGE: 110

ENTER FREQUENCY (HZ): 60

ENTER DC OUTPUT VOLTAGE: 6

ENTER LOAD RESISTANCE (OHMS): 20


THE VALUE FOR 'C' SHOULD BE CLOSE TO
7.25 MICROFARADS. SELECT
THE NEAREST STANDARD VALUE

ENTER C (MICROFARADS): 6.8


WITH A CAPACITOR OF 6.8 MICROFARADS
THE OUTPUT VOLTAGE WILL BE 5.63 VOLTS

DO YOU WANT TO TRY ANOTHER DESIGN? NO
```

8.5 TWO-DIODE FULL-WAVE REGULATED POWER SUPPLY

A full-wave rectified power supply that uses only two diodes and a center-tapped transformer is a must for low voltage outputs. It has fewer components than the bridge rectifier supply and does not have the additional two diode voltage drops of the bridge circuit, an important factor in low voltage designs.

This program makes designing full-wave supplies a snap. The design takes into account factors often ignored, such as high and low line voltages. To use the program, the high, low, and nominal line voltages must be entered along with the voltage regulator drop, peak-to-peak ripple voltage, desired output voltage, and load current. All voltages are entered in volts, and the load current is entered in amperes.

The program will then indicate what the transformer secondary voltage must be, giving the voltage for each half of the secondary, indicating the secondary current and the volt-amperes of the transformer, and suggesting a value for the filter capacitor.

The generalized circuit for this power supply is shown in Fig. 8.4. The regulator, indicated as a block, can be either a discrete regulator or an integrated circuit.

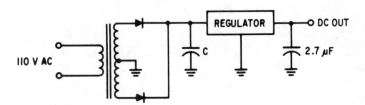

Fig. 8.4 Two-diode full-wave regulated power supply

```
0   CALL  - 936
1   PRINT : PRINT : PRINT : PRINT "WRITTEN BY JULES H. GILDER"
2   PRINT : PRINT "COPYRIGHT (C) HAYDEN BOOK CO. 1978"
3   FOR X = 1 TO 4000: NEXT X
4   PRINT : PRINT : PRINT : PRINT
5   PRINT  TAB( 4)"FULL WAVE REGULATED POWER SUPPLY"
10  PRINT : PRINT : PRINT : PRINT
20  PRINT "THIS PROGRAM DESIGNS A TWO-DIODE FULL"
25  PRINT "WAVE RECTIFIED, REGULATED POWER SUPPLY."
30  PRINT "ENTER ALL VOLTAGES IN VOLTS."
35  PRINT : PRINT : PRINT
40  INPUT "ENTER OUTPUT VOLTAGE: ";VO
60  INPUT "ENTER VOLTAGE REGULATOR DROP: ";VR
80  INPUT "ENTER RIPPLE VOLTAGE (P-P): ";RV
100 INPUT "ENTER NOMINAL LINE VOLTAGE: ";VN
120 INPUT "ENTER LINE VOLTAGE LOW: ";VL
140 INPUT "ENTER LINE VOLTAGE HIGH: ";VH
160 VAC = (VO + VR + 1.25 + RV / 2) * VN / .92 / VL /  SQR (2)
170 INPUT "ENTER REQUIRED CURRENT (AMPS): ";I
180 PRINT
190 IO =  INT (1.2 * I * 10 + .5) / 10
200 C = IO / RV * 6E - 3
```

```
205 C =  INT (1E7 * C + .5) / 10
210  IF  I > 1  THEN  C = C * 3
220  PRINT : PRINT : PRINT
230  PRINT "   2-DIODE FULL WAVE REGULATED SUPPLY"
240  PRINT : PRINT : PRINT
250  PRINT "FOR A ";VO;" VOLT, ";I;" AMP POWER SUPPLY:"
252  PRINT
260 VAC =  INT (10 * VAC + .5) / 10
265  PRINT : PRINT "TOTAL SECONDARY VOLTAGE = ";2 * VAC;" VOLTS"
270  PRINT : PRINT "EACH HALF OF THE SECONDARY = ";VA;" VOLTS"
275  PRINT : PRINT "TRANSFORMER SECONDARY CURRENT = ";I0;" AMP"
276  PRINT : PRINT "TRANSFORMER POWER RATING = "; INT (10 * VAC *
     2 + .5);" VA"
280  PRINT : PRINT "RECOMMENDED CAPACITANCE = ";C;" MFD"
285  PRINT : PRINT
290  PRINT : PRINT "FOR LIGHT LOADS AND HIGH LINE VOLTAGE"
300  PRINT "THE VOLTAGE DROP ACROSS THE REGULATOR"
310  PRINT "WILL BE "; INT (10 * VH / VL * VAC / 2 + .5) / 10;" V
     OLTS."
320  END
```

```
FULL WAVE REGULATED POWER SUPPLY


THIS PROGRAM DESIGNS A TWO-DIODE FULL
WAVE RECTIFIED, REGULATED POWER SUPPLY.
ENTER ALL VOLTAGES IN VOLTS.


ENTER OUTPUT VOLTAGE: 12
ENTER VOLTAGE REGULATOR DROP: 3
ENTER RIPPLE VOLTAGE (P-P): 1.2
ENTER NOMINAL LINE VOLTAGE: 110
ENTER LINE VOLTAGE LOW: 95
ENTER LINE VOLTAGE HIGH: 130
ENTER REQUIRED CURRENT (AMPS): 2


   2-DIODE FULL WAVE REGULATED SUPPLY


FOR A 12 VOLT, 2 AMP POWER SUPPLY:

TOTAL SECONDARY VOLTAGE = 30 VOLTS

EACH HALF OF THE SECONDARY = 15 VOLTS

TRANSFORMER SECONDARY CURRENT = 2.4 AMP

TRANSFORMER POWER RATING = 72 VA

RECOMMENDED CAPACITANCE = 36000 MFD


FOR LIGHT LOADS AND HIGH LINE VOLTAGE
THE VOLTAGE DROP ACROSS THE REGULATOR
WILL BE 10.3 VOLTS.
```

8.6 BRIDGE-RECTIFIED REGULATED POWER SUPPLY

As mentioned earlier, a bridge-rectified power supply (Fig. 8.5) is not a good choice for low-voltage supplies because the extra two diodes in the bridge circuit cause an additional voltage drop that may not always be tolerable. For most other applications, however, the bridge rectifier is an excellent choice. Two reasons for this are that center-tapped secondary transformers are not needed and the voltage of the secondary winding is lower with the bridge circuit. Of course the current will have to be higher to get the same output power.

Like the previous program, this one also requires high, low, and nominal values of the line voltage to be entered, as well as the minimum voltage regulator drop, load voltage, and current.

The output consists of the transformer secondary voltage, current and volt-ampere ratings, and a value for the filter capacitor.

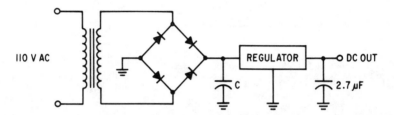

Fig. 8.5 Bridge-rectified regulated power supply

```
0   CALL  - 936
1   PRINT : PRINT : PRINT : PRINT "WRITTEN BY JULES H. GILDER"
2   PRINT : PRINT "COPYRIGHT (C) HAYDEN  BOOK CO. 1978"
3   FOR X = 1 TO 4000: NEXT X
4   PRINT : PRINT : PRINT : PRINT
5   PRINT  TAB( 5)"BRIDGE REGULATED POWER SUPPLY"
10   PRINT : PRINT : PRINT : PRINT
20   PRINT "THIS PROGRAM DESIGNS A BRIDGE FULL-WAVE"
25   PRINT "RECTIFIED, REGULATED POWER SUPPLY."
30   PRINT : PRINT : PRINT
40   INPUT "ENTER OUTPUT VOLTAGE: ";VO
50   PRINT
60   INPUT "ENTER VOLTAGE REGULATOR DROP: ";VR
70   PRINT
80   INPUT "ENTER RIPPLE VOLTAGE (P-P): ";RV
90   PRINT
100   INPUT "ENTER NOMINAL LINE VOLTAGE: ";VN
110   PRINT
120   INPUT "ENTER LINE VOLTAGE LOW: ";VL
130   PRINT
140   INPUT "ENTER LINE VOLTAGE HIGH: ";VH
150   PRINT
160   VAC = ( VO + VR + 2.50 + RV / 2) * VN / .92 / VL /  SQR (2)
170   INPUT "ENTER REQUIRED CURRENT (AMPS): ";I
180   PRINT
190   IO =   INT (1.8 * I * 10 + .5) / 10
200   C = IO / RV * 6E - 3
205   C =   INT ( 1E7 * C + .5) / 10
210   IF  I > 1  THEN  C = C * 3
220   PRINT : PRINT : PRINT
```

```
230    PRINT "      REGULATED POWER SUPPLY DESIGN"
240    PRINT : PRINT : PRINT
250    PRINT "FOR A ";VO;" VOLT, ";I;" AMP POWER SUPPLY:"
252    PRINT
260 VAC =  INT (10 * VAC + .5) / 10
270    PRINT : PRINT "TRANSFORMER SECONDARY VOLTAGE = ";VAC;" V "
275    PRINT : PRINT "TRANSFORMER SECONDARY CURRENT = ";I0;" AMP"
276    PRINT : PRINT "TRANSFORMER POWER RATING = "; INT (I0 * VAC +
       .5);" VA"
280    PRINT : PRINT "RECOMMENDED CAPACITANCE = ";C;" MFD"
285    PRINT : PRINT
290    PRINT : PRINT "FOR LIGHT LOADS AND HIGH LINE VOLTAGE"
300    PRINT "THE VOLTAGE DROP ACROSS THE REGULATOR"
310    PRINT "WILL BE "; INT (10 * VH / VL * VAC / 2 + .5) / 10;" V
       OLTS."
```

```
          BRIDGE REGULATED POWER SUPPLY


THIS PROGRAM DESIGNS A BRIDGE FULL-WAVE
RECTIFIED, REGULATED POWER SUPPLY.

ENTER OUTPUT VOLTAGE: 5

ENTER VOLTAGE REGULATOR DROP: 3

ENTER RIPPLE VOLTAGE (P-P): 1

ENTER NOMINAL LINE VOLTAGE: 110

ENTER LINE VOLTAGE LOW: 95

ENTER LINE VOLTAGE HIGH: 130

ENTER REQUIRED CURRENT (AMPS): 10


          REGULATED POWER SUPPLY DESIGN


FOR A 5 VOLT, 10 AMP POWER SUPPLY:

TRANSFORMER SECONDARY VOLTAGE = 9.8 V

TRANSFORMER SECONDARY CURRENT = 18 AMP

TRANSFORMER POWER RATING = 176 VA

RECOMMENDED CAPACITANCE = 324000 MFD


FOR LIGHT LOADS AND HIGH LINE VOLTAGE
THE VOLTAGE DROP ACROSS THE REGULATOR
WILL BE 6.7 VOLTS.
```

8.7 DUAL-OUTPUT REGULATED POWER SUPPLY

While most digital circuits require only a single supply voltage, a few linear integrated circuits must have symmetrical output voltages that are +V and –V. A power supply to meet these requirements could simply be composed of two supplies in series. But a more effective way of building such a supply is to use a full-wave complementary rectifier design. This circuit combines both the two-diode and bridge full-wave rectifiers into a circuit that will supply both positive and negative voltages.

The circuit in Fig. 8.6 requires a center-tapped secondary transformer. The two voltages of opposite polarity are developed across the bridge and measured with reference to the ground, where the center tap of the transformer secondary is connected.

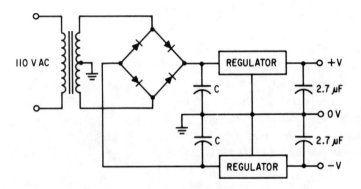

Fig. 8.6 Dual-output regulated power supply

```
0   CALL  - 936
1   PRINT : PRINT : PRINT : PRINT "WRITTEN BY JULES H. GILDER"
2   PRINT : PRINT "COPYRIGHT (C) HAYDEN BOOK CO. 1978"
3   FOR X = 1 TO 4000: NEXT X
4   PRINT : PRINT : PRINT : PRINT
5   PRINT  TAB( 6)"DUAL REGULATED POWER SUPPLY"
10  PRINT : PRINT : PRINT : PRINT
20  PRINT "THIS PROGRAM DESIGNS A DUAL REGULATED"
25  PRINT "POWER SUPPLY."
30  PRINT : PRINT : PRINT
40  INPUT "ENTER SYMMETRICAL OUTPUT VOLTAGE: ";VO
50  PRINT
60  INPUT "ENTER VOLTAGE REGULATOR DROP: ";VR
70  PRINT
80  INPUT "ENTER RIPPLE VOLTAGE (P-P): ";RV
90  PRINT
100 INPUT "ENTER NOMINAL LINE VOLTAGE: ";VN
110 PRINT
120 INPUT "ENTER LINE VOLTAGE LOW: ";VL
130 PRINT
140 INPUT "ENTER LINE VOLTAGE HIGH: ";VH
150 PRINT
160 VAC = ( VO + VR + 1.25 + RV / 2 ) * VN / .92 / VL /  SQR (2)
170 INPUT "ENTER REQUIRED CURRENT: ";I
```

```
180   PRINT
190   IO =   INT (1.8 * I * 10 + .5) / 10

200   C = IO / RV * 6E - 3
205   C =   INT (1E7 * C + .5) / 10
210   IF  I > 1  THEN  C = C * 3
220   PRINT : PRINT : PRINT
230   PRINT "     REGULATED POWER SUPPLY DESIGN"
240   PRINT : PRINT : PRINT
250   PRINT "FOR A ";VO;" VOLT, ";I;" AMP POWER SUPPLY:"
252   PRINT
260   VAC =   INT (10 * VAC + .5) / 10
270   PRINT : PRINT "TRANSFORMER SECONDARY VOLTAGE = ";VAC * 2;" C
      T"
275   PRINT : PRINT "TRANSFORMER SECONDARY CURRENT = ";IO;" AMP"
276   PRINT : PRINT "TRANSFORMER POWER RATING = "; INT (IO * VAC *
      2 + .5);" VA"
280   PRINT : PRINT "RECOMMENDED CAPACITANCE = ";C;" MFD"
285   PRINT : PRINT
290   PRINT : PRINT "FOR LIGHT LOADS AND HIGH LINE VOLTAGE"
300   PRINT "THE VOLTAGE DROP ACROSS THE REGULATOR"
310   PRINT "WILL BE "; INT (10 * VH / VL * VAC / 2 + .5) / 10;" V
      OLTS."
```

DUAL REGULATED POWER SUPPLY

THIS PROGRAM DESIGNS A DUAL REGULATED
POWER SUPPLY.

ENTER SYMMETRICAL OUTPUT VOLTAGE: 18

ENTER VOLTAGE REGULATOR DROP: 3

ENTER RIPPLE VOLTAGE (P-P): 1.5

ENTER NOMINAL LINE VOLTAGE: 110

ENTER LINE VOLTAGE LOW: 95

ENTER LINE VOLTAGE HIGH: 130

ENTER REQUIRED CURRENT: 1

       REGULATED POWER SUPPLY DESIGN

FOR A 18 VOLT, 1 AMP POWER SUPPLY:

TRANSFORMER SECONDARY VOLTAGE = 41 CT

TRANSFORMER SECONDARY CURRENT = 1.8 AMP

TRANSFORMER POWER RATING = 74 VA

RECOMMENDED CAPACITANCE = 7200 MFD

FOR LIGHT LOADS AND HIGH LINE VOLTAGE
THE VOLTAGE DROP ACROSS THE REGULATOR
WILL BE 14 VOLTS.

9 Active Filter Design

In the processing of analog signals, it is invariably necessary to filter the signal to separate desired information from unwanted noise. Active filters are very attractive for this application because with them it is possible to tailor the filter cutoff characteristics and gain to any specific set of requirements.

The first three programs in this chapter design active bandpass filters. The specific instances when a particular one of these should or should not be used are indicated in the text accompanying the programs.

The next two programs design notch filters, which are generally used to remove a specific noise component, such as 6Ø Hz hum from audio signals. The final three programs design various active low-pass filters, including a FET input version.

9.1 ACTIVE BANDPASS FILTER[1]

The bandpass filter in Fig. 9.1 is of simple design and can be fabricated with a conventional 741 operational amplifier. Like the program for active low-pass filter No. 2 (see Fig. 9.7), this program contains a data statement (line 23Ø) with nine standard values for C1, enabling nine different designs for the same circuit parameters. The program also contains two routines for selecting the proper string descriptors for the capacitors and resistors. Lines 166 to 175 select the proper capacitor descriptors, and lines 21Ø to 215 select the proper resistor descriptors.

When run, the program requests the center frequency, bandwidth, and magnitude of the gain in the passband.

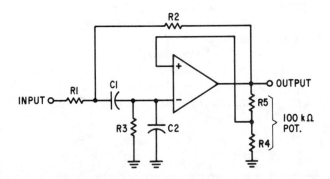

Fig. 9.1 Active bandpass filter

```
0   CALL  - 936
1   PRINT : PRINT : PRINT : PRINT "WRITTEN BY JULES H. GILDER"
2   PRINT : PRINT "COPYRIGHT (C) HAYDEN BOOK CO. 1978"
3   FOR X = 1 TO 4000: NEXT X
4   PRINT : PRINT : PRINT
5   PRINT  TAB( 11 )"ACTIVE BANDPASS FILTER"
10   PRINT : PRINT : PRINT : PRINT
20   PRINT "THIS PROGRAM DESIGNS A BANDPASS ACTIVE"
30   PRINT "FILTER. YOU MUST ENTER THE CENTER"
40   PRINT "FREQUENCY, THE BANDWIDTH AND THE DESIRED"
50   PRINT "GAIN. THE PROGRAM WILL SUPPLY COM-"
60   PRINT "PONENT VALUES FOR NINE STANDARD VALUES"
70   PRINT "OF C1.  YOU CAN THEN SELECT THE MOST"
80   PRINT "CONVENIENT SET OF VALUES TO USE."
90   PRINT : PRINT : PRINT
100   INPUT "ENTER FREQUENCY (HZ): ";F
104   PRINT : INPUT "ENTER GAIN: ";G
106   PRINT : INPUT "ENTER BANDWIDTH (HZ): ";BW
108 Q = F / BW
110   PRINT : PRINT : PRINT
115 A( 6 ) = 10
120   FOR XX = 1 TO 9
130 D$ = " MICROFARADS":E$ = " NANOFARADS"
```

[1]Adapted from H. Minuskin, "Active Filter Design Uses Basic Language," *Electronic Design* 5 (March 1, 1970): p. 83.

```
140   READ  C1
150 K = C1 * 6.28 * F
160 M = .333 * (6.5 - (1 / Q))
164 CA = C1 * 1E6
165 C1 =  INT (CA + .5)
166  IF  C1 < 1  THEN  D$ = " NANOFARADS"
167  IF  C1 < 1  THEN  C1 =  INT (CA * 1E3 + .5)
170 C2 = .5 * C1
171  IF  C2 =  > 1000  OR  D$ = " MICROFARADS"  THEN  E$ = " MICR
     OFARADS"
172  IF C2 =  > 1000  AND D$ = " MICROFARADS" THEN 180
175  IF C2 =  > 1000 THEN C2 =  INT (C2 / 100 + .5) / 10
180 R(2) = .666 / K
190 R(1) = 3 * R(2)
200 R(3) = 4 / K
202 R(5) = 1E5 / M
204 R(4) = R(5) * (M - 1)
205  GOTO 220
210  REM
212  IF R(J) =  > 1E6 THEN R(J) = R(J) / 1E6:R$(J) = " MEGOHMS": GOTO
     218
213  IF R(J) =  > 1E3 THEN R(J) = R(J) / 1E3:R$(J) = " KILOHMS": GOTO
     218
215 R$(J) = " OHMS"
218  RETURN
220  PRINT "C1 = ";C1;D$
221  PRINT "C2 = ";C2;E$
222  PRINT
223  FOR J = 1 TO 5
224  GOSUB 210
225 X = R(J): GOSUB 300:R(J) = X
226  NEXT J
227  FOR J = 1 TO 5
228  PRINT "R";J;" = ";R(J);R$(J)
229  NEXT J
230  DATA   1E-9,1E-8,2.2E-8,4.7E-8,1E-7,2.2E-7,4.7E-7,1E-6,1E-5

235  IF XX = 9 THEN 270
237  PRINT
240  PRINT : INPUT "ANOTHER SET OF VALUES? ";A$
245  PRINT : PRINT : PRINT
250  IF  LEFT$ (A$,1) = "N" THEN 270
260  NEXT XX
270  END
300  IF J > 3 THEN X =  INT (R(J) + .5): RETURN
305 A(4) = 1.19927E - 2 *  INT (1 + 1.5 * A(6) + .004 * A(6) ↑ 2)

310 A(3) =  INT ( LOG (X) /  LOG (10) -  INT (2.2 - 3 * A(4)))
320 X = X / 10 ↑ A(3)
330  FOR K = 1 TO 2
340 A(K) =  INT ( EXP (A(4) * ( INT ( LOG (X) / A(4)) + K - 1)) +
     .5)
350 A(5) = 1.88E - 5 * A(K) ↑ 3 - .00335 * A(K) ↑ 2 + .164 * A(K)
     - 1.284
360 A(K) = A(K) +  INT (A(5) *  INT (3 * A(4) + .8))
370  NEXT K
380 X = 10 ↑ A(3) * A(X /  SQR (A(1) * A(2)) + 1)
390 X =  INT (X + .5)
400  RETURN
```

ACTIVE BANDPASS FILTER

THIS PROGRAM DESIGNS A BANDPASS ACTIVE
FILTER. YOU MUST ENTER THE CENTER
FREQUENCY, THE BANDWIDTH AND THE DESIRED
GAIN. THE PROGRAM WILL SUPPLY COM-
PONENT VALUES FOR NINE STANDARD VALUES
OF C1. YOU CAN THEN SELECT THE MOST
CONVENIENT SET OF VALUES TO USE.

ENTER FREQUENCY (HZ): 3000

ENTER GAIN: 10

ENTER BANDWIDTH (HZ): 1000

C1 = 1 NANOFARADS
C2 = .5 NANOFARADS

R1 = 100 KILOHMS
R2 = 33 KILOHMS
R3 = 220 KILOHMS
R4 = 51 KILOHMS
R5 = 49 KILOHMS

ANOTHER SET OF VALUES? YES

C1 = 10 NANOFARADS
C2 = 5 NANOFARADS

R1 = 10 KILOHMS
R2 = 3 KILOHMS
R3 = 22 KILOHMS
R4 = 51 KILOHMS
R5 = 49 KILOHMS

ANOTHER SET OF VALUES? NO

9.2 STATE VARIABLE BANDPASS FILTER

This program calculates the component values required for a state variable bandpass filter. This particular one is built with three operational amplifiers as shown in Fig. 9.2. This active filter has several advantages over other types of filters. It can provide circuit Qs of over 1∅∅. It is stable and insensitive to passive component drift.

Components used in the filter should be of high quality. Carbon resistors are suitable, but capacitors designed for bypass and coupling applications are not. Their tolerance and stability are generally poor.

To use the program, the frequency characteristics of the op amp must be known. The popular 741 op amp can easily be used.

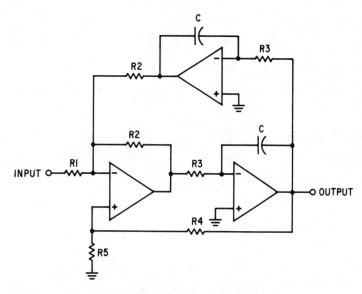

Fig. 9.2 State variable bandpass filter

```
0   CALL  - 936
1   PRINT : PRINT : PRINT : PRINT "WRITTEN BY JULES H. GILDER"
2   PRINT : PRINT "COPYRIGHT (C) HAYDEN BOOK CO. 1978"
3   FOR X = 1 TO 4000: NEXT X
4   PRINT : PRINT : PRINT : PRINT
5   PRINT  TAB( 5)"STATE VARIABLE BANDPASS FILTER"
10  PRINT : PRINT : PRINT : PRINT
20  PRINT "THIS PROGRAM WILL DESIGN A STATE"
30  PRINT "VARIABLE ACTIVE BANDPASS FILTER."
40  PRINT "USING AN OPERATIONAL AMPLIFIER"
45  PRINT "AS THE ACTIVE ELEMENT. "
50  PRINT : PRINT : PRINT : PRINT
```

```
140   INPUT "ENTER F(T) OF THE OP AMP (MHZ): ";FT
142 FT = FT * 1E6
145   PRINT
150   INPUT "ENTER DESIRED GAIN (DB): ";G
155   PRINT
160   INPUT "ENTER DESIRED Q: ";Q
165   PRINT
170   INPUT "ENTER CENTER FREQUENCY (HZ): ";F
180   PRINT : PRINT : PRINT
190   R(2) = 1E5
200   R(4) = 1E5
260   C = 1 / (6.2832 * F * 1E - 4)
265   C = INT (C + .5)
270   PRINT "THE CAPACITORS SHOULD HAVE A VALUE OF"
280   PRINT "ABOUT ";C;" NANOFARADS."
290   PRINT
300   INPUT "ENTER NEAREST STANDARD VALUE: ";C
302 CC = C
305   C = C * 1E - 9
310   R(1) = R(2) * Q / (10 ↑ (G / 20))
315 PI = 3.1415927
320   R(3) = (1 - (F / FT)) / (2 * PI * F * C)
324 V = 10 ↑ (G / 20)
325 X = 2 * (Q + V)
329 ZZ = 1 + (2 * X) / (FT / F)
330   R(5) = R(4) / (X / ZZ - 1)
355   PRINT : PRINT
360   FOR I = 1 TO 5
361 B$ = " KILOHMS "
362 RR = R(I)
364   R(I) = INT (R(I) / 100 + .5) / 10
366   IF R(I) < 1 THEN B$ = " OHMS "
368   IF R(I) < 1 THEN R(I) = INT (RR + .5)
370   PRINT "R";I;" = ";R(I);B$
375   NEXT I
376   PRINT
380   FOR I = 1 TO 2
390   PRINT "C";I;" = ";CC;" NANOFARADS"
410   NEXT I
420   PRINT
430   INPUT "WANT TO TRY AGAIN? ";A$
435   PRINT : PRINT
440   IF LEFT$ (A$,1) = "Y" THEN 140
450   END
```

```
        STATE VARIABLE BANDPASS FILTER


THIS PROGRAM WILL DESIGN A STATE
VARIABLE ACTIVE BANDPASS FILTER,
USING AN OPERATIONAL AMPLIFIER
AS THE ACTIVE ELEMENT.


ENTER F(T) OF THE OP AMP (MHZ): 1

ENTER DESIRED GAIN (DB): 12

ENTER DESIRED Q: 20

ENTER CENTER FREQUENCY (HZ): 3000


THE CAPACITORS SHOULD HAVE A VALUE OF
ABOUT 1 NANOFARADS.
```

```
ENTER NEAREST STANDARD VALUE: 1

R1 = 502.4 KILOHMS
R2 = 100 KILOHMS
R3 = 52.9 KILOHMS
R4 = 100 KILOHMS
R5 = 2.8 KILOHMS

C1 = 1 NANOFARADS
C2 = 1 NANOFARADS

WANT TO TRY AGAIN? NO
```

9.3 MULTIPLE FEEDBACK BANDPASS FILTER

Where high circuit Qs are not essential (values of 1∅ or less), the multiple feedback bandpass filter should be considered. It requires the use of only one operational amplifier and only five other passive components.

Most of the time it is possible to use the 741. op amp for this circuit. However, if the parameters entered indicate that an amplifier with an F(T) of more than 1 MHz is needed, the program will indicate that a 741 is not suitable and will state what the required F(T) should be.

The schematic for the circuit is shown in Fig. 9.3.

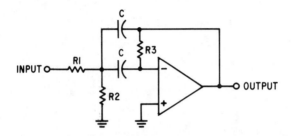

Fig. 9.3 Multiple feedback bandpass filter

```
0    CALL  - 936
1    PRINT : PRINT : PRINT : PRINT "WRITTEN BY JULES H. GILDER"
2    PRINT : PRINT "COPYRIGHT (C) HAYDEN BOOK CO. 1978"
3    FOR X = 1 TO 4000: NEXT X
4    PRINT : PRINT : PRINT : PRINT
5    PRINT  TAB( 4)"MULTIPLE FEEDBACK BANDPASS FILTER"
10   PRINT : PRINT : PRINT : PRINT
20   PRINT "THIS PROGRAM WILL DESIGN A MULTIPLE"
30   PRINT "FEEDBACK ACTIVE BANDPASS FILTER. THE"
40   PRINT "'Q' OF THIS FILTER IS LIMITED TO 10"
140  PRINT : PRINT : PRINT
150  INPUT "ENTER DESIRED GAIN (DB): ";G
155  PRINT
160  INPUT "ENTER DESIRED Q: ";Q
162  IF Q > 10 THEN 155
165  PRINT
170  INPUT "ENTER CENTER FREQUENCY (HZ): ";F
175  FT =  INT (100 * F + .5)
180  PRINT : PRINT : PRINT
190  PRINT "FOR A BANDPASS FREQUENCY OF ";F;" HERTZ"
200  PRINT "YOU NEED AN OP AMP WITH A AN F(T)"
210  PRINT "OF AT LEAST ";FT;" HERTZ"
220  PRINT
225  Z$ = "MAY"
230  IF  FT > 1E6  THEN  Z$ = "MAY NOT"
240  PRINT "YOU ";Z$;" USE A 741 TYPE OF AMP."
250  PRINT
260  C = 1 / (6.2832 * F * 1E - 5)
265  C =  INT (C + .5)
270  PRINT "THE CAPACITORS SHOULD HAVE A VALUE OF"
280  PRINT "ABOUT ";C;" NANOFARADS."
290  PRINT
300  INPUT "ENTER NEAREST STANDARD VALUE: ";C
```

```
302 CC = C
305 C = C * 1E - 3
310 R(3) = Q / (3.1416 * F * C * 1E - 6)
320 R(1) = R(3) / (2 * 10 ↑ (G / 20))
322 PI = 3.1415927
325 ZZ = (2 * PI * F * C * 1E - 6) ↑ 2
329 X = R(3) - (1 / R(1))
330 R(2) = 1 / (ZZ * X)
340   PRINT : PRINT : PRINT
350   PRINT "THE COMPONENT VALUES ARE:"
355   PRINT : PRINT
360   FOR  I = 1  TO  3
361 B$ = " KILOHMS "
362 RR = R(I)
364 R(I) =  INT (R(I) / 100 + .5) / 10
366   IF R(I) < 1 THEN B$ = " OHMS "
368   IF  R(I) < 1  THEN  R(I) =  INT (RR + .5)
370   PRINT "R";I;" = ";R(I);B$
375   NEXT  I
376   PRINT
380   FOR  I = 1  TO  2
390   PRINT "C";I;" = ";CC;" NANOFARADS"
410   NEXT  I
420   PRINT
430   INPUT "WANT TO TRY AGAIN? ";A$
440   IF   LEFT$ (A$,1) = "Y"     THEN  140
450   END



        MULTIPLE FEEDBACK BANDPASS FILTER


THIS PROGRAM WILL DESIGN A MULTIPLE
FEEDBACK ACTIVE BANDPASS FILTER. THE
'Q' OF THIS FILTER IS LIMITED TO 10


ENTER DESIRED GAIN (DB): 10

ENTER DESIRED Q: 8

ENTER CENTER FREQUENCY (HZ): 2000


FOR A BANDPASS FREQUENCY OF 2000 HERTZ
YOU NEED AN OP AMP WITH A AN F(T)
OF AT LEAST 200000 HERTZ

YOU MAY USE A 741 TYPE OP AMP.

THE CAPACITORS SHOULD HAVE A VALUE OF
ABOUT 8 NANOFARADS.

ENTER NEAREST STANDARD VALUE: 8


THE COMPONENT VALUES ARE:

R1 = 25.2 KILOHMS
R2 = 622 OHMS
R3 = 159.2 KILOHMS

C1 = 8 NANOFARADS
C2 = 8 NANOFARADS

WANT TO TRY AGAIN? NO
```

9.4 WIEN BRIDGE NOTCH FILTER [1]

In applications requiring deep notches and high Qs, a Wien bridge filter is a good choice. Its design is simple. Since it has few frequency-determining components, it's easy to adjust the desired notch frequency.

Qs with the Wien bridge filter are higher than those for twin tee filters because there is no need for critical balancing between two parallel branch networks. Tuning is simple because there is no interaction between null- and frequency-determining components.

The program calculates component values and allows entry of the nearest standard value.

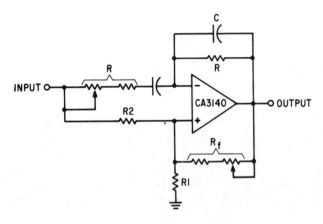

Fig. 9.4 Wien bridge notch filter

```
0    CALL  - 936
1    PRINT : PRINT : PRINT : PRINT "WRITTEN BY JULES H. GILDER"
2    PRINT : PRINT "COPYRIGHT (C) HAYDEN BOOK CO. 1978"
3    FOR X = 1 TO 4000: NEXT X
4    PRINT : PRINT : PRINT : PRINT
5    PRINT  TAB( 4)"WIEN BRIDGE NOTCH FILTER DESIGN"
10   PRINT : PRINT : PRINT
30   PRINT : PRINT : INPUT "ENTER CENTER FREQUENCY (HZ): ";F
40   PRINT : INPUT "ENTER BANDWIDTH (HZ): ";BW
60   PRINT : PRINT : PRINT
70   FBW = BW / F
80   PRINT "YOU MUST ENTER A VALUE FOR R1 IN THE"
90   PRINT "RANGE OF 100 KILOHMS TO 1 MEGOHM. YOUR"
100  PRINT "PARTICULAR APPLICATION REQUIRES A VALUE"
110  IF  FBW < = 0.1  THEN  130
120  PRINT "NEAR THE LOW END OF THE RESISTANCE RANGE"
125  GOTO  140
130  PRINT "NEAR THE HIGH END OF THE RANGE."
```

[1] G. Darilek and O. Tranbarger, "Try a Wien Bridge Network," *Electronic Design* 3 (Feb. 1, 1978): p. 80.

```
135   PRINT
140   INPUT "ENTER R1 (KILOHMS): ";R1
150 R1 = R1 * 1000
160 C = 1 / (62831.854 * F)
165   PRINT
170   PRINT "THE VALUE FOR 'C' SHOULD BE CLOSE TO"
180   PRINT   INT (C * 1E10 + .5) / 10;" NANOFARADS."
184   PRINT : PRINT
185   PRINT "ENTER THE NEAREST STANDARD VALUE IN"
190   INPUT "NANOFARADS: ";C
195   PRINT
200 C = C * 1E - 9
210 R2 = FBW * R1 / (3 - FBW)
220 RF = FBW * R1 / (3 * (2 - FBW))
230 R = 1 / (6.2831854 * F * C)
250 X = R1
260   GOSUB 400
270 R1 = X
280 X = R2
290   GOSUB 400
300 R2 = X
310 X = RF
320   GOSUB 400
330 RF = X
340 X = R
350   GOSUB 400
360 R = X
370 C =   INT (C * 1E10 + .5) / 10
375   PRINT : PRINT
380   PRINT : PRINT "FOR A WIEN BRIDGE NOTCH FILTER WITH A"
385   PRINT "CENTER FREQUENCY OF ";F;" HERTZ"
386   PRINT "AND A NOTCH BANDWIDTH OF ";BW;" HERTZ"
387   PRINT "COMPONENT VALUES ARE AS FOLLOWS:" : PRINT
388   PRINT "R1 = ";R1;" KILOHMS"
389   PRINT "R2 = ";R2;" KILOHMS"
390   PRINT "RF = ";RF;" KILOHMS"
391   PRINT "R  = ";R;" KILOHMS"
392   PRINT "C  = ";C;" NANOFARADS"
398   PRINT
399   GOTO 450
400 X =   INT (X / 100 + .5) / 10
420   RETURN
450   PRINT
460   INPUT "DO YOU WANT TO TRY ANOTHER DESIGN? ";A$
470   IF   LEFT$ (A$,1) = "Y" THEN 10
480   END


     WIEN BRIDGE NOTCH FILTER DESIGN




ENTER CENTER FREQUENCY (HZ): 3000

ENTER BANDWIDTH (HZ): 500


YOU MUST ENTER A VALUE FOR R1 IN THE
RANGE OF 100 KILOHMS TO 1 MEGOHM. YOUR
PARTICULAR APPLICATION REQUIRES A VALUE
NEAR THE LOW END OF THE RESISTANCE RANGE
ENTER R1 (KILOHMS): 100

THE VALUE FOR 'C' SHOULD BE CLOSE TO
5.3 NANOFARADS.

ENTER THE NEAREST STANDARD VALUE IN
NANOFARADS: 5
```

```
FOR A WIEN BRIDGE NOTCH FILTER WITH A
CENTER FREQUENCY OF 3000 HERTZ
AND A NOTCH BANDWIDTH OF 500 HERTZ
COMPONENT VALUES ARE AS FOLLOWS:

R1  =  100 KILOHMS
R2  =  5.9 KILOHMS
RF  =  3 KILOHMS
R   =  10.6 KILOHMS
C   =  5 NANOFARADS

DO YOU WANT TO TRY ANOTHER DESIGN? NO
```

9.5 TWIN TEE NOTCH FILTER

Twin tee filters are generally inconvenient to work with because they are difficult to adjust. Normal variable capacitors have values too low for use below 5 kHz, and fixed capacitors limit adjustment flexibility. The circuit in Fig. 9.5 overcomes these problems by using a capacitance multiplier in which the effective capacitance can be adjusted with a potentiometer.[1]

The circuit below can be adjusted to achieve a rejection of more than 70 dB. The operational amplifier used in this circuit should be of the FET input variety since high output offset voltage would result from input bias current in the feedback network. This, in turn, would decrease the amplifier's signal swing capability.

At high frequencies, C4 is needed to make the pass-frequency more uniform. Otherwise, it can be eliminated.

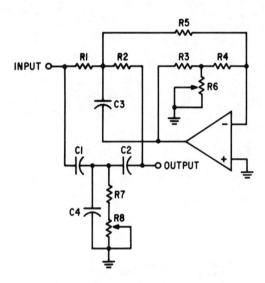

Fig. 9.5 Twin tee notch filter

```
0   CALL  - 936
1   PRINT : PRINT : PRINT : PRINT "WRITTEN BY JULES H. GILDER"
2   PRINT : PRINT "COPYRIGHT (C) HAYDEN BOOK CO. 1978"
3   FOR X = 1 TO 4000: NEXT X
4   PRINT : PRINT : PRINT : PRINT
5   PRINT  TAB( 10 )"TWIN TEE NOTCH FILTER"
10  PRINT : PRINT : PRINT
40  PRINT "THIS PROGRAM CALCULATES THE VALUES OF"
50  PRINT "THE COMPONENTS FOR A TWIN-TEE NOTCH"
```

---

[1] J. Graeme, "Twin Tee Filter Rejects More Than 70 dB with Capacitance Multiplier Circuit," *Electronic Design* 2 (Jan. 18, 1978): p. 104.

```
60    PRINT "FILTER. YOU MUST ENTER THE FREQUENCY"
70    PRINT "OF THE NOTCH AND A VALUE FOR 'C'."
80    PRINT
90    INPUT "ENTER FREQUENCY (HERTZ): ";F
95    PRINT
100   INPUT "ENTER CAPACITANCE (MICROFARADS): ";C
110 C = C * 1E - 6
120   PRINT
125 B$ = " KILOHMS"
130 R = 1 / (3.1416 * F * C * 2 ↑ .5)
131 RR = R
135 C = C * 1E6
140 R = INT (R / 1000 + .5)
141   IF  R > 0  THEN  150
142 R =  INT (   RR + .5)
144 B$ = " OHMS"
150 R(1) = R
160 R(2) = R
170 R(3) = 10 * R
180 R(4) = 10 * R
190 R(5) = 100 * R
200 R(6) = 1.5 * R
210 R(7) = .2 * R
220 R(8) = .1 * R
230 C(1) = C
240 C(2) = C
250 C(3) = .7 * C
255 C(4) = C / 100
256   PRINT : PRINT : PRINT : PRINT : PRINT
260   PRINT "FOR A NOTCH FREQUENCY OF ";F;" HERTZ"
270   PRINT "AND A VALUE 'C' OF ";C;" MICROFARADS"
280   PRINT "THE COMPONENT VALUES ARE:"
285   PRINT : PRINT
290   FOR  I = 1  TO  8
300   PRINT "R";I;" = ";R(I);B$;
310   IF  I > 4  THEN  330
320   PRINT "    C";I;" = ";C(I);" MFD"
325   GOTO 340
330   PRINT
340   NEXT  I
342   PRINT
344   PRINT "* C4 IS ONLY NEEDED FOR HIGH FREQUENCIES"
345   PRINT
350   INPUT "DO YOU WANT TO CHANGE 'C'? ";Z$
360   IF   LEFT$ (Z$,1) = "Y"  THEN   95
370   PRINT
380   INPUT "NEW FREQUENCY? ";Z$
390   IF   LEFT$ (Z$,1) = "Y"  THEN  80
```

```
                 TWIN TEE NOTCH FILTER


THIS PROGRAM CALCULATES THE VALUES OF
THE COMPONENTS FOR A TWIN-TEE NOTCH
FILTER. YOU MUST ENTER THE FREQUENCY
OF THE NOTCH AND A VALUE FOR 'C'.

ENTER FREQUENCY (HERTZ): 60

ENTER CAPACITANCE (MICROFARADS): .1
```

```
FOR A NOTCH FREQUENCY OF 60 HERTZ
AND A VALUE 'C' OF .1 MICROFARADS
THE COMPONENT VALUES ARE:

R1 = 38 KILOHMS     C1 = .1 MFD
R2 = 38 KILOHMS     C2 = .1 MFD
R3 = 380 KILOHMS    C3 = .07 MFD
R4 = 380 KILOHMS    C4 = 1E-03 MFD
R5 = 3800 KILOHMS
R6 = 57 KILOHMS
R7 = 7.6 KILOHMS
R8 = 3.8 KILOHMS

* C4 IS ONLY NEEDED FOR HIGH FREQUENCIES

DO YOU WANT TO CHANGE 'C'? NO

NEW FREQUENCY? NO
```

9.6 ACTIVE LOW-PASS FILTER NO. 1

A two-pole active low-pass filter that is built with a FET input operational amplifier (like the CA313Ø or CA314Ø) can be designed for upper cutoff frequencies ranging from hundredths of hertz to tens of kilohertz.[1]

The circuit in Fig. 9.6 uses a single amplifier and four other passive components. The program is structured so that the user may enter in component values that are available and close to those desired. The program then uses these component values to calculate the others. As a result, the filter can be designed to operate with components on hand.

If a value chosen is not of the proper value, the program will instruct the user to select another value.

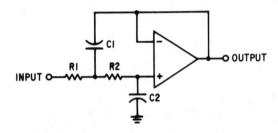

Fig. 9.6 Active low-pass filter No. 1 (FET input)

```
0   CALL  - 936
1   PRINT : PRINT : PRINT : PRINT "WRITTEN BY JULES H. GILDER"
2   PRINT : PRINT "COPYRIGHT (C) HAYDEN BOOK CO. 1978"
3   FOR X = 1 TO 4000: NEXT X
4   PRINT : PRINT : PRINT : PRINT
5   PRINT  TAB( 7)"ACTIVE LOW PASS FILTER #1"
10   PRINT : PRINT : PRINT : PRINT
20   PRINT "THIS PROGRAM DESIGNS ACTIVE LOW-PASS"
30   PRINT "FILTERS. FOR BEST RESULTS USE A FET"
40   PRINT "INPUT OP AMP (E.G.  CA 3140). YOU MUST"
50   PRINT "ENTER VALUES FOR THE DAMPING FACTOR"
60   PRINT "(PSI) AND THE RATIO OF THE UNDAMPED"
70   PRINT "NATURAL FREQUENCY TO THE CUTOFF FRE-"
80   PRINT "QUENCY (WO/WC)."
90   PRINT
100   PRINT "AMPLIFIER INPUT CURRENT DRIFT IS "
110   PRINT "ASSUMED TO BE 10 NA, RESULTING IN A"
120   PRINT "1 MV CHANGE IN VOLTAGE. DO YOU WANT TO"
130   PRINT "CHANGE THESE VALUES? ";
140   INPUT "";A$
```

---

[1]K. Timothy, "Design Active Low-Pass Filters," *Electronic Design* 18 (Sept. 1, 1977): p. 144.

```
145 IC = 1E - 8
146 VC = 1E - 3
150  IF   LEFT$ (A$,1) = "N"   THEN  170
155  PRINT
160  INPUT "ENTER CURRENT DRIFT (NA) : ";IC
162 IC = IC * 1E - 9
165  INPUT "ENTER VOLTAGE DRIFT (MV); ";VC
166 VC = VC * 1E - 3
170  PRINT
180 RMAX = VC / IC
190  INPUT "ENTER PSI: ";PSI
200  INPUT "ENTER WO/WC: ";W
210  PRINT
220  INPUT "ENTER CUTOFF FREQUENCY: ";F
230  PRINT
240 WO = 2 * 3.1416 * W * F
250 C(1) = 2 / (PSI * WO * RMAX) * 1E9
255 C(1) =  INT (100 * C(1) + .5) / 100
260  PRINT "C 1  SHOULD BE ABOUT ";C(1);" NANOFARADS."
270  PRINT
280  INPUT "ENTER NEXT HIGHEST STANDARD VALUE: ";C(1)
290 C(1) = C(1) * 1E - 9
300  PRINT
310 C(2) = PSI ↑ 2 * C(1) * 1E9
315 C(2) =  INT (100 * C(2) + .5) / 100
320  PRINT "C 2  SHOULD BE ABOUT ";C(2);" NANOFARADS,"
330  PRINT "BUT NOT LESS THAN 1 NF."
340  PRINT
350  INPUT "ENTER THE NEXT LOWEST STANDARD VALUE: ";C(2)
360 C(2) = C(2) * 1E - 9
370  PRINT
380 R(1) = (PSI +  SQR (PSI ↑ 2 - C(2) / C(1))) / (WO * C(2))
390 R(2) = 1 / (WO ↑ 2 * R(1) * C(1) * C(2))
400  FOR  I = 1 TO  2
410  R(I) =  INT (R(I) / 100 + .5) / 10
420  PRINT "R";I;" SHOULD BE ABOUT ";R(I);" KILOHMS"
430  INPUT "ENTER CLOSEST STANDARD VALUE: ";R(I)
445 R(I) = R(I) * 1E3
450  PRINT
455 C(I) =  INT (C(I) * 1E9 + .5)
460  NEXT  I
470 RR = R(1) + R(2)
480  IF  RR > RMAX  THEN  500
490  GOTO  522
500  PRINT "C(1) IS TO SMALL, ENTER NEXT LARGEST"
510  INPUT "STANDARD VALUE: ";C(1)
520  GOTO 290
522 R(1) =  INT (R(1) / 100 + .5) / 10
523 R(2) =  INT (R(2) / 100 + .5) / 10
530  PRINT : PRINT : PRINT
535 B$ = " KILOHMS "
540  PRINT "FOR A ";F;" HERTZ LOW PASS FILTER"
550  PRINT "THE COMPONENT VALUES ARE:"
560  PRINT : PRINT
570  PRINT "R(1) = ";R(1);B$
580  PRINT "R(2) = ";R(2);B$
585  PRINT
590  PRINT "C(1) = ";C(1);" NANOFARADS"
600  PRINT "C(2) = ";C(2);" NANOFARADS"
```

THIS PROGRAM DESIGNS ACTIVE LOW-PASS
FILTERS. FOR BEST RESULTS USE A FET
INPUT OP AMP (E.G. CA 3140). YOU MUST
ENTER VALUES FOR THE DAMPING FACTOR
(PSI) AND THE RATIO OF THE UNDAMPED
NATURAL FREQUENCY TO THE CUTOFF FRE-
QUENCY (WO/WC).

AMPLIFIER INPUT CURRENT DRIFT IS
ASSUMED TO BE 10 NA, RESULTING IN A
1 MV CHANGE IN VOLTAGE. DO YOU WANT TO
CHANGE THESE VALUES? NO

ENTER PSI: .866
ENTER WO/WC: 1.732

ENTER CUTOFF FREQUENCY: 100

C 1   SHOULD BE ABOUT 21.22 NANOFARADS.

ENTER NEXT HIGHEST STANDARD VALUE: 27

C 2   SHOULD BE ABOUT 20.25 NANOFARADS,
BUT NOT LESS THAN 1 NF.

ENTER THE NEXT LOWEST STANDARD VALUE: 20

R1 SHOULD BE ABOUT 44.2 KILOHMS
ENTER CLOSEST STANDARD VALUE: 43

R2 SHOULD BE ABOUT 35.4 KILOHMS
ENTER CLOSEST STANDARD VALUE: 33

FOR A 100 HERTZ LOW PASS FILTER
THE COMPONENT VALUES ARE:

R(1) = 43 KILOHMS
R(2) = 33 KILOHMS

C(1) = 27 NANOFARADS
C(2) = 20 NANOFARADS

9.7 ACTIVE LOW-PASS FILTER NO. 2[1]

The low-pass filter in Fig. 9.7 is very similar to the previous one with two exceptions. It uses a conventional operational amplifier instead of a FET input and has a feedback network connected to the output. This network is designed to be implemented as a 100-kilohm potentiometer.

The program contains a data statement (line 230) that contains nine standard capacitor values for C1. This makes it possible to produce nine different circuit designs for the same parameters so that the most convenient set of components can be chosen.

The program requests a value for the damping ratio. A value of 1.41 will result in an overdamped design to ensure that the phase shift of the circuit never exceeds 170 degrees. This results in a stable filter design.

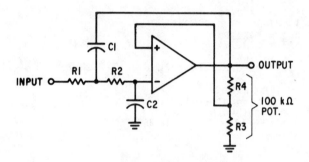

Fig. 9.7   Active low-pass filter No. 2

```
0    CALL  - 936
1    PRINT : PRINT : PRINT : PRINT "WRITTEN BY JULES H. GILDER"
2    PRINT : PRINT "COPYRIGHT (C) HAYDEN BOOK CO. 1978"
3    FOR X = 1 TO 4000: NEXT X
4    PRINT : PRINT : PRINT : PRINT
5    PRINT  TAB( 10 )"ACTIVE LOW PASS FILTER #2"
10   PRINT : PRINT : PRINT : PRINT
20   PRINT "THIS PROGRAM DESIGNS A LOW PASS ACTIVE"
30   PRINT "FILTER.  YOU MUST ENTER THE FREQUENCY"
40   PRINT "OF THE 3 DB POINT AND THE DESIRED FIL-"
50   PRINT "TER GAIN.  THE PROGRAM WILL SUPPLY COM-"
60   PRINT "PONENT VALUES FOR NINE STANDARD VALUES"
70   PRINT "OF C1.  YOU CAN THEN SELECT THE MOST"
80   PRINT "CONVENIENT SET OF VALUES TO USE."
90   PRINT : PRINT : PRINT
100  INPUT "ENTER FREQUENCY (HZ): ";F
104  PRINT : INPUT "ENTER GAIN: ";G
106  PRINT : INPUT "ENTER DAMPING RATIO (OVERDAMPED=1.41): ";PSI
110  PRINT : PRINT : PRINT
120  FOR X = 1 TO 9
130  A$ = " KILOHMS":B$ = " KILOHMS":C$ = " KILOHMS"
135  D$ = " MICROFARADS":E$ = " NANOFARADS"
```

---

[1]Adapted from H. Minuskin, "Active Filter Design Uses Basic Language," *Electronic Design* 5 (March 1, 1970): p. 83.

```
140  READ  C1
150  K = C1 * 6.28 * F
160  M = G
164  CA = C1 * 1E6
165  C1 =  INT (CA + .5)
166  IF  C1 < 1  THEN  D$ = " NANOFARADS"
167  IF  C1 < 1  THEN  C1 =  INT (CA * 1E3 + .5)
170  C2 =  INT (M * C1 + .5)
171  IF  C2 =  > 1000  OR  D$ = " MICROFARADS"  THEN  E$ = " MICR
     OFARADS"
172  IF C2 =  > 1000 AND D$ = " MICROFARADS" THEN 180
175  IF C2 =  > 1000 THEN C2 =  INT (C2 / 100 + .5) / 10
180  R1 =  INT (2 / (PSI * K * 100) + .5) / 10
184  IF  R1 < 1  THEN  A$ = " OHMS"
185  IF  R1 < 1 THEN R1 =  INT (2 / (PSI * K) + .5)
190  R2 =  INT (PSI / (2 * M * K * 100) + .5) / 10
194  IF  R2 < 1  THEN  B$ = " OHMS"
195  IF R2 < 1 THEN R2 =  INT (PSI / (2 * M * K) + .5)
200  R3 =  INT (100 / G + .5)
204  IF  R3 < 1  THEN  C$ = " OHMS"
205  IF  R3 < 1  THEN  R3 =  INT (100000 / G + .5)
210  R4 =  INT (R3 * (G - 1) + .5)
220  PRINT "C1 = ";C1;D$
221  PRINT "C2 = ";C2;E$
222  PRINT : PRINT "R1 = ";R1;A$
223  PRINT "R2 = ";R2;B$
224  PRINT "R3 = ";R3;C$
225  PRINT "R4 = ";R4;C$
230  DATA  1E-9,1E-8,2.2E-8,4.7E-8,1E-7,2.2E-7,4.7E-7,1E-6,1E-5

235  IF X = 9 THEN 300
240  PRINT : INPUT "ANOTHER SET OF VALUES? ";A$
245  PRINT : PRINT : PRINT
250  IF  LEFT$ (A$,1) = "N" THEN 300
260  NEXT X
300  END
```

ACTIVE LOW PASS FILTER #2

THIS PROGRAM DESIGNS A LOW PASS ACTIVE
FILTER. YOU MUST ENTER THE FREQUENCY
OF THE 3 DB POINT AND THE DESIRED FIL-
TER GAIN. THE PROGRAM WILL SUPPLY COM-
PONENT VALUES FOR NINE STANDARD VALUES
OF C1. YOU CAN THEN SELECT THE MOST
CONVENIENT SET OF VALUES TO USE.

ENTER FREQUENCY (HZ): 100

ENTER GAIN: 100

ENTER DAMPING RATIO (OVERDAMPED=1.41): 1.41

C1 = 1 NANOFARADS
C2 = 100 NANOFARADS

R1 = 2258.7 KILOHMS
R2 = 11.2 KILOHMS
R3 = 1 KILOHMS
R4 = 99 KILOHMS

ANOTHER SET OF VALUES? YES

C1 = 10 NANOFARADS
C2 = 1 MICROFARADS

R1 = 225.9 KILOHMS
R2 = 1.1 KILOHMS
R3 = 1 KILOHMS
R4 = 99 KILOHMS

ANOTHER SET OF VALUES? NO

174   BASIC Computer Programs in Science and Engineering

9.8 BUTTERWORTH-THOMPSON LOW-PASS FILTER

The active low-pass transitional Butterworth-Thompson filter in Fig. 9.8 actually includes two designs in one. By changing the value of MU, the type of filter designed is changed. For a MU = ∅, the filter designed is a Butterworth filter. For MU = 1, it is a linear-phase Thompson filter. If MU is somewhere in between, the filter designed is a compromise between the flat amplitude response of the Butterworth filter and the flat time delay of the Thompson filter.

The program contains a standard resistor selection subroutine that starts on line 5∅∅ and requires manual entering of the nearest standard value for capacitors. It then takes the actual component values and calculates the real corner frequency, dc gain, and MU.

In addition, the program permits the user to change any or all component values to see what effect the change will have on the circuit design.

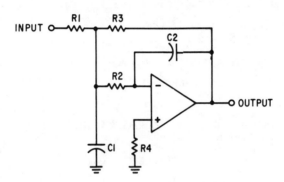

Fig. 9.8 Butterworth-Thompson low-pass filter

```
0    CALL  - 936
1    PRINT : PRINT : PRINT : PRINT "WRITTEN BY JULES H  GILDER"
2    PRINT : PRINT "COPYRIGHT (C) HAYDEN BOOK CO. 1978"
3    FOR X = 1 TO 4000: NEXT X
4    PRINT : PRINT : PRINT : PRINT
5    PRINT "  BUTTERWORTH-THOMPSON LOW PASS FILTER"
10   PRINT : PRINT : PRINT
20   PRINT "THIS PROGRAM DESIGNS A LOW-PASS TRANSI-"
30   PRINT "TIONAL BUTTERWORTH-THOMPSON FILTER."
35   PRINT "YOU MUST ENTER THE CORNER FREQUENCY, DC"
40   PRINT "GAIN,INPUT IMPEDANCE AND MU.  MU VARIES"
50   PRINT "BETWEEN '0' AND '1'. WHEN MU=0 IT COR-"
60   PRINT "RESPONDS TO A BUTTERWORTH FILTER"
70   PRINT "WHEN MU=1 IT CORRESPONDS TO A LINEAR"
80   PRINT "PHASE THOMPSON FILTER."
90   PRINT : PRINT : PRINT
95 A( 6 ) = 5
100  INPUT "ENTER CORNER FREQUENCY (HZ): ";F
105  INPUT "ENTER DC GAIN: ";A
107  INPUT "ENTER INPUT IMPEDANCE (OHMS): ";R( 1 )
108  INPUT "ENTER MU: ";M
110  PRINT
115 F1 = 6.2832 * F
```

```
120  R(3) = A * R(1)
121  X = R(3): GOSUB 500:R(3) = X
122  R = R(1) * R(3) / (R(1) + R(3))
140  C = (1 + A) / F1 / R(3)
145   PRINT "C1 SHOULD BE LARGER THAN "; INT (1E11 * C + .5) / 1E2

146   INPUT "NANOFARADS. ENTER C1: ";C1
147   PRINT
148  C1 = C1 * 1E - 9
149  R(2) = R / (F1 * R * C1 *  SQR (2 + M) - 1)
150  X = R(2): GOSUB 500:R(2) = X
151  C2$ = " NANOFARADS"
152  C2 = 1 / (R(2) * R(3) * C1 * (F1 ↑ 2))
155  C2 =  INT (1E13 * C2 + .5) / 1E4
159   PRINT "C2 SHOULD BE ABOUT ";C2;C2$
160   INPUT "ENTER NEAREST STANDARD VALUE: ";C2
161  C2 = C2 * 1E - 9
165   PRINT
170  R(4) = R(2) + R
175  X = R(4): GOSUB 500:R(4) = X
185   PRINT
215  F =  INT (100 * (1 /  SQR (R(2) * R(3) * C1 * C2) / 6.2832) +
      .5) / 100
216  A =  INT (100 * A + .5) / 100
217  M = ((R(2) * C2 / R(3) / C1) * ((1 + A + R(3) / R(2)) ↑ 2) -
      2)
218  M =  INT (100 * M + .5) / 100
219  C1 = C1 * 1E9:C2 = C2 * 1E9
220   GOSUB 400: FOR J = 1 TO 4
221   PRINT "R";J;" = ";R(J);R$(J)
222   NEXT J
223   PRINT "C1 = ";C1;" NANOFARADS"
224   PRINT "C2 = ";C2;C2$
227   PRINT
228   PRINT "THE GAIN IS ";A
230   PRINT : PRINT "THE ACTUAL CORNER FREQUENCY IS"
232   PRINT F;" HERTZ."
235   PRINT : PRINT "THE REAL VALUE OF MU IS ";M
240   PRINT : INPUT "WANT TO CHANGE COMPONENT VALUES? ";A$
242   PRINT
245   IF  LEFT$ (A$,1) = "N" THEN 300
247   PRINT
250   PRINT "ENTER RESISTANCES IN KILOHMS AND"
255   PRINT "CAPACITANCES IN NANOFARADS."
257   PRINT : PRINT
260   FOR J = 1 TO 4
265   PRINT "ENTER R";J;" = ";: INPUT "";R(J)
270  R(J) = 1E3 * R(J)
272   NEXT J
274   PRINT
275   INPUT "ENTER C1 = ";C1
276  C1 = C1 * 1E - 9
280   INPUT "ENTER C2 = ";C2
282  C2 = C2 * 1E - 9
285   PRINT : INPUT "ENTER GAIN: ";A
286   PRINT
290   GOTO  216
300   END
400   FOR J = 1 TO 4
410   IF R(J) > 1E6 THEN R(J) = R(J) / 1E6:R$(J) = " MEGOHMS": GOTO
      440
420   IF R(J) > 1E3 THEN R(J) = R(J) / 1E3:R$(J) = " KILOHMS": GOTO
      440
430  R$(J) = " OHMS"
440   NEXT
450   RETURN
500  A(4) = 1.19927E - 2 *  INT (1 + 1.5 * A(6) + .004 * A(6) ↑ 2)
```

```
510 A(3) =  INT ( LOG (X) /  LOG (10) -  INT (2.2 - 3 * A(4)))
520 X = X / 10 ↑ A(3)
530  FOR K = 1 TO 2
540 A(K) =  INT ( EXP (A(4) * ( INT ( LOG (X) / A(4)) + K - 1)) +
     .5)
550 A(5) = 1.88E - 5 * A(K) ↑ 3 - .00335 * A(K) ↑ 2 + .164 * A(K)
     - 1.284
560 A(K) = A(K) +  INT (A(5) *  INT (3 * A(4) + .8))
570  NEXT K
580 X = 10 ↑ A(3) * A(X /  SQR (A(1) * A(2)) + 1)
590 X =  INT (X + .5)
600  RETURN
```

BUTTERWORTH-THOMPSON LOW PASS FILTER

THIS PROGRAM DESIGNS A LOW-PASS TRANSI-
TIONAL BUTTERWORTH-THOMPSON FILTER.
YOU MUST ENTER THE CORNER FREQUENCY, DC
GAIN, INPUT IMPEDANCE AND MU. MU VARIES
BETWEEN '0' AND '1'. WHEN MU=0 IT COR-
RESPONDS TO A BUTTERWORTH FILTER
WHEN MU=1 IT CORRESPONDS TO A LINEAR
PHASE THOMPSON FILTER.

ENTER CORNER FREQUENCY (HZ): 100
ENTER DC GAIN: 10
ENTER INPUT IMPEDANCE (OHMS): 10000
ENTER MU: .5

C1 SHOULD BE LARGER THAN 175.07
NANOFARADS. ENTER C1: 180

C2 SHOULD BE ABOUT 9.3815 NANOFARADS
ENTER NEAREST STANDARD VALUE: 10

R1 = 10 KILOHMS
R2 = 15 KILOHMS
R3 = 100 KILOHMS
R4 = 24 KILOHMS
C1 = 180 NANOFARADS
C2 = 10 NANOFARADS

THE GAIN IS 10

THE ACTUAL CORNER FREQUENCY IS
96.86 HERTZ.

THE REAL VALUE OF MU IS .6

WANT TO CHANGE COMPONENT VALUES? NO

10 Communications

The programs in this chapter will be helpful in designing communications circuits. In program 10.1, the computer is used to calculate the bandwidth required in a communications channel so that a digital pulse of a specified shape, amplitude, and width can pass.

In programs 10.2 and 10.3, microwave circuit elements, microstrips, and strip-lines are designed. The fourth program in this section greatly simplifies transmission line calculations. Even with the help of the well-known Smith chart, these calculations are generally quite cumbersome. With this program, however, they are reduced to trivial exercises. The program calculates the impedance of a line as well as its normalized impedance. In addition, it calculates the SWR of the line referenced to a particular impedance.

The next two programs calculate the impedance of a line as well as its linear resistance, inductance, and capacitance, given the wire's diameter, length, and the frequency at which it will be used. Still in the field of RF, program 10.7 determines the diameter of wire and coil required to produce an inductance of a specific value. It also calculates the number of turns required. The last two programs calculate the voltage standing wave ratio and transform voltage, current, and power ratios to decibels.

10.1   GAUSSIAN PULSE BANDWIDTH CALCULATION

When digital pulses are sent over communications channels, the sharpness of the pulse received is determined by the bandwidth of the channel.[1]

For mathematical analysis, it is often possible to assume that the received pulse has a Gaussian wave shape. With this assumption, it is easy to calculate the bandwidth required to pass a pulse with a specified amplitude and pulse width.

The bandwidth calculated by this program contains over 95 percent of the pulse power. To use the program, the pulse width in nanoseconds and the normalized amplitude must be entered. The frequency is rounded off to the nearest megahertz.

```
0    CALL  - 936
1    PRINT : PRINT : PRINT : PRINT "WRITTEN BY JULES H. GILDER"
2    PRINT : PRINT "COPYRIGHT (C) HAYDEN BOOK CO. 1978"
3    FOR X = 1 TO 4000: NEXT X
4    PRINT : PRINT : PRINT : PRINT
5    PRINT   TAB( 5)"BANDWIDTH FOR A GAUSSIAN PULSE"
6    PRINT : PRINT : PRINT : PRINT
10   PRINT "THIS PROGRAM DETERMINES THE BANDWIDTH"
20   PRINT "REQUIRED TO FOR A GAUSSIAN SHAPED PULSE"
30   PRINT "IN A SYSTEM WITH A GIVEN TIME SLOT(T)"
40   PRINT "AND A NORMALIZED PULSE AMPLITUDE (A)."
50   PRINT
90   PRINT "YOU MUST ENTER THE TIME SLOT AND"
92   PRINT "THE NORMALIZED AMPLITUDE DESIRED AT THE"
94   PRINT "EDGE OF THE SLOT."
95   PRINT : INPUT "ENTER TIME SLOT (NANOSECONDS): ";TT
96   PRINT : INPUT "ENTER AMPLITUDE (NORMALIZED): ";P
97   PRINT
98   T = TT * 1E - 9
100  F = (.6366198 / T) * (2 *  LOG (1 / P)) ^ .5
110  F =  INT (F / 1E6 + .5)
115  PRINT : PRINT : PRINT : PRINT
120  PRINT "THE BANDWIDTH REQUIRED TO PASS A PULSE"
130  PRINT "WITH A TIME SLOT OF ";TT;" NANOSECONDS"
140  PRINT "AND A NORMALIZED AMPLITUDE OF ";P
150  PRINT "AT THE EDGE OF THE SLOT IS:"
160  PRINT
170  PRINT F;" MEGAHERTZ"
175  PRINT
180  INPUT "DO YOU HAVE MORE DATA? ";Z$
185  PRINT
190  IF  LEFT$ (Z$,1) = "Y"  THEN  90
200  END
```

---

[1]F. E. Noel and J. S. Kolodzey, "Nomograph Shows Bandwidth for Specified Pulse Shape," *Electronics* (April 1, 1976): p. 102.

BANDWIDTH FOR A GAUSSIAN PULSE

THIS PROGRAM DETERMINES THE BANDWIDTH
REQUIRED TO FOR A GAUSSIAN SHAPED PULSE
IN A SYSTEM WITH A GIVEN TIME SLOT(T)
AND A NORMALIZED PULSE AMPLITUDE (A).

YOU MUST ENTER THE TIME SLOT AND
THE NORMALIZED AMPLITUDE DESIRED AT THE
EDGE OF THE SLOT.

ENTER TIME SLOT (NANOSECONDS): 10

ENTER AMPLITUDE (NORMALIZED): .135

THE BANDWIDTH REQUIRED TO PASS A PULSE
WITH A TIME SLOT OF 10 NANOSECONDS
AND A NORMALIZED AMPLITUDE OF .135
AT THE EDGE OF THE SLOT IS:

127 MEGAHERTZ

DO YOU HAVE MORE DATA? NO

10.2 MICROSTRIP DESIGN

A microstrip is a low-loss transmission line used in microwave circuits. It consists of a conductor above a ground plane (see Fig. 10.1) and is analogous to a two-wire line in which one of the wires is represented by the ground plane.

When the characteristic impedance of the line, the substrate thickness, and the conductor thickness are entered, along with the dielectric constant of the material separating the conductor, the program will determine the width of the microstrip and the velocity factor of the line.

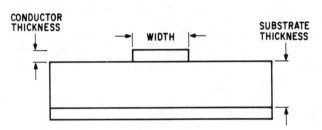

Fig. 10.1 Microstrip cross-section

```
0    CALL  - 936
1    PRINT : PRINT : PRINT : PRINT "WRITTEN BY JULES H. GILDER"
2    PRINT : PRINT "COPYRIGHT (C) HAYDEN BOOK CO. 1978"
3    FOR X = 1 TO 4000: NEXT X
4    PRINT : PRINT : PRINT : PRINT
5    PRINT  TAB( 11 )"MICROSTRIP DESIGN"
10   PRINT : PRINT : PRINT : PRINT
40   PRINT "THIS PROGRAM WILL CALCULATE THE DIMEN-"
50   PRINT "SIONS NEEDED TO PRODUCE A MICROSTRIP"
60   PRINT "WITH THE DESIRED CHARACTERISTICS.YOU"
70   PRINT "MUST ENTER THE:"
80   PRINT
90   INPUT "LINE IMPEDANCE (ZO): ";ZO
100  INPUT "SUBSTRATE THICKNESS (INCH): ";H
110  INPUT "CONDUCTOR THICKNESS (INCH): ";T
120  INPUT "DIELECTRIC CONSTANT: ";ER
130  PRINT
140  X =  EXP (ZO * ((ER + 1.41) ↑ .5) / 87)
150  W = 1.25 * (5.98 * H / X - T)
155  W =  INT (1E3 * W + .5) / 1E3
160  V = 1 / (0.475 * ER + .67) ↑ .5
165  V =  INT (1E3 * V + .5) / 1E3
169  PRINT : PRINT : PRINT : PRINT
170  PRINT "FOR A LINE IMPEDANCE OF ";ZO;" OHMS, A"
180  PRINT "SUBSTRATE THICKNESS OF ";H;" INCH, A"
185  PRINT "CONDUCTOR THICKNESS OF ";T;" INCH"
190  PRINT "AND A DIELECTRIC CONSTANT OF ";ER
195  PRINT
200  PRINT    "A MICROSTRIP WITH A WIDTH"
220  PRINT "OF ";W;" INCH IS REQUIRED."
230  PRINT
235  PRINT "THE VELOCITY FACTOR IS ";V
236  PRINT
240  INPUT "DO YOU HAVE MORE DATA? ";Z$
245  PRINT
250  IF   LEFT$ (Z$,1) = "Y"  THEN   90
260  END
```

MICROSTRIP DESIGN

THIS PROGRAM WILL CALCULATE THE DIMEN-
SIONS NEEDED TO PRODUCE A MICROSTRIP
WITH THE DESIRED CHARACTERISTICS.YOU
MUST ENTER THE:

LINE IMPEDANCE (ZO): 70
SUBSTRATE THICKNESS (INCH): .05
CONDUCTOR THICKNESS (INCH): .001
DIELECTRIC CONSTANT: 4.7

FOR A LINE IMPEDANCE OF 70 OHMS, A
SUBSTRATE THICKNESS OF .05 INCH, A
CONDUCTOR THICKNESS OF 1E-03 INCH
AND A DIELECTRIC CONSTANT OF 4.7

A MICROSTRIP WITH A WIDTH
OF .05 INCH IS REQUIRED.

THE VELOCITY FACTOR IS .587

DO YOU HAVE MORE DATA? NO

10.3   STRIP-LINE DESIGN

Like the microstrip, a strip-line is also a low-loss transmission line used in micro-wave circuits. It differs from the microstrip, however, in that it has a second ground plane placed above the conductor (see Fig. 10.2).

To use the program, values must be entered for the desired characteristic impedance of the line, the substrate thickness, the conductor thickness, and the dielectric constant of the material separating the conductors. The units used for the thickness are not important so long as they are consistent.

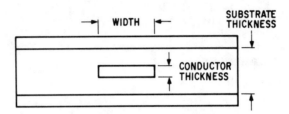

Fig. 10.2   Microstrip cross-section

```
0    CALL  - 936
1    PRINT : PRINT : PRINT : PRINT "WRITTEN BY JULES H. GILDER"
2    PRINT : PRINT "COPYRIGHT (C) HAYDEN BOOK CO. 1978"
3    FOR X = 1 TO 4000: NEXT X
4    PRINT : PRINT : PRINT : PRINT
5    PRINT  TAB( 11 )"STRIP-LINE DESIGN"
10   PRINT : PRINT : PRINT : PRINT
40   PRINT "THIS PROGRAM WILL CALCULATE THE DIMEN-"
50   PRINT "SIONS NEEDED TO PRODUCE A STRIP-LINE"
70   PRINT  "YOU MUST ENTER THE:"
80   PRINT
90   INPUT "LINE IMPEDANCE (ZO): ";ZO
100  INPUT "SUBSTRATE THICKNESS ( INCH): ";H
110  INPUT "CONDUCTOR THICKNESS ( INCH): ";T
120  INPUT "DIELECTRIC CONSTANT: ";ER
130  PRINT
140  X =  EXP (ZO *  (ER ↑ .5) / 60 )
150  W = .59 * (4 * H / X - 2.1 * T)
155  W =  INT ( 1E3 * W + .5) / 1E3
160  V = 1 / ER ↑ .5
165  V =  INT ( 1E3 * V + .5) / 1E3
168  PRINT : PRINT : PRINT : PRINT
170  PRINT "FOR A LINE IMPEDANCE OF ";ZO;" OHMS, A"
180  PRINT "SUBSTRATE THICKNESS OF ";H;" INCH, A"
185  PRINT "CONDUCTOR THICKNESS OF ";T
190  PRINT "INCH AND A DIELECTRIC CONSTANT OF ";ER
195  PRINT
200  PRINT    "A STRIP-LINE WITH A WIDTH"
220  PRINT "OF ";W;" INCH IS REQUIRED."
230  PRINT
235  PRINT "THE VELOCITY FACTOR IS ";V
236  PRINT
240  INPUT "DO YOU HAVE MORE DATA? ";Z$
245  PRINT
250  IF  LEFT$ (Z$,1 ) = "Y"  THEN  90
260  END
```

STRIP-LINE DESIGN

THIS PROGRAM WILL CALCULATE THE DIMEN
SIONS NEEDED TO PRODUCE A STRIP-LINE
YOU MUST ENTER THE:

LINE IMPEDANCE (ZO): 70
SUBSTRATE THICKNESS (INCH): .05
CONDUCTOR THICKNESS (INCH): .001
DIELECTRIC CONSTANT: 4.7

FOR A LINE IMPEDANCE OF 70 OHMS, A
SUBSTRATE THICKNESS OF .05 INCH, A
CONDUCTOR THICKNESS OF 1E-03
INCH AND A DIELECTRIC CONSTANT OF 4.7

A STRIP-LINE WITH A WIDTH
OF 8E-03 INCH IS REQUIRED.

THE VELOCITY FACTOR IS .461

DO YOU HAVE MORE DATA? NO

10.4 LOSSLESS TRANSMISSION LINES

Solving lossless RF transmission-line problems with equations and a calculator can be tedious. Even with a Smith chart, you don't always get the accuracy you need. This program combines speed and accuracy to solve these problems.[1]

The program calculates the impedance of the line as well as its normalized impedance. It also yields the SWR referenced to a particular impedance.

To use the program, the characteristic impedance of the line, the reference impedance for the SWR, and the velocity factor must be entered. In addition, the input resistance and reactance, the frequency, and the length of the line must be entered.

When entering the length of the line, a sign must also be given. If the load is at the far end of the line, the sign is negative; if the generator is at the far end, the sign is positive. The length of the line should be entered in meters.

```
0   CALL  - 936
1   PRINT : PRINT : PRINT : PRINT "WRITTEN BY JULES H. GILDER"
2   PRINT : PRINT "COPYRIGHT (C)  HAYDEN BOOK CO. 1978"
3   FOR X = 1 TO 4000: NEXT X
5   REM ADAPTED FROM "TRANSMISSION LINE PROBLEMS SOLVED FAST WITH
        BASIC"
6   REM  R.J. FINGER, ELEC. DESIGN 17, AUG 16, 1971, P.76
10  PRINT : PRINT : PRINT : PRINT
20  PRINT  TAB( 6)"LOSSLESS TRANSMISSION LINES"
30  PRINT : PRINT : PRINT : PRINT
40  PRINT "THIS PROGRAM CAN BE USED INSTEAD OF A"
50  PRINT "SMITH CHART TO SOLVE LOSSLESS TRANSMIS-"
60  PRINT "SION LINE PROBLEMS."
62  PRINT
65  PRINT "ALL RESISTANCES AND IMPEDANCES SHOULD"
66  PRINT "BE ENTERED IN OHMS."
70  PRINT : PRINT : PRINT
80  INPUT "ENTER LINE IMPEDANCE: ";Z1
90  INPUT "ENTER REFERENCE IMPEDANCE: ";Z2
100 INPUT "ENTER VELOCITY FACTOR: ";K
110 PRINT : PRINT "ENTER LENGTH OF LINE IN METERS. IT IS"
120 PRINT "NEGATIVE IF LOAD IS AT FAR END AND"
130 INPUT "POSITIVE IF GENERATOR IS THERE: ";L
140 PRINT
150 T1 = 1.2 * L * 1.74532925E - 2 / K
160 A = 1E3
170 B = 5E - 4
180 C = Z1 / Z2
190 INPUT "ENTER FREQUENCY (MHZ): ";F
200 INPUT "ENTER INPUT RESISTANCE: ";R1
210 INPUT "ENTER INPUT REACTANCE: ";X1
220 PRINT : PRINT : PRINT
225 T =  TAN (T1 * F)
```

---

[1] Adapted from R. J. Finger, "Transmission-line Problems Solved Fast with BASIC," *Electronic Design* 17 (Aug. 17, 1971): p. 76.

```
230 R = R1 / Z1
240 X = X1 / Z1
250 D1 = ((1 - (T * X)) ↑ 2) + ((R * T) ↑ 2)
260 R0 = (R * (1 + T ↑ 2)) * C / D1
270 X0 = ((T * (1 - X ↑ 2 - (X * T) - R ↑ 2)) + X) * C / D1
280 D2 = R0 ↑ 2 + (2 * R0) + X0 ↑ 2 + 1
290 R1 = SQR (((R0 ↑ 2 + X0 ↑ 2 - 1) ↑ 2) + (4 * X0 ↑ 2)) / D2
300 S = (1 + R1) / (1 - R1)
310 A$ = " + ":B$ = " + "
320    PRINT "FREQUENCY (MHZ) = ";F
330    PRINT
340 AA =  INT (A * ((R0 * Z2) + B)) / A
350    IF X0 < 0 THEN A$ = " - "
360 BB =  ABS ( INT (A * ((X0 * Z2) + B)) / A)
370    PRINT "OUTPUT IMPEDANCE = ";AA;A$;"J ";BB
375    PRINT
380 CC =  INT (A * (R0 + B)) / A
390 DD =  ABS ( INT (A * (X0 + B)) / A)
400 SWR =  INT (A * (S + B)) / A
410    PRINT "NORMALIZED  ZO = ";CC;A$;"J ";DD
420    PRINT : PRINT "SWR = ";SWR
430    END
```

LOSSLESS TRANSMISSION LINES

THIS PROGRAM CAN BE USED INSTEAD OF A
SMITH CHART TO SOLVE LOSSLESS TRANSMIS-
SION LINE PROBLEMS.

ALL RESISTANCES AND IMPEDANCES SHOULD
BE ENTERED IN OHMS.

ENTER LINE IMPEDANCE: 75
ENTER REFERENCE IMPEDANCE: 50
ENTER VELOCITY FACTOR: .6

ENTER LENGTH OF LINE IN METERS. IT IS
NEGATIVE IF LOAD IS AT FAR END AND
POSITIVE IF GENERATOR IS THERE: -2

ENTER FREQUENCY (MHZ): 100
ENTER INPUT RESISTANCE: 100
ENTER INPUT REACTANCE: 80

FREQUENCY (MHZ) = 100

OUTPUT IMPEDANCE = 35.187 + J 29.78

NORMALIZED ZO = .704 + J .596

SWR = 2.167

10.5 SINGLE-WIRE TRANSMISSION LINE

This program calculates the characteristics of a single-wire transmission line located near the ground.

The diameter of the wire, its distance above the ground, and the frequency at which it is to be used must be entered. The output is the characteristic impedance and the inductance, capacitance, and resistance per meter.

```
0   CALL  - 936
1   PRINT : PRINT : PRINT : PRINT "WRITTEN BY JULES H. GILDER"
2   PRINT : PRINT "COPYRIGHT (C)  HAYDEN BOOK CO. 1978"
3   FOR X = 1 TO 4000: NEXT X
10   PRINT : PRINT : PRINT : PRINT
20   PRINT "      SINGLE-WIRE TRANSMISSION LINE"
30   PRINT : PRINT : PRINT : PRINT
40   PRINT "THIS PROGRAM DESIGNS ABOVE GROUND"
50   PRINT "SINGLE-WIRE TRANSMISSION LINES. IT CAL-"
60   PRINT "CULATES THE LINE'S CHARACTERISTIC IMPE-"
65   PRINT "DANCE, INDUCTANCE, CAPACITANCE AND RE-"
70   PRINT "SISTANCE."
80   PRINT : PRINT : PRINT
90   INPUT "ENTER WIRE DIAMETER (CM): ";D
100   INPUT "ENTER DISTANCE ABOVE GROUND (CM): ";DD
105   INPUT "ENTER FREQUENCY (MHZ): ";F
110   F = F * 1E6
115   PRINT : PRINT : PRINT
120   Z = 138 * LOG (4 * DD / D) / LOG (10)
125   Z = INT (100 * Z + .5) / 100
130   L = .460 * LOG (4 * DD / D) / LOG (10)
132   L = INT (1E2 * L + .5) / 100
135   C = 24.12 / ( LOG (4 * DD / D) / LOG (10))
140   C = INT (100 * C + .5) / 100
150   R = 8.3 * SQR (F) / (D) / 1E6
160   R = INT (1E3 * R + .5) / 1E3
200   PRINT "LINE COMPONENT VALUES ARE:"
210   PRINT : PRINT
220   PRINT : PRINT "ZO = ";Z;" OHMS"
225   PRINT : PRINT "L = ";L;" MICROHENRIES/METER"
230   PRINT : PRINT "C = ";C;" PICOFARADS/METER"
240   PRINT : PRINT "R = ";R;" OHMS/METER"
```

```
        SINGLE-WIRE TRANSMISSION LINE

THIS PROGRAM DESIGNS ABOVE GROUND
SINGLE-WIRE TRANSMISSION LINES. IT CAL-
CULATES THE LINE'S CHARACTERISTIC IMPE-
DANCE, INDUCTANCE, CAPACITANCE AND RE-
SISTANCE.

ENTER WIRE DIAMETER (CM): .016
ENTER DISTANCE ABOVE GROUND (CM): 2
ENTER FREQUENCY (MHZ): 1


LINE COMPONENT VALUES ARE:


ZO = 372.46 OHMS

L = 1.24 MICROHENRIES/METER

C = 8.94 PICOFARADS/METER

R = .519 OHMS/METER
```

10.6 TWO-WIRE TRANSMISSION LINE

This program calculates the characteristics of a two-wire open transmission line. Details of the line (such as the wire diameter, the distance between the wires, and the frequency at which it is to be used) are entered. The program then calculates the characteristic impedance of the line and its inductance, capacitance, and resistance per meter.

Although the program specifies that the diameter and distance between wires be entered in centimeters, any consistent units can be used since the units cancel out in the calculation.

```
0   CALL  - 936
1   PRINT : PRINT : PRINT : PRINT "WRITTEN BY JULES H. GILDER"
2   PRINT : PRINT "COPYRIGHT (C)  HAYDEN BOOK CO. 1978"
3   FOR X = 1 TO 4000: NEXT X
10    PRINT : PRINT : PRINT : PRINT
20    PRINT "     OPEN TWO-WIRE TRANSMISSION LINE"
30    PRINT : PRINT : PRINT : PRINT
40    PRINT "THIS PROGRAM DESIGNS OPEN TWO-WIRE "
50    PRINT "TRANSMISSION LINES. IT CALCULATES THE"
60    PRINT "LINE'S CHARACTERISTIC IMPEDANCE, INDUC-"
65    PRINT "TANCE AND CAPACITANCE."
80    PRINT : PRINT : PRINT
90    INPUT "ENTER WIRE DIAMETER (CM): ";D
100   INPUT "ENTER DISTANCE BETWEEN WIRES (CM): ";DD
105   INPUT "ENTER FREQUENCY (MHZ): ";F
110 F = F * 1E6
115   PRINT : PRINT : PRINT
120 Z = 276 *  LOG (2 * DD / D) /  LOG (10)
125 Z =   INT (100 * Z + .5) / 100
130 L = .921 *  LOG (2 * DD / D) /  LOG (10)
132 L  =   INT (1E2 * L  + .5) / 100
135 C = 12.06 / ( LOG (2 * DD / D) /  LOG (10))
140 C =   INT (100 * C + .5) / 100
150 R = 8.3 *  SQR (F) / (D / 2) / 1E6
160 R =   INT (R * 1E3 + .5) / 1E3
200   PRINT "LINE COMPONENT VALUES ARE:"
210   PRINT : PRINT
220   PRINT : PRINT "ZO = ";Z;" OHMS"
225   PRINT : PRINT "L = ";L;" MICROHENRIES/METER"
230   PRINT : PRINT "C = ";C;" PICOFARADS/METER"
240   PRINT : PRINT "R = ";R;" OHMS/METER"
```

OPEN TWO-WIRE TRANSMISSION LINE

THIS PROGRAM DESIGNS OPEN TWO-WIRE
TRANSMISSION LINES. IT CALCULATES THE
LINE'S CHARACTERISTIC IMPEDANCE, INDUC-
TANCE AND CAPACITANCE.

ENTER WIRE DIAMETER (CM): .016
ENTER DISTANCE BETWEEN WIRES (CM): 3
ENTER FREQUENCY (MHZ): 100

LINE COMPONENT VALUES ARE:

ZO = 710.43 OHMS

L = 2.37 MICROHENRIES/METER

C = 4.69 PICOFARADS/METER

R = 10.375 OHMS/METER

10.7 RF AIR-CORE INDUCTOR DESIGN

Amateur radio operators and communications engineers find a lot of use for air-core inductors, especially at VHF frequencies. This program will design such inductors, given the diameter of the coil form, the diameter of the wire (both in inches), and the desired inductance (in microhenries).

The program is based on the formula shown below, where N is the number of turns, R is the radius of the coil in inches, and D is the diameter of the wire in inches. The equation is then solved for N. This form of the equation is used in the program (line 18Ø).

$$N = \frac{10DL + [100D^2L^2 + 4R^2L(9R + 100)]^{\frac{1}{2}}}{2R^2}$$

```
0   CALL  - 936
1   PRINT : PRINT : PRINT : PRINT "WRITTEN BY JULES H. GILDER"
2   PRINT : PRINT "COPYRIGHT (C) HAYDEN BOOK CO. 1978"
3   FOR X = 1 TO 4000: NEXT X
4   PRINT : PRINT : PRINT : PRINT
5   PRINT  TAB( 6)"RF AIR-CORE INDUCTOR DESIGN"
10    PRINT : PRINT : PRINT : PRINT
20    PRINT "THIS PROGRAM DESIGNS AIR-CORE INDUCTORS"
30    PRINT "FOR RF CIRCUITRY. YOU MUST ENTER THE"
40    PRINT "THE DIAMETER OF THE WIRE AND THE DIA-"
50    PRINT "METER OF THE COIL FORM, BOTH IN INCHES,"
60    PRINT "AND THE DESIRED INDUCTANCE IN MICRO-"
70    PRINT "HENRIES."
80    PRINT : PRINT
90    INPUT "ENTER WIRE DIAMETER (INCHES): ";D
100   PRINT
110   INPUT "ENTER COIL FORM DIAMETER (INCHES): ";CD
120   PRINT
130   INPUT "ENTER INDUCTANCE (MICROHENRIES): ";L
140 R = CD / 2
150 A = 100 * D ↑ 2 * L ↑ 2
160 B = 4 * R ↑ 2 * L * (9 * R + 10 * D)
170 C =  SQR (A + B)
180 N = (10 * D * L + C) / (2 * R ↑ 2)
185 N =  INT (100 * N + .5) / 100
190   PRINT : PRINT : PRINT : PRINT : PRINT
200   PRINT "   CLOSE-WOUND COIL DESIGN"
210   PRINT : PRINT : PRINT : PRINT : PRINT
220   PRINT "FOR A ";L;" MICROHENRY INDUCTOR"
230   PRINT : PRINT : PRINT
235 D =  INT (10000 * D + .5) / 10
240   PRINT "WIRE DIAMETER = ";D ;" MILS"
250   PRINT
260   PRINT "COIL DIAMETER = ";CD;" INCH"
270   PRINT : PRINT : PRINT
280   PRINT "NUMBER OF TURNS REQUIRED = ";N
290 END
```

RF AIR-CORE INDUCTOR DESIGN

THIS PROGRAM DESIGNS AIR-CORE INDUCTORS
FOR RF CIRCUITRY. YOU MUST ENTER THE
THE DIAMETER OF THE WIRE AND THE DIA-
METER OF THE COIL FORM, BOTH IN INCHES,
AND THE DESIRED INDUCTANCE IN MICRO-
HENRIES.

ENTER WIRE DIAMETER (INCHES): .0403

ENTER COIL FORM DIAMETER (INCHES): .25

ENTER INDUCTANCE (MICROHENRIES): .4

    CLOSE-WOUND COIL DESIGN

FOR A .4 MICROHENRY INDUCTOR

WIRE DIAMETER = 40.3 MILS

COIL DIAMETER = .25 INCH

NUMBER OF TURNS REQUIRED = 13.27

10.8   VOLTAGE STANDING WAVE RATIO CALCULATION

Ham and CB operators, as well as communications engineers, are always interested in knowing the VSWR of their antenna feed lines. The VSWR is the ratio of the maximum voltage to the minimum voltage along the line. It is a measure of the mismatch between the line and its load. When the line and the load are perfectly matched, the VSWR is equal to 1.

For mismatch conditions, the VSWR increases in value. As it does, the power loss in the line increases, limiting the amount of power radiated by the transmitter.

In order to calculate the VSWR, the incident power and the reflected power of the line must be entered.

```
0   CALL  - 936
1   PRINT : PRINT : PRINT : PRINT "WRITTEN BY JULES H. GILDER"
2   PRINT : PRINT "COPYRIGHT (C)  HAYDEN BOOK CO. 1978"
3   FOR X = 1 TO 4000: NEXT X
10   PRINT : PRINT : PRINT : PRINT
20   PRINT  TAB( 12)"VSWR CALCULATION"
30   PRINT : PRINT : PRINT : PRINT
40   PRINT "THIS PROGRAM CALCULATES THE VOLTAGE "
50   PRINT "STANDING WAVE RATIO WHEN THE POWERS OF"
60   PRINT "THE REFLECTED AND INCIDENT WAVES ARE"
70   PRINT "KNOWN."
80   PRINT : PRINT : PRINT
90   INPUT "ENTER REFLECTED WAVE POWER: ";PR
100   INPUT "ENTER INCIDENT WAVE POWER: ";PI
110   PRINT : PRINT : PRINT
120 A = 1 +  SQR (PR / PI)
130 B = 1 -  SQR (PR / PI)
140 VSWR = A / B
150   PRINT "VSWR = ";VSWR
160   END
```

```
        VSWR CALCULATION



THIS PROGRAM CALCULATES THE VOLTAGE
STANDING WAVE RATIO WHEN THE POWERS OF
THE REFLECTED AND INCIDENT WAVES ARE
KNOWN.


ENTER REFLECTED WAVE POWER: 2.5
ENTER INCIDENT WAVE POWER: 180


VSWR = 1.26719102
```

10.9   DECIBEL CONVERSION

The conversion of voltage, current, and power ratios to decibels (dB) is performed by this program.

When run, the program presents a menu. The desired conversion must be selected by entering a number from 1 to 3. Based on this selection, the program then branches to line 132 (voltage), line 14Ø (current), or line 15Ø (power).

The program automatically inverts the current values to calculate the correct sign.

```
0    CALL  - 936
1    PRINT : PRINT : PRINT : PRINT "WRITTEN BY JULES H. GILDER"
2    PRINT : PRINT "COPYRIGHT (C)  HAYDEN BOOK CO. 1978"
3    FOR X = 1 TO 4000: NEXT X
10   PRINT : PRINT : PRINT : PRINT
20   PRINT  TAB( 13)"DB CONVERSION"
30   PRINT : PRINT : PRINT : PRINT
40   PRINT "THIS PROGRAM CONVERTS VOLTAGE, CURRENT"
50   PRINT "OR POWER RATIOS TO DB. SELECT MODE:"
60   PRINT
70   PRINT "   1. VOLTAGE"
80   PRINT "   2. CURRENT"
90   PRINT "   3. POWER"
100  PRINT : PRINT
110  INPUT "ENTER CHOICE: ";N
115  PRINT
120  IF  N = 3  THEN  150
130  IF  N = 2  THEN  140
132  INPUT "ENTER V2,V1: ";X2,X1
134  DB = 20 *  LOG (X2 / X1) /  LOG (10)
135  A$ = "VOLTAGE"
136  GOTO 175
140  INPUT "ENTER I2,I1: ";X1,X2
144  DB = 20 *  LOG (X2 / X1) /  LOG (10)
145  A$ = "CURRENT"
146  GOTO 175
150  INPUT "ENTER P2,P1: ";X2,X1
160  DB = 10 *  LOG (X2 / X1) /  LOG (10)
170  A$ = "POWER"
175  DB =  INT (100 * DB + .5) / 100
180  PRINT : PRINT : PRINT
190  PRINT "THE ";A$;" RATIO ";X2;"/";X1
195  PRINT
200  PRINT "IS EQUAL TO ";DB;" DB."
```

```
            DB CONVERSION

THIS PROGRAM CONVERTS VOLTAGE, CURRENT
OR POWER RATIOS TO DB. SELECT MODE:

    1. VOLTAGE
    2. CURRENT
    3. POWER

ENTER CHOICE: 2

ENTER I2,I1: 3,10


THE CURRENT RATIO 10/3

IS EQUAL TO 10.46 DB.
```

11 Passive Filters

For noncritical filtering applications, passive filters are frequently used. The advantage of passive filters is higher reliability. They do not use active devices that can burn out or otherwise be damaged by incorrectly applied voltages or transients.

The filters designed by the programs in this chapter are passive filters of various configurations that are built from inductors and capacitors. Given the desired frequency, the program calculates the values of the capacitors and inductors indicated in the accompanying circuit diagrams.

The filters include six types of low-pass filters, four different high-pass filters, and two each of bandpass and band-elimination filters.

11.1 LOW-PASS, CONSTANT-K π FILTER

The filter in Fig. 11.1 is composed of two capacitors with a coil connected between them in a π configuration. The filter has a passband frequency range from dc to the cutoff frequency. The program calculates the values of the inductance and the two capacitors, which are equal in value.

To use the program, it is only necessary to enter the terminating resistance of the filter in ohms and the cutoff frequency in hertz.

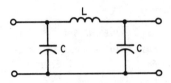

Fig. 11.1 Low-pass, constant-K π filter

```
0    CALL  - 936
1    PRINT : PRINT : PRINT : PRINT "WRITTEN BY JULES H. GILDER"
2    PRINT : PRINT "COPYRIGHT (C)  HAYDEN BOOK CO, 1978"
3    FOR X = 1 TO 4000: NEXT X
10   PRINT : PRINT : PRINT : PRINT
20   PRINT   TAB( 4)"LOW-PASS CONSTANT-K 'PI' FILTERS"
30   PRINT : PRINT : PRINT : PRINT
40   PRINT "THIS PROGRAM DESIGNS LOW-PASS 'PI' CON-"
50   PRINT "FIGURATION, CONSTANT-K FILTERS, YOU"
60   PRINT "MUST ENTER THE CUTOFF FREQUENCY."
75   PRINT "YOU ALSO HAVE TO ENTER THE TERMINATING"
76   PRINT "RESISTANCE IN OHMS,"
80   PRINT : PRINT : PRINT
85   INPUT "ENTER TERMINATING RESISTANCE (OHMS): ";R
90   INPUT "ENTER CUTOFF FREQUENCY (HZ): ";F
110  PRINT : PRINT : PRINT
120  PI = 3.14159
130  L = R / (PI * F)
140  C = 1E6 / (PI * R * F * 2)
150  C =   INT (100 * C + .5) / 100
160  LA =   INT (1E5 * L + .5) / 100
200  PRINT "FILTER COMPONENT VALUES ARE:"
210  PRINT : PRINT
220  PRINT : PRINT "L = ";LA;" MILLIHENRIES"
230  PRINT : PRINT "C = ";C;" MICROFARADS"
```

LOW-PASS CONSTANT-K 'PI' FILTERS

THIS PROGRAM DESIGNS LOW-PASS 'PI' CON-
FIGURATION, CONSTANT-K FILTERS. YOU
MUST ENTER THE CUTOFF FREQUENCY.
YOU ALSO HAVE TO ENTER THE TERMINATING
RESISTANCE IN OHMS.

ENTER TERMINATING RESISTANCE (OHMS): 75
ENTER CUTOFF FREQUENCY (HZ): 3000

FILTER COMPONENT VALUES ARE:

L = 7.96 MILLIHENRIES

C = .71 MICROFARADS

11.2 LOW-PASS, CONSTANT-K T FILTER

The filter in Fig. 11.2 is very similar to the previous one except that it is composed of two inductors and one capacitor arranged in a T configuration. As with the previous filter, the passband is from dc to the cutoff frequency, after which a sharp attenuation occurs. The values of the inductors are identical.

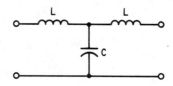

Fig. 11.2   Low-pass, constant-K T filter

```
0    CALL  - 936
1    PRINT : PRINT : PRINT : PRINT "WRITTEN BY JULES H. GILDER"
2    PRINT : PRINT "COPYRIGHT (C)  HAYDEN BOOK CO. 1978"
3    FOR X = 1 TO 4000: NEXT X
10   PRINT : PRINT : PRINT : PRINT
20   PRINT  TAB( 4)"LOW-PASS CONSTANT-K 'T' FILTERS"
30   PRINT : PRINT : PRINT : PRINT
40   PRINT "THIS PROGRAM DESIGNS LOW-PASS 'T' CON-"
50   PRINT "FIGURATION, CONSTANT-K FILTERS. YOU"
60   PRINT "MUST ENTER THE CUTOFF FREQUENCY."
75   PRINT "YOU ALSO HAVE TO ENTER THE TERMINATING"
76   PRINT "RESISTANCE IN OHMS."
80   PRINT : PRINT : PRINT
85   INPUT "ENTER TERMINATING RESISTANCE (OHMS): ";R
90   INPUT "ENTER CUTOFF FREQUENCY (HZ): ";F
110  PRINT : PRINT : PRINT
120 PI = 3.14159
130 L = R / (PI * F) / 2
140 C = 1E6 / (PI * R * F)
150 C =  INT (100 * C + .5) / 100
160 LA =  INT (1E5 * L + .5) / 100
200  PRINT "FILTER COMPONENT VALUES ARE:"
210  PRINT : PRINT
220  PRINT : PRINT "L = ";LA;" MILLIHENRIES"
230  PRINT : PRINT "C = ";C;" MICROFARADS"
```

LOW-PASS CONSTANT-K 'T' FILTERS

THIS PROGRAM DESIGNS LOW-PASS 'T' CON-
FIGURATION, CONSTANT-K FILTERS. YOU
MUST ENTER THE CUTOFF FREQUENCY.
YOU ALSO HAVE TO ENTER THE TERMINATING
RESISTANCE IN OHMS.

ENTER TERMINATING RESISTANCE (OHMS): 1000
ENTER CUTOFF FREQUENCY (HZ): 100

FILTER COMPONENT VALUES ARE:

L = 1591.55 MILLIHENRIES

C = 3.18 MICROFARADS

11.3 LOW-PASS, M-DERIVED T FILTER

Like the other low-pass filters previously described, this one has a passband from dc to the cutoff frequency. What differentiates it from the constant-K type of filter, among other things, is that the cutoff frequency and the frequency at which maximum attenuation is desired are specified when the filter is designed.

As can be seen in Fig. 11.3, the T filter is composed of three inductors and a single capacitor. The two series inductors of the input and output lines are identical in value.

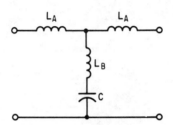

Fig. 11.3 Low-pass, M-derived T filter

```
0   CALL  - 936
1   PRINT : PRINT : PRINT : PRINT "WRITTEN BY JULES H. GILDER"

2   PRINT : PRINT "COPYRIGHT (C)  HAYDEN BOOK CO. 1978"
3   FOR X = 1 TO 4000: NEXT X

10   PRINT : PRINT : PRINT : PRINT
20   PRINT  TAB( 5)"LOW-PASS M-DERIVED 'T' FILTERS"

30   PRINT : PRINT : PRINT : PRINT
40   PRINT "THIS PROGRAM DESIGNS LOW-PASS 'T' CON-"

50   PRINT "FIGURATION, M-DERIVED FILTERS. YOU"
60   PRINT "MUST ENTER THE CUTOFF FREQUENCY AND THE"

70   PRINT "FREQUENCY OF MAXIMUM ATTENUATION (HZ)"
75   PRINT "YOU ALSO HAVE TO ENTER THE TERMINATING"

76   PRINT "RESISTANCE IN OHMS."
80   PRINT : PRINT : PRINT

85   INPUT "ENTER TERMINATING RESISTANCE (OHMS): ";R
90   INPUT "ENTER CUTOFF FREQUENCY (HZ): ";F

100  INPUT "ENTER MAXIMUM ATTENUATION FREQ.: ";FM
110  PRINT : PRINT : PRINT

120 PI = 3.14159
130 M =  SQR (1 - ( F / FM) ↑ 2)

135 L = R / (PI * F)
140 C = 1E6 / (PI * R * F)

145 C =  INT (100 * M * C + .5) / 100
150 LA =  INT (M * L * 100000 / 2 + .5) / 100

160 LB =  INT.((1 - M ↑ 2) * L / 4 / M * 100000 + .5) / 100
200  PRINT "FILTER COMPONENT VALUES ARE:"

210  PRINT : PRINT
220  PRINT : PRINT "LA = ";LA;" MILLIHENRIES"

225  PRINT : PRINT "LB = ";LB;" MILLIHENRIES"
230  PRINT : PRINT "C = ";C;" MICROFARADS"
```

LOW-PASS M-DERIVED 'T' FILTERS

THIS PROGRAM DESIGNS LOW-PASS 'T' CON-
FIGURATION, M-DERIVED FILTERS. YOU
MUST ENTER THE CUTOFF FREQUENCY AND THE
FREQUENCY OF MAXIMUM ATTENUATION (HZ)
YOU ALSO HAVE TO ENTER THE TERMINATING
RESISTANCE IN OHMS.

ENTER TERMINATING RESISTANCE (OHMS): 100
ENTER CUTOFF FREQUENCY (HZ): 3000
ENTER MAXIMUM ATTENUATION FREQ.: 3500

FILTER COMPONENT VALUES ARE:

LA = 2.73 MILLIHENRIES

LB = 3.78 MILLIHENRIES

C = .55 MICROFARADS

11.4   LOW-PASS, M-DERIVED L FILTER

The L configuration filter is used as an end element in a compound filter design. Thus, when several filter sections are stacked to produce a sharper cutoff, the terminating element in the chain is often an L filter.

The L filter in Fig. 11.4 is used as a terminating element when T filter elements are stacked. As with the T filter, the cutoff frequency and the frequency of maximum attenuation must be entered when the program is run.

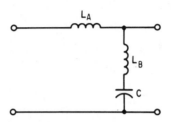

Fig. 11.4   Low-pass, M-derived L filter

```
0    CALL  - 936
1    PRINT : PRINT : PRINT : PRINT "WRITTEN BY JULES H. GILDER"
2    PRINT : PRINT "COPYRIGHT (C)  HAYDEN BOOK CO. 1978"
3    FOR X = 1 TO 4000: NEXT X
10     PRINT : PRINT : PRINT : PRINT
20     PRINT   TAB( 5)"LOW-PASS M-DERIVED 'L' FILTERS"
30     PRINT : PRINT : PRINT : PRINT
40     PRINT "THIS PROGRAM DESIGNS LOW-PASS 'L' CON-"
50     PRINT "FIGURATION, M-DERIVED FILTERS. YOU"
60     PRINT "MUST ENTER THE CUTOFF FREQUENCY AND THE"
70     PRINT "FREQUENCY OF MAXIMUM ATTENUATION (HZ)"
75     PRINT "YOU ALSO HAVE TO ENTER THE TERMINATING"
76     PRINT "RESISTANCE IN OHMS."
80     PRINT : PRINT : PRINT
85     INPUT "ENTER TERMINATING RESISTANCE (OHMS): ";R
90     INPUT "ENTER CUTOFF FREQUENCY (HZ): ";F
100    INPUT "ENTER MAXIMUM ATTENUATION FREQ.: ";FM
110     PRINT : PRINT : PRINT
120  PI = 3.14159
130  M =  SQR (1 - ( F / FM) ↑ 2)
135  L = R / (PI * F)
140  C = 1E6 / (PI * R * F)
145  C =   INT (100 * M * C / 2 + .5) / 100
150  LA =   INT (M * L * 100000 / 2 + .5) / 100
160  LB =   INT ((1 - M ↑ 2) * L / 2 / M * 100000 + .5) / 100
200    PRINT "FILTER COMPONENT VALUES ARE:"
210    PRINT : PRINT
220    PRINT : PRINT "LA = ";LA;" MILLIHENRIES"
225    PRINT : PRINT "LB = ";LB;" MILLIHENRIES"
230    PRINT : PRINT "C = ";C;" MICROFARADS"
```

LOW-PASS M-DERIVED 'L' FILTERS

THIS PROGRAM DESIGNS LOW-PASS 'L' CON-
FIGURATION, M-DERIVED FILTERS. YOU
MUST ENTER THE CUTOFF FREQUENCY AND THE
FREQUENCY OF MAXIMUM ATTENUATION (HZ)
YOU ALSO HAVE TO ENTER THE TERMINATING
RESISTANCE IN OHMS.

ENTER TERMINATING RESISTANCE (OHMS): 75
ENTER CUTOFF FREQUENCY (HZ): 1000
ENTER MAXIMUM ATTENUATION FREQ.: 1100

FILTER COMPONENT VALUES ARE:

LA = 4.97 MILLIHENRIES

LB = 23.68 MILLIHENRIES

C = .88 MICROFARADS

11.5   LOW-PASS, SHUNT, M-DERIVED L FILTER

Just as the M-derived L filter was used with the T filter, the shunt M-derived L filter is used with the shunt M-derived π filter.

As indicated in Fig. 11.5, the filter consists of only two capacitors and a single inductor.

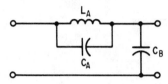

Fig. 11.5 Low-pass, shunt, M-derived L filter

```
0   CALL  - 936
1   PRINT : PRINT : PRINT : PRINT "WRITTEN BY JULES H. GILDER"

2   PRINT : PRINT "COPYRIGHT (C)  HAYDEN BOOK CO. 1978"
3   FOR X = 1 TO 4000: NEXT X

10  PRINT : PRINT : PRINT : PRINT
20  PRINT "  LOW-PASS SHUNT M-DERIVED 'L' FILTER"

30  PRINT : PRINT : PRINT : PRINT
40  PRINT "THIS PROGRAM DESIGNS LOW-PASS 'L' CON-"

50  PRINT "FIGURATION, SHUNT M-DERIVED FILTERS YOU"
60  PRINT "MUST ENTER THE CUTOFF FREQUENCY AND THE"

70  PRINT "FREQUENCY OF MAXIMUM ATTENUATION (HZ)"
75  PRINT "YOU ALSO HAVE TO ENTER THE TERMINATING"

76  PRINT "RESISTANCE IN OHMS."
80  PRINT : PRINT : PRINT

85  INPUT "ENTER TERMINATING RESISTANCE (OHMS): ";R
90  INPUT "ENTER CUTOFF FREQUENCY (HZ): ";F

100  INPUT "ENTER MAXIMUM ATTENUATION FREQ.: ";FM
110  PRINT : PRINT : PRINT

120 PI = 3.14159
130 M =  SQR (1 - ( F / FM) ↑ 2)

135 L = R / (PI * F)
140 C = 1E6 / (PI * R * F)

145 CB = M * C / 2
150 LA =  INT (M * L * 100000 / 2 + .5) / 100

160 CA = (1 - M ↑ 2) * C / (4 * M) * 2
170 CA =  INT (100 * CA + .5) / 100

180 CB =  INT (100 * CB + .5) / 100
200  PRINT "FILTER COMPONENT VALUES ARE:"

210  PRINT : PRINT
220  PRINT : PRINT "LA = ";LA;" MILLIHENRIES"

225  PRINT : PRINT "CA = ";CA;" MICROFARADS"
230  PRINT : PRINT "CB = ";CB;" MICROFARADS"
```

LOW-PASS SHUNT M-DERIVED 'L' FILTER

THIS PROGRAM DESIGNS LOW-PASS 'L' CON-
FIGURATION, SHUNT M-DERIVED FILTERS YOU
MUST ENTER THE CUTOFF FREQUENCY AND THE
FREQUENCY OF MAXIMUM ATTENUATION (HZ)
YOU ALSO HAVE TO ENTER THE TERMINATING
RESISTANCE IN OHMS.

ENTER TERMINATING RESISTANCE (OHMS): 90
ENTER CUTOFF FREQUENCY (HZ): 2000
ENTER MAXIMUM ATTENUATION FREQ.: 2100

FILTER COMPONENT VALUES ARE:

LA = 2.18 MILLIHENRIES

CA = 2.63 MICROFARADS

CB = .27 MICROFARADS

11.6 LOW-PASS, SHUNT, M-DERIVED π FILTER

When the use of capacitors is preferred to the use of inductors in a filter circuit, the shunt, M-derived π filter can be used instead of the T configuration. As seen in Fig. 11.6, this filter contains one inductor and three capacitors.

The input and output impedances are identical, as would be assumed by the symmetrical configuration of the filter. This makes it ideal for a middle element in a chain of filter elements.

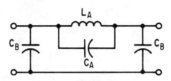

Fig. 11.6 Low-pass, shunt, M-derived π filter

```
0    CALL  - 936
1    PRINT : PRINT : PRINT : PRINT "WRITTEN BY JULES H. GILDER"
2    PRINT : PRINT "COPYRIGHT (C)  HAYDEN BOOK CO. 1978"
3    FOR X = 1 TO 4000: NEXT X
10   PRINT : PRINT : PRINT : PRINT
20   PRINT "   LOW-PASS SHUNT M-DERIVED PI FILTER"
30   PRINT : PRINT : PRINT : PRINT
40   PRINT "THIS PROGRAM DESIGNS LOW-PASS PI CON-"
50   PRINT "FIGURATION, SHUNT M-DERIVED FILTERS YOU"
60   PRINT "MUST ENTER THE CUTOFF FREQUENCY AND THE"
70   PRINT "FREQUENCY OF MAXIMUM ATTENUATION (HZ)"
75   PRINT "YOU ALSO HAVE TO ENTER THE TERMINATING"
76   PRINT "RESISTANCE IN OHMS."
80   PRINT : PRINT : PRINT
85   INPUT "ENTER TERMINATING RESISTANCE (OHMS): ";R
90   INPUT "ENTER CUTOFF FREQUENCY (HZ): ";F
100   INPUT "ENTER MAXIMUM ATTENUATION FREQ.: ";FM
110   PRINT : PRINT : PRINT
120  PI = 3.14159
130  M =  SQR (1 - ( F / FM) ↑ 2)
135  L = R / (PI * F)
140  C = 1E6 / (PI * R * F)
145  CB = M * C / 2
150  LA =  INT (M * L * 100000 + .5) / 100
160  CA = (1 - M ↑ 2) * C / (4 * M)
170  CA =  INT (CA * 100 + .5) / 100
180  CB =  INT (CB * 100 + .5) / 100
200   PRINT "FILTER COMPONENT VALUES ARE:"
210   PRINT : PRINT
220   PRINT : PRINT "LA = ";LA;" MILLIHENRIES"
225   PRINT : PRINT "CA = ";CA;" MICROFARADS"
230   PRINT : PRINT "CB = ";CB;" MICROFARADS"
```

LOW-PASS SHUNT M-DERIVED PI FILTER

THIS PROGRAM DESIGNS LOW-PASS PI CON-
FIGURATION, SHUNT M-DERIVED FILTERS YOU
MUST ENTER THE CUTOFF FREQUENCY AND THE
FREQUENCY OF MAXIMUM ATTENUATION (HZ)
YOU ALSO HAVE TO ENTER THE TERMINATING
RESISTANCE IN OHMS.

ENTER TERMINATING RESISTANCE (OHMS): 1000
ENTER CUTOFF FREQUENCY (HZ): 5000
ENTER MAXIMUM ATTENUATION FREQ.: 5200

FILTER COMPONENT VALUES ARE:

LA = 17.49 MILLIHENRIES

CA = .05 MICROFARADS

CB = .01 MICROFARADS

11.7 HIGH-PASS, CONSTANT-K FILTER

High-pass filters pass all frequencies above the cutoff frequency but attenuate all frequencies from dc to the cutoff.

    This particular filter consists of two inductors, one each across the input and output of the filter, with a capacitor connected between them (see Fig. 11.7). This is the π configuration. Since both inductors have the same value, the terminating impedance on the input and output are identical.

    To use the program, the termination resistance and cutoff frequency must be entered.

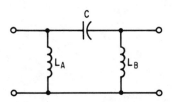

Fig. 11.7 High-pass, constant-K π filter

```
0   CALL - 936
1   PRINT : PRINT : PRINT : PRINT "WRITTEN BY JULES H. GILDER"
2   PRINT : PRINT "COPYRIGHT (C)  HAYDEN BOOK CO. 1978"
3   FOR X = 1 TO 4000: NEXT X
10    PRINT : PRINT : PRINT : PRINT
20    PRINT "   HIGH-PASS CONSTANT-K PI FILTER"
30    PRINT : PRINT : PRINT
40    PRINT "THIS PROGRAM DESIGNS HIGH-PASS PI CON-"
50    PRINT "FIGURATION, CONSTANT-K FILTERS. YOU"
60    PRINT "MUST ENTER THE CUTOFF FREQUENCY AND THE"
70    PRINT "TERMINATING RESISTANCE."
76    PRINT "RESISTANCE IN OHMS."
80    PRINT : PRINT : PRINT
85    INPUT "ENTER TERMINATING RESISTANCE (OHMS): ";R
90    INPUT "ENTER CUTOFF FREQUENCY (HZ): ";F
110   PRINT : PRINT : PRINT
120 PI = 3.14159
130 L = R / (4 * PI * F)
135 L =  INT (1E5 * L + .5) / 100
140 C = 1 / (4 * PI * F * R)
150 C = C * 1E6
160 C =  INT (100 * C + .5) / 100
170 LA = 2 * L
180 LB = 2 * L
200   PRINT "FILTER COMPONENT VALUES ARE:"
210   PRINT : PRINT
220   PRINT : PRINT "LA = ";LA;" MILLIHENRIES"
225   PRINT : PRINT "LB = ";LB;" MILLIHENRIES"
230   PRINT : PRINT "C = ";C;" MICROFARADS"
```

HIGH-PASS CONSTANT-K PI FILTER

THIS PROGRAM DESIGNS HIGH-PASS PI CON-
FIGURATION, CONSTANT-K FILTERS. YOU
MUST ENTER THE CUTOFF FREQUENCY AND THE
TERMINATING RESISTANCE.
RESISTANCE IN OHMS.

ENTER TERMINATING RESISTANCE (OHMS): 90
ENTER CUTOFF FREQUENCY (HZ): 1000

FILTER COMPONENT VALUES ARE:

LA = 14.32 MILLIHENRIES

LB = 14.32 MILLIHENRIES

C = .88 MICROFARADS

11.8 HIGH-PASS, CONSTANT-K T FILTER

The filter in Fig. 11.8 has a similar frequency response to that of the previous filter. It has series capacitors in the input and output arms with a parallel-connected inductor between them. The two capacitors and the input and output impedances have identical values.

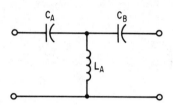

Fig. 11.8 High-pass, constant-K T filter

```
0   CALL  - 936
1   PRINT : PRINT : PRINT : PRINT "WRITTEN BY JULES H. GILDER"
2   PRINT : PRINT "COPYRIGHT (C)  HAYDEN BOOK CO. 1978"
3   FOR X = 1 TO 4000: NEXT X
10  PRINT : PRINT : PRINT : PRINT
20  PRINT "   HIGH-PASS CONSTANT-K 'T' FILTER"
30  PRINT : PRINT : PRINT : PRINT
40  PRINT "THIS PROGRAM DESIGNS HIGH-PASS 'T' CON-"
50  PRINT "FIGURATION, CONSTANT-K FILTERS. YOU"
60  PRINT "MUST ENTER THE CUTOFF FREQUENCY AND THE"
70  PRINT "TERMINATING RESISTANCE."
76  PRINT "RESISTANCE IN OHMS."
80  PRINT : PRINT : PRINT
85  INPUT "ENTER TERMINATING RESISTANCE (OHMS): ";R
90  INPUT "ENTER CUTOFF FREQUENCY (HZ): ";F
110 PRINT : PRINT : PRINT
120 PI = 3.14159
130 L = R / (4 * PI * F)
135 L = INT (1E5 * L + .5) / 100
140 C = 1 / (4 * PI * F * R)
150 C = 2 * C * 1E6
160 CA = INT (100 * C + .5) / 100
170 CB = CA
200 PRINT "FILTER COMPONENT VALUES ARE:"
210 PRINT : PRINT
220 PRINT : PRINT "LA = ";L;" MILLIHENRIES"
225 PRINT : PRINT "CA = ";CA;" MICROFARADS"
230 PRINT : PRINT "CB = ";CB;" MICROFARADS"
```

HIGH-PASS CONSTANT-K 'T' FILTER

THIS PROGRAM DESIGNS HIGH-PASS 'T' CON-
FIGURATION, CONSTANT-K FILTERS. YOU
MUST ENTER THE CUTOFF FREQUENCY AND THE
TERMINATING RESISTANCE.
RESISTANCE IN OHMS.

ENTER TERMINATING RESISTANCE (OHMS): 1000
ENTER CUTOFF FREQUENCY (HZ): 60

FILTER COMPONENT VALUES ARE:

LA = 1326.29 MILLIHENRIES

CA = 2.65 MICROFARADS

CB = 2.65 MICROFARADS

11.9 HIGH-PASS, SERIES, M-DERIVED T FILTER

This filter is used to pass only those frequencies above a certain specified frequency. As with the low-pass M-derived filters, the maximum attenuation frequency must be entered. But unlike the low-pass filters where the maximum attenuation frequency was higher than the cutoff frequency, the maximum attenuation for high-pass filters is lower than the cutoff frequency.

The high-pass series, M-derived T filter is relatively simple. It is built from three capacitors and one inductor (see Fig. 11.9).

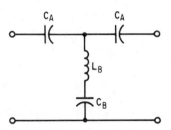

Fig. 11.9 High-pass, series, M-derived T filter

```
0    CALL  - 936
1    PRINT : PRINT : PRINT : PRINT "WRITTEN BY JULES H. GILDER"
2    PRINT : PRINT "COPYRIGHT (C)  HAYDEN BOOK CO. 1978"
3    FOR X = 1 TO 4000: NEXT X

10   PRINT : PRINT : PRINT : PRINT
20   PRINT "HIGH-PASS SERIES M-DERIVED 'T' FILTER"

30   PRINT : PRINT : PRINT : PRINT
40   PRINT "THIS PROGRAM DESIGNS HIGH-PASS 'T' CON-"

50   PRINT "FIGURATION, SERIES M-DERIVED FILTERS."
60   PRINT "YOU MUST ENTER THE CUTOFF FREQUENCY AND"

65   PRINT "THE FREQUENCY OF MAXIMUM ATTENUATION "
70   PRINT "TERMINATING RESISTANCE."

80   PRINT : PRINT : PRINT
85   INPUT "ENTER TERMINATING RESISTANCE (OHMS): ";R

90   INPUT "ENTER CUTOFF FREQUENCY (HZ): ";F
100  INPUT "ENTER MAX. ATTENUATION FREQUENCY: ";FM

105  M =  SQR (1 - (FM / F) ↑ 2)
110   PRINT : PRINT : PRINT

120  PI = 3.14159
130  L = R / (4 * PI * F )

135  LB =  INT (1E5 * L / M + .5) / 100
140  C = 1 / (4 * PI * F * R)

142  C = C * 1E6
150  CA = C / M * 2

160  CB = 4 * M / (1 - M ↑ 2) * C
170  CA =  INT (100 * CA + .5) / 100

180  CB =  INT (100 * CB + .5) / 100
200   PRINT "FILTER COMPONENT VALUES ARE:"

210   PRINT : PRINT
220   PRINT : PRINT "LB = ";LB;" MILLIHENRIES"

225   PRINT : PRINT "CA = ";CA;" MICROFARADS"
230   PRINT : PRINT "CB = ";CB;" MICROFARADS"
```

HIGH-PASS SERIES M-DERIVED 'T' FILTER

THIS PROGRAM DESIGNS HIGH-PASS 'T' CON-
FIGURATION, SERIES M-DERIVED FILTERS.
YOU MUST ENTER THE CUTOFF FREQUENCY AND
THE FREQUENCY OF MAXIMUM ATTENUATION
TERMINATING RESISTANCE.

ENTER TERMINATING RESISTANCE (OHMS): 300
ENTER CUTOFF FREQUENCY (HZ): 1000
ENTER MAX. ATTENUATION FREQUENCY: 950

FILTER COMPONENT VALUES ARE:

LB = 76.46 MILLIHENRIES

CA = 1.7 MICROFARADS

CB = .37 MICROFARADS

11.10 HIGH-PASS, SHUNT, M-DERIVED π FILTER

The shunt, M-derived π filter is made from three inductors and one capacitor. Two inductors are connected in parallel across the input and output. The other inductor is connected in parallel with a capacitor and located between the two termination inductors (see Fig. 11.10).

To use the program, the termination resistance, cutoff frequency, and maximum attenuation frequency must be entered.

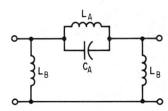

Fig. 11.10 High-pass, shunt, M-derived π filter

```
0    CALL   - 936
1    PRINT : PRINT : PRINT : PRINT "WRITTEN BY JULES H. GILDER"

2    PRINT : PRINT "COPYRIGHT (C)  HAYDEN BOOK CO. 1978"
3    FOR X = 1 TO 4000: NEXT X

10   PRINT : PRINT : PRINT : PRINT
20   PRINT "HIGH-PASS SHUNT M-DERIVED PI FILTER"

30   PRINT : PRINT : PRINT : PRINT
40   PRINT "THIS PROGRAM DESIGNS HIGH-PASS PI CON-"

50   PRINT "FIGURATION, SHUNT M-DERIVED FILTERS."
60   PRINT "YOU MUST ENTER THE CUTOFF FREQUENCY AND"

65   PRINT "THE FREQUENCY OF MAXIMUM ATTENUATION "
70   PRINT "TERMINATING RESISTANCE."

80   PRINT : PRINT : PRINT
85   INPUT "ENTER TERMINATING RESISTANCE (OHMS): ";R

90   INPUT "ENTER CUTOFF FREQUENCY (HZ): ";F
100  INPUT "ENTER MAX. ATTENUATION FREQUENCY: ";FM

105  M =  SQR (1 - (FM / F) ↑ 2)
110  PRINT : PRINT : PRINT
120  PI = 3.14159
130  L = R / (4 * PI * F)
135  LB =  INT (1E5 * L / M + .5) / 100
137  LB = 2 * LB
140  C = 1 / (4 * PI * F * R)
142  C = C * 1E6
150  CA = C / M
160  LA =  INT (4 * M * L * 1E5 / (1 - M ↑ 2) + .5) / 100
170  CA =  INT (100 * CA + .5) / 100
200  PRINT "FILTER COMPONENT VALUES ARE:"
210  PRINT : PRINT
220  PRINT : PRINT "LA = ";LA;" MILLIHENRIES"
225  PRINT : PRINT "LB = ";LB;" MILLIHENRIES"
230  PRINT : PRINT "CA = ";CA;" MICROFARADS"
```

HIGH-PASS SHUNT M-DERIVED PI FILTER

THIS PROGRAM DESIGNS HIGH-PASS PI CON-
FIGURATION, SHUNT M-DERIVED FILTERS.
YOU MUST ENTER THE CUTOFF FREQUENCY AND
THE FREQUENCY OF MAXIMUM ATTENUATION
TERMINATING RESISTANCE.

ENTER TERMINATING RESISTANCE (OHMS): 90
ENTER CUTOFF FREQUENCY (HZ): 60
ENTER MAX. ATTENUATION FREQUENCY: 55

FILTER COMPONENT VALUES ARE:

LA = 227.09 MILLIHENRIES

LB = 597.36 MILLIHENRIES

CA = 36.87 MICROFARADS

11.11 BANDPASS, CONSTANT-K π FILTER

The bandpass filter in Fig. 11.11 is a combination of both a low-pass filter and a high-pass filter, where the cutoff frequency of the low-pass filter is higher than the cutoff frequency of the high-pass filter. Bandpass filters permit a specific band of frequencies to be passed. Above and below this band of frequencies, the signal is significantly attenuated.

This particular filter has two parallel arms in the input and output portions of the circuit, with a series arm connected between them. To use the program, you must enter the upper and lower limits of the passband and the terminating resistance.

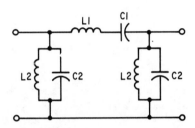

Fig. 11.11 Bandpass, constant-K π filter

```
0   CALL  - 936
1   PRINT : PRINT : PRINT : PRINT "WRITTEN BY JULES H. GILDER"
2   PRINT : PRINT "COPYRIGHT (C)  HAYDEN BOOK CO. 1978"
3   FOR X = 1 TO 4000: NEXT X
10   PRINT : PRINT : PRINT : PRINT
20   PRINT "    BAND-PASS CONSTANT-K PI FILTER"
30   PRINT : PRINT : PRINT
40   PRINT "THIS PROGRAM DESIGNS BAND-PASS CONSTANT"
50   PRINT "K PI FILTERS. YOU MUST ENTER THE TER-"
60   PRINT "MINATING RESISTANCE AND UPPER AND LOWER"
70   PRINT "PASSBAND FREQUENCIES."
80   PRINT : PRINT : PRINT
85   INPUT "ENTER TERMINATING RESISTANCE (OHMS): ";R
90   INPUT "ENTER LOW FREQUENCY (HZ): ";F1
100   INPUT "ENTER HIGH FREQUENCY: ";F2
110   PRINT : PRINT : PRINT
120 PI = 3.14159
130 L1 = R / (PI * (F2 - F1))
132 L1 =  INT (1E5 * L1 + .5) / 100
135 L2 = (F2 - F1) * R / (2 * PI * F1 * F2)
136 L2 =  INT (1E5 * L2 + .5) / 100
140 C1 = (F2 - F1) / (4 * PI * F1 * F2 * R)
142 C1 = C1 * 1E6
145 C1 =  INT (C1 * 100 + .5) / 100
150 C2 = 1 / (PI * (F2 - F1) * R) / 2
160 C2 = C2 * 1E6
170 C2 =  INT (100 * C2 + .5) / 100
```

```
200   PRINT "FILTER COMPONENT VALUES ARE:"
210   PRINT : PRINT
220   PRINT : PRINT "L1 = ";L1;" MILLIHENRIES"
225   PRINT : PRINT "L2 = ";L2;" MILLIHENRIES"
230   PRINT : PRINT "C1 = ";C1;" MICROFARADS"
240   PRINT : PRINT "C2 = ";C2;" MICROFARADS"
```

BAND-PASS CONSTANT-K PI FILTER

THIS PROGRAM DESIGNS BAND-PASS CONSTANT
K PI FILTERS. YOU MUST ENTER THE TER-
MINATING RESISTANCE AND UPPER AND LOWER
PASSBAND FREQUENCIES.

ENTER TERMINATING RESISTANCE (OHMS): 75
ENTER LOW FREQUENCY (HZ): 2500
ENTER HIGH FREQUENCY: 3500

FILTER COMPONENT VALUES ARE:

L1 = 23.87 MILLIHENRIES

L2 = 1.36 MILLIHENRIES

C1 = .12 MICROFARADS

C2 = 2.12 MICROFARADS

11.12 BANDPASS, CONSTANT-K T FILTER

The filter in Fig. 11.12 differs from the previous one in that it has series input and output elements instead of parallel ones. The frequency response curve of this filter is similar to the earlier bandpass filter.

As with the other program, frequency must be entered in hertz and the terminating resistance, in ohms. The component values are given in microfarads and millihenries.

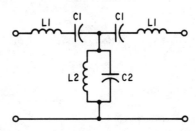

Fig. 11.12 Bandpass, constant-K T filter

```
0    CALL  - 936
1    PRINT : PRINT : PRINT : PRINT "WRITTEN BY JULES H. GILDER"
2    PRINT : PRINT "COPYRIGHT (C)  HAYDEN BOOK CO. 1978"
3    FOR X = 1 TO 4000: NEXT X
10    PRINT : PRINT : PRINT : PRINT
20    PRINT "     BAND-PASS CONSTANT-K 'T' FILTER"
30    PRINT : PRINT : PRINT : PRINT
40    PRINT "THIS PROGRAM DESIGNS BAND-PASS CONSTANT"
50    PRINT "K 'T' FILTERS. YOU MUST ENTER THE TER-"
60    PRINT "MINATING RESISTANCE AND UPPER AND LOWER"
70    PRINT "PASSBAND FREQUENCIES."
80    PRINT : PRINT : PRINT
85    INPUT "ENTER TERMINATING RESISTANCE (OHMS): ";R
90    INPUT "ENTER LOW FREQUENCY (HZ): ";F1
100   INPUT "ENTER HIGH FREQUENCY: ";F2
110    PRINT : PRINT : PRINT
120 PI = 3.14159
130 L1 = R / (PI * (F2 - F1) * 2)
132 L1 =   INT (1E5 * L1 + .5) / 100
135 L2 = (F2 - F1) * R / (4 * PI * F1 * F2)
136 L2 =   INT (1E5 * L2 + .5) / 100
140 C1 = (F2 - F1) / (2 * PI * F1 * F2 * R)
142 C1 = C1 * 1E6
145 C1 =   INT (C1 * 100 + .5) / 100
150 C2 = 1 / (PI * (F2 - F1) * R)
160 C2 = C2 * 1E6
170 C2 =   INT (100 * C2 + .5) / 100
200    PRINT "FILTER COMPONENT VALUES ARE:"
210    PRINT : PRINT
220    PRINT : PRINT "L1 = ";L1;" MILLIHENRIES"
225    PRINT : PRINT "L2 = ";L2;" MILLIHENRIES"
230    PRINT : PRINT "C1 = ";C1;" MICROFARADS"
240    PRINT : PRINT "C2 = ";C2;" MICROFARADS"
```

BAND—PASS CONSTANT—K 'T' FILTER

THIS PROGRAM DESIGNS BAND—PASS CONSTANT
K 'T' FILTERS. YOU MUST ENTER THE TER-
MINATING RESISTANCE AND UPPER AND LOWER
PASSBAND FREQUENCIES.

ENTER TERMINATING RESISTANCE (OHMS): 75
ENTER LOW FREQUENCY (HZ): 900
ENTER HIGH FREQUENCY: 1100

FILTER COMPONENT VALUES ARE:

L1 = 59.68 MILLIHENRIES

L2 = 1.21 MILLIHENRIES

C1 = .43 MICROFARADS

C2 = 21.22 MICROFARADS

11.13 BAND-ELIMINATION, CONSTANT-K π FILTER

Like the bandpass filter, the band-elimination filter can be thought of as a combination of a low-pass filter and a high-pass filter. In this case, however, the cutoff frequency of the low-pass filter would be lower than the cutoff frequency of the high-pass filter, leaving a frequency gap between the two where the frequency is attenuated. Thus, the band-elimination filter is able to attenuate a specific frequency selectively.

As can be seen in Fig. 11.13, this filter has a π configuration. The input and output impedances are identical.

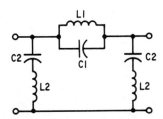

Fig. 11.13 Band-elimination, constant-K π filter

```
0    CALL  - 936
1    PRINT : PRINT : PRINT : PRINT "WRITTEN BY JULES H. GILDER"
2    PRINT : PRINT "COPYRIGHT (C)  HAYDEN BOOK CO. 1978"
3    FOR X = 1 TO 4000: NEXT X

10   PRINT : PRINT : PRINT : PRINT
20   PRINT "BAND-ELIMINATION CONSTANT-K 'PI' FILTER"

30   PRINT : PRINT : PRINT
40   PRINT "THIS PROGRAM DESIGNS BAND-ELIMINATION"

50   PRINT "CONSTANT-K 'PI' FILTERS. YOU MUST ENTER"
60   PRINT "THE TERMINATING RESISTANCE AND UPPER"

70   PRINT "AND LOWER ELIMINATION BAND FREQUENCIES"
80   PRINT : PRINT : PRINT

85   INPUT "ENTER TERMINATING RESISTANCE (OHMS): ";R
90   INPUT "ENTER LOW FREQUENCY (HZ): ";F1

100  INPUT "ENTER HIGH FREQUENCY: ";F2
110  PRINT : PRINT : PRINT

120  PI = 3.14159
130  L2 = R / (PI * (F2 - F1)) / 2

132  L2 =  INT (1E5 * L2 + .5) / 100
135  L1 = (F2 - F1) * R / (PI * F1 * F2)

136  L1 =  INT (1E5 * L1 + .5) / 100
140  C2 = (F2 - F1) / (2 * PI * F1 * F2 * R)

142  C2 = C2 * 1E6
150  C1 = 1 / (PI * (F2 - F1) * R * 4)

160  C1 = C1 * 1E6
170  C1 =  INT (100 * C1 + .5) / 100

180  C2 =  INT (100 * C2 + .5) / 100
200  PRINT "FILTER COMPONENT VALUES ARE:"

210  PRINT : PRINT
220  PRINT : PRINT "L1 = ";L1;" MILLIHENRIES"

225  PRINT : PRINT "L2 = ";L2;" MILLIHENRIES"
230  PRINT : PRINT "C1 = ";C1;" MICROFARADS"

240  PRINT : PRINT "C2 = ";C2;" MICROFARADS"
```

BAND-ELIMINATION CONSTANT-K 'PI' FILTER

THIS PROGRAM DESIGNS BAND-ELIMINATION
CONSTANT-K 'PI' FILTERS. YOU MUST ENTER
THE TERMINATING RESISTANCE AND UPPER
AND LOWER ELIMINATION BAND FREQUENCIES

ENTER TERMINATING RESISTANCE (OHMS): 75
ENTER LOW FREQUENCY (HZ): 45
ENTER HIGH FREQUENCY: 55

FILTER COMPONENT VALUES ARE:

L1 = 96.46 MILLIHENRIES

L2 = 1193.66 MILLIHENRIES

C1 = 106.1 MICROFARADS

C2 = 8.57 MICROFARADS

11.14 BAND-ELIMINATION, CONSTANT-K T FILTER

This T filter is similar to the π filter previously described, except for its physical layout. Like the π filter, this one will permit all frequencies to pass except for a specific band designated by the low and high frequencies entered by the user.

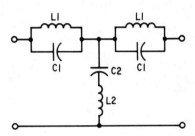

Fig. 11.14 Band-elimination, constant-K T filter

```
0   CALL - 936
1   PRINT : PRINT : PRINT : PRINT "WRITTEN BY JULES H. GILDER"
2   PRINT : PRINT "COPYRIGHT (C)  HAYDEN BOOK CO. 1978"
3   FOR X = 1 TO 4000: NEXT X
10  PRINT : PRINT : PRINT : PRINT
20  PRINT "BAND-ELIMINATION CONSTANT-K 'T' FILTER"
30  PRINT : PRINT : PRINT : PRINT
40  PRINT "THIS PROGRAM DESIGNS BAND-ELIMINATION"
50  PRINT "CONSTANT-K 'T' FILTERS. YOU MUST ENTER"
60  PRINT "THE TERMINATING RESISTANCE AND UPPER"
70  PRINT "AND LOWER ELIMINATION BAND FREQUENCIES"
80  PRINT : PRINT : PRINT
85  INPUT "ENTER TERMINATING RESISTANCE (OHMS): ";R
90  INPUT "ENTER LOW FREQUENCY (HZ): ";F1
100  INPUT "ENTER HIGH FREQUENCY: ";F2
110  PRINT : PRINT : PRINT
120 PI = 3.14159
130 L2 = R / (PI * (F2 - F1)) / 4
132 L2 =   INT (1E5 * L2 + .5) / 100
135 L1 = (F2 - F1) * R / (PI * F1 * F2) / 2
136 L1 =   INT (1E5 * L1 + .5) / 100
140 C2 = (F2 - F1) / (PI * F1 * F2 * R)
142 C2 = C2 * 1E6
150 C1 = 1 / (PI * (F2 - F1) * R) / 2
160 C1 = C1 * 1E6
170 C1 =   INT (100 * C1 + .5) / 100
180 C2 =   INT (100 * C2 + .5) / 100
200  PRINT "FILTER COMPONENT VALUES ARE:"
210  PRINT : PRINT
220  PRINT : PRINT "L1 = ";L1;" MILLIHENRIES"
225  PRINT : PRINT "L2 = ";L2;" MILLIHENRIES"
230  PRINT : PRINT "C1 = ";C1;" MICROFARADS"
240  PRINT : PRINT "C2 = ";C2;" MICROFARADS"
```

BAND-ELIMINATION CONSTANT-K 'T' FILTER

THIS PROGRAM DESIGNS BAND-ELIMINATION
CONSTANT-K 'T' FILTERS. YOU MUST ENTER
THE TERMINATING RESISTANCE AND UPPER
AND LOWER ELIMINATION BAND FREQUENCIES

ENTER TERMINATING RESISTANCE (OHMS): 50
ENTER LOW FREQUENCY (HZ): 55
ENTER HIGH FREQUENCY: 65

FILTER COMPONENT VALUES ARE:

L1 = 22.26 MILLIHENRIES

L2 = 397.89 MILLIHENRIES

C1 = 318.31 MICROFARADS

C2 = 17.81 MICROFARADS

12   Attenuator Pads

When feeding analog signals from one circuit to another, a situation sometimes arises where the signal applied is too strong and its application to a particular circuit causes it to overload and malfunction. Situations such as this commonly arise in RF, audio, and video applications. For example, if you live near a television transmitter, it is possible that the gain produced by your antenna will result in a signal overload, preventing proper reception.

Another application arises when interfacing various sources of audio signals to an amplifier. Too strong a signal on the input will cause distortion in the output of the amplifier.

To overcome these overloading problems, resistor networks, known as attenuator pads, are used. The eleven programs in this chapter design different types of attenuators. Some are for balanced (ungrounded) lines, and some are for unbalanced lines. Some are for symmetrical inputs and outputs, while others are for unsymmetrical inputs and outputs. Still others are for a combination of these. In addition, the last two programs design attenuators that will introduce a minimum of loss when connected between the two systems.

12.1 BALANCED-BRIDGED H ATTENUATOR PAD

For attenuation of signals on balanced transmission lines with symmetrical input and output impedances, the bridged H attenuator is applicable (see Fig. 12.1).

The attenuator is composed of seven resistors. To use the program, it is necessary only to enter the desired symmetrical impedance and the loss introduced by the attenuator.

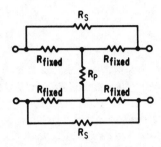

Fig. 12.1 Balanced-bridged H attenuator

```
0    CALL  - 936
1    PRINT : PRINT : PRINT : PRINT "WRITTEN BY JULES H. GILDER"

2    PRINT : PRINT "COPYRIGHT (C) HAYDEN BOOK CO. 1978"
3    FOR X = 1 TO 4000: NEXT X

4    PRINT : PRINT : PRINT : PRINT
5    PRINT "BALANCED BRIDGED 'H' ATTENUATOR"

10   PRINT : PRINT : PRINT : PRINT
20   PRINT "THIS PROGRAM WILL DESIGN BALANCED"

30   PRINT "BRIDGED 'H' ATTENUATOR PADS. YOU"
40   PRINT "MUST ENTER THE DESIRED IMPEDANCE"

50   PRINT "IN OHMS AND THE REQUIRED VOLTAGE"
60   PRINT "OR CURRENT LOSS IN DECIBELS."

70   PRINT : PRINT
80   INPUT "WHAT IS THE DESIRED IMPEDANCE? ";A

100  INPUT "WHAT IS THE DESIRED LOSS IN DB? ";L
110  PRINT

120  Z = A
130  K =  EXP (L *  LOG (10) / 20)

140  Y =  INT (Z / 2 + .5)
145  V =  INT (Z * (K - 1) / 2 + .5)

150  W =  INT (Z / (K - 1) + .5)
160  PRINT : PRINT : PRINT

170  PRINT "FOR BALANCED SYMMETRICAL PADS OF ";Z
180  PRINT "OHMS AND ";L;" DB LOSS:"

190  PRINT : PRINT
200  PRINT "BRIDGED 'H' SERIES RESISTORS 'S' ARE"

210  PRINT V;" OHMS."
220  PRINT

230  PRINT "THE SHUNT RESISTOR 'P' IS ";W;" OHMS."
235  PRINT : PRINT "THIS PAD USES ";Y;" OHM FIXED RESISTORS"

237  PRINT "FOR ALL VALUES OF LOSS."
240  PRINT

250  PRINT "MULTIPLY SERIES RESISTOR VALUES BY 2"
260  PRINT "FOR THE UNBALANCED PAD VALUES."

270  PRINT : PRINT
280  INPUT "ANOTHER DESIGN? ";Z$

290  IF  LEFT$ (Z$,1) = "Y" THEN 70
300  END
```

BALANCED BRIDGED 'H' ATTENUATOR

THIS PROGRAM WILL DESIGN BALANCED
BRIDGED 'H' ATTENUATOR PADS. YOU
MUST ENTER THE DESIRED IMPEDANCE
IN OHMS AND THE REQUIRED VOLTAGE
OR CURRENT LOSS IN DECIBELS.

WHAT IS THE DESIRED IMPEDANCE? 600
WHAT IS THE DESIRED LOSS IN DB? 6

FOR BALANCED SYMMETRICAL PADS OF 600
OHMS AND 6 DB LOSS:

BRIDGED 'H' SERIES RESISTORS 'S' ARE
299 OHMS.

THE SHUNT RESISTOR 'P' IS 603 OHMS.

THIS PAD USES 300 OHM FIXED RESISTORS
FOR ALL VALUES OF LOSS.

MULTIPLY SERIES RESISTOR VALUES BY 2
FOR THE UNBALANCED PAD VALUES.

ANOTHER DESIGN? NO

12.2 SYMMETRICAL, UNBALANCED-BRIDGED T ATTENUATOR

The bridged T attenuator (Fig. 12.2) is designed to be used on unbalanced transmission lines (where one side is grounded). The input and output impedances are symmetrical, and the attenuator itself consists of only four resistors.

To use the program, enter the termination impedance and the desired signal loss in dB.

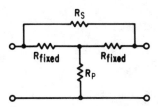

Fig. 12.2 Symmetrical, unbalanced-bridged T attenuator

```
0    CALL  - 936
1    PRINT : PRINT : PRINT : PRINT "WRITTEN BY JULES H. GILDER"
2    PRINT : PRINT "COPYRIGHT (C) HAYDEN BOOK CO. 1978"
3    FOR X = 1 TO 4000: NEXT X
4    PRINT : PRINT : PRINT : PRINT
5    PRINT  TAB( 5)"SYMMETRICAL BRIDGED 'T' ATTENUATOR"
10   PRINT : PRINT : PRINT : PRINT
20   PRINT "THIS PROGRAM WILL DESIGN UNBALANCED"
30   PRINT "SYMMETRICAL BRIDGED 'T' ATTENUATORS YOU"
40   PRINT "MUST ENTER THE INPUT AND OUTPUT IMPE-"
50   PRINT "DANCES IN OHMS AND THE DESIRED VOLTAGE"
60   PRINT "OR CURRENT LOSS IN DECIBELS."
70   PRINT : PRINT
90   INPUT "WHAT IS THE DESIRED IMPEDANCE? ";A
100  INPUT "WHAT IS THE DESIRED LOSS IN DB? ";L
110  PRINT
120  Z = A
130  K =  EXP (L *  LOG (10) / 20)
140  S =  INT (Z * (K - 1) + .5)
150  P =  INT (Z / (K - 1) + .5)
160  PRINT : PRINT : PRINT
170  PRINT "FOR SYMMETRICAL PADS OF ";Z
180  PRINT "OHMS AND ";L;" DB LOSS:"
190  PRINT : PRINT
200  PRINT "BRIDGED 'T' SERIES RESISTOR 'S' IS"
202  PRINT S;" OHMS."
204  PRINT
206  PRINT "SHUNT RESISTOR 'P' IS ";P;" OHMS."
220  PRINT
230  PRINT "FIXED RESISTORS R1 AND R2 ARE ";Z;" OHMS"
240  PRINT : PRINT
250  INPUT "ANOTHER DESIGN? ";Z$
260  IF  LEFT$ (Z$,1) = "Y" THEN 70
270  END
```

SYMMETRICAL BRIDGED 'T' ATTENUATOR

THIS PROGRAM WILL DESIGN UNBALANCED
SYMMETRICAL BRIDGED 'T' ATTENUATORS YOU
MUST ENTER THE INPUT AND OUTPUT IMPE-
DANCES IN OHMS AND THE DESIRED VOLTAGE
OR CURRENT LOSS IN DECIBELS.

WHAT IS THE DESIRED IMPEDANCE? 300
WHAT IS THE DESIRED LOSS IN DB? 10

FOR SYMMETRICAL PADS OF 300
OHMS AND 10 DB LOSS:

BRIDGED 'T' SERIES RESISTOR 'S' IS
649 OHMS.

SHUNT RESISTOR 'P' IS 139 OHMS.

FIXED RESISTORS R1 AND R2 ARE 300 OHMS

ANOTHER DESIGN? NO

12.3 UNSYMMETRICAL H-PAD ATTENUATOR

The H-pad attenuator in Fig. 12.3 is composed of five resistors. For unsymmetrical attenuators, the input series resistors have a different value than the output series.

The H attenuator designed by the program is a balanced attenuator. For unbalanced attenuators, it is necessary to multiply the series resistors by 2.

Input and output impedance values should be entered in ohms. One of the first things the program does is calculate the minimum impedance possible, given the input and output impedances. If this value is larger than the desired loss in decibels, the program terminates execution and prints out a message indicating the minimum loss. If attenuator design is still desired, the value for loss in dB must be made equal to or greater than the minimum loss.

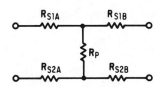

Fig. 12.3 Unsymmetrical H-pad attenuator

```
0   CALL  - 936
1   PRINT : PRINT : PRINT : PRINT "WRITTEN BY JULES H. GILDER"
2   PRINT : PRINT "COPYRIGHT (C) HAYDEN BOOK CO. 1978"
3   FOR X = 1 TO 4000: NEXT X
4   PRINT : PRINT : PRINT : PRINT
5   PRINT  TAB( 5)"UNSYMMETRICAL H PAD ATTENUATOR"
10   PRINT : PRINT : PRINT : PRINT
20   PRINT "THIS COMPUTER PROGRAM WILL DESIGN"
30   PRINT "UNSYMMETRICAL 'H' ATTENUATOR PADS. YOU"
40   PRINT "MUST ENTER THE INPUT AND OUTPUT IMPE-"
50   PRINT "DANCES IN OHMS AND THE DESIRED VOLTAGE"
60   PRINT "OR CURRENT LOSS IN DECIBELS."
70   PRINT : PRINT
80   INPUT "WHAT IS THE INPUT IMPEDANCE? ";A
90   INPUT "WHAT IS THE OUTPUT IMPEDANCE? ";B
100   INPUT "WHAT IS THE DESIRED LOSS IN DB? ";L
110   PRINT
130   IF  B > A  THEN 180
140  C = 1
150  D = 2
160  Z1 = A:  Z2 = B
170   GOTO  230
180  Z1 = B
190  Z2 = A
210  C = 2
220  D = 1
230  K5 = (Z1 +  SQR ((Z1 ↑ 2) - (Z1 * Z2))) / Z2
240  L5 =  LOG (K5 /  SQR (Z1 / Z2)) / ( LOG (10) / 20)
250   IF  L < L5  THEN  440
260  K = ( EXP (L * ( LOG (10) / 20))) *  SQR (Z1 / Z2)
270  N =  EXP (L * ( LOG (10) / 10))
280  S(1) = Z1 * ((K * Z2) * (K - 2) + Z1) / (((K ↑ 2) * Z2) - Z1)

290  S(2) = Z2 * ((K ↑ 2 * Z2) - Z1 * (2 * K - 1)) / (((K ↑ 2) * Z
     2) - Z1)
```

```
300 P3 = (2 *  SQR (N * Z1 * Z2)) / (N - 1)
310  PRINT : PRINT : PRINT
320  PRINT "FOR UNSYMMETRICAL BALANCED PADS WHERE"
330  PRINT "Z1 = "; A;" OHMS, Z2 = ";B;" OHMS"
340  PRINT "AND LOSS = ";L;" DB THE COMPONENT "
350  PRINT "VALUES FOR AN 'H' ATTENUATOR ARE:"
360  PRINT : PRINT
370  PRINT "THE INPUT SERIES RESISTORS S1A AND S1B"
380  PRINT "ARE "; INT (S(3 - D) / 2 + .5);" OHMS."
390  PRINT
400  PRINT "THE OUTPUT SERIES RESISTORS S2A AND"
410  PRINT "S2B ARE "; INT (S(3 - C) / 2 + .5);" OHMS."
420  PRINT
430  PRINT "THE SHUNT RESISTOR  P  IS "; INT (P3 + .5);" OHMS."
440  PRINT
450  PRINT "MINIMUM LOSS FOR THESE IMPEDANCES IS"
460  PRINT    INT (10 * L5 + .5) / 10;" DB."
470  PRINT
480  PRINT "FOR UNBALANCED PAD VALUES MULTIPLY"
490  PRINT "SERIES RESISTOR VALUES BY 2."
500  PRINT : PRINT : INPUT "ANOTHER DESIGN? ";Z$
510  IF  LEFT$ (Z$,1) = "Y" THEN 70
520  END
```

```
    UNSYMMETRICAL H PAD ATTENUATOR


THIS COMPUTER PROGRAM WILL DESIGN
UNSYMMETRICAL 'H' ATTENUATOR PADS. YOU
MUST ENTER THE INPUT AND OUTPUT IMPE-
DANCES IN OHMS AND THE DESIRED VOLTAGE
OR CURRENT LOSS IN DECIBELS.

WHAT IS THE INPUT IMPEDANCE? 300
WHAT IS THE OUTPUT IMPEDANCE? 150
WHAT IS THE DESIRED LOSS IN DB? 20


FOR UNSYMMETRICAL BALANCED PADS WHERE
Z1 = 300 OHMS, Z2 = 150 OHMS
AND LOSS = 20 DB THE COMPONENT
VALUES FOR AN 'H' ATTENUATOR ARE:

THE INPUT SERIES RESISTORS S1A AND S1B
ARE 132 OHMS.

THE OUTPUT SERIES RESISTORS S2A AND
S2B ARE 55 OHMS.

THE SHUNT RESISTOR  P  IS 43 OHMS.

MINIMUM LOSS FOR THESE IMPEDANCES IS
7.7 DB.

FOR UNBALANCED PAD VALUES MULTIPLY
SERIES RESISTOR VALUES BY 2.


ANOTHER DESIGN? NO
```

12.4   UNSYMMETRICAL SQUARE-PAD ATTENUATOR

The square attenuator in Fig. 12.4 is composed of four resistors. For unsymmetrical attenuators, the input parallel resistor has a different value from the output parallel resistor. The two series resistors are identical in value.

The square attenuator designed in this program is a balanced attenuator. For unbalanced attenuators, it is necessary to multiply the series resistors by 2.

Input and output impedance values should be entered in ohms. One of the first things the program does is calculate the minimum impedance possible, given the input and output impedances. If this value is larger than the desired loss in decibels, the program terminates execution and prints out a message indicating the minimum loss. If attenuator design is still desired, the value for loss in dB must be made equal to or greater than the minimum loss.

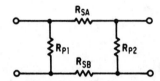

Fig. 12.4 Unsymmetrical square-pad attenuator

```
0    CALL  - 936
1    PRINT : PRINT : PRINT : PRINT "WRITTEN BY JULES H. GILDER"
2    PRINT : PRINT "COPYRIGHT (C) HAYDEN BOOK CO. 1978"
3    FOR X = 1 TO 4000: NEXT X
4    PRINT : PRINT : PRINT : PRINT
5    PRINT "  UNSYMMETRICAL SQUARE PAD ATTENUATOR"
10   PRINT : PRINT : PRINT : PRINT
20   PRINT "THIS PROGRAM WILL DESIGN UNSYMMETRICAL"
30   PRINT "SQUARE ATTENUATOR PADS. TO USE YOU"
40   PRINT "MUST ENTER THE INPUT AND OUTPUT IMPE-"
50   PRINT "DANCES IN OHMS AND THE DESIRED VOLTAGE"
60   PRINT "OR CURRENT LOSS IN DECIBELS."
70   PRINT : PRINT
80   INPUT "WHAT IS THE INPUT IMPEDANCE? ";A
90   INPUT "WHAT IS THE OUTPUT IMPEDANCE? ";B
100  INPUT "WHAT IS THE DESIRED LOSS IN DB? ";L
110  PRINT
130  IF   B > A    THEN  180
140  C = 1
150  D = 2
160  Z1 = A:  Z2 = B
170  GOTO 230
180  Z1 = B
190  Z2 = A
210  C = 2
220  D = 1
230  K5 = (Z1 +  SQR ((Z1 ↑ 2) - (Z1 * Z2))) / Z2
240  L5 =  LOG (K5 /  SQR (Z1 / Z2)) / ( LOG (10) / 20)
250  IF  L < L5  THEN  440
260  K = ( EXP (L * ( LOG (10) / 20))) *  SQR (Z1 / Z2)
270  N =  EXP (L * ( LOG (10) / 20))
280  P(1) = (Z1 * (((K ↑ 2) * Z2) - Z1)) / (((K ↑ 2) * Z2) - (2 *
     K * Z1) + Z1)
290  P(2) = (((K ↑ 2) * (Z2 ↑ 2)) - (Z1 * Z2)) / ((K * Z2 * (K - 2
     ) + Z1))
```

```
300 S3 = (P(2) * Z2 * (K - 1)) / (P(2) + Z2)
310   PRINT : PRINT : PRINT
320   PRINT "FOR UNSYMMETRICAL BALANCED PADS WHERE"
330   PRINT "Z1 = "; A;" OHMS, Z2 = ";B;" OHMS"
340   PRINT "AND LOSS = ";L;" DB THE COMPONENT "
350   PRINT "VALUES FOR A SQUARE ATTENUATOR ARE:"
360   PRINT : PRINT
370   PRINT "THE INPUT SHUNT RESISTOR P1 IS "
380   PRINT   INT (P(3 - D) + .5);" OHMS.
390   PRINT
400   PRINT "THE OUTPUT SHUNT RESISTOR P2 IS "
410   PRINT   INT (P(3 - C) + .5);" OHMS."
420   PRINT
430   PRINT "SERIES RESISTORS SA AND SB ARE "; INT (S3 / 2 + .5);"
      OHMS."
440   REM
445   PRINT
450   PRINT "MINIMUM LOSS FOR THESE IMPEDANCES IS"
460   PRINT   INT (10 * L5 + .5) / 10;" DB."
470   PRINT
480   PRINT "MULTIPLY SERIES RESISTOR VALUES BY 2"
490   PRINT "FOR THE UNBALANCED PAD VALUES."
500   PRINT : PRINT
510   INPUT "ANOTHER DESIGN? ";Z$
520   IF  LEFT$ (Z$,1) = "Y" THEN 70
530   END
```

```
UNSYMMETRICAL SQUARE PAD ATTENUATOR


THIS PROGRAM WILL DESIGN UNSYMMETRICAL
SQUARE ATTENUATOR PADS. TO USE YOU
MUST ENTER THE INPUT AND OUTPUT IMPE-
DANCES IN OHMS AND THE DESIRED VOLTAGE
OR CURRENT LOSS IN DECIBELS.


WHAT IS THE INPUT IMPEDANCE? 300
WHAT IS THE OUTPUT IMPEDANCE? 75
WHAT IS THE DESIRED LOSS IN DB? 15


FOR UNSYMMETRICAL BALANCED PADS WHERE
Z1 = 300 OHMS, Z2 = 75 OHMS
AND LOSS = 15 DB THE COMPONENT
VALUES FOR A SQUARE ATTENUATOR ARE:


THE INPUT SHUNT RESISTOR P1 IS
907 OHMS.

THE OUTPUT SHUNT RESISTOR P2 IS
85 OHMS.

SERIES RESISTORS SA AND SB ARE 204 OHMS.

MINIMUM LOSS FOR THESE IMPEDANCES IS
11.4 DB.

MULTIPLY SERIES RESISTOR VALUES BY 2
FOR THE UNBALANCED PAD VALUES.


ANOTHER DESIGN? NO
```

12.5 SYMMETRICAL SQUARE-PAD ATTENUATOR

The attenuator designed in this program (Fig. 12.5) is very similar to the one in the previous program. In a symmetrical attenuator, the input and output resistances are identical.

Like the former design, this one is also for a balanced attenuator. For an unbalanced design, multiply the series resistor values by 2.

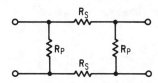

Fig. 12.5 Symmetrical square-pad attenuator

```
0    CALL  - 936
1    PRINT : PRINT : PRINT "WRITTEN BY JULES H. GILDER"
2    PRINT : PRINT "COPYRIGHT (C) HAYDEN BOOK CO. 1978"
3    FOR X = 1 TO 4000: NEXT X
4    PRINT : PRINT : PRINT : PRINT
5    PRINT "   SYMMETRICAL SQUARE PAD ATTENUATOR"
10   PRINT : PRINT : PRINT
20   PRINT "THIS PROGRAM WILL DESIGN BALANCED"
30   PRINT "SYMMETRICAL SQUARE ATTENUATOR PADS. YOU"
40   PRINT "MUST ENTER THE INPUT AND OUTPUT IMPE-"
50   PRINT "DANCES IN OHMS AND THE DESIRED VOLTAGE"`
60   PRINT "OR CURRENT LOSS IN DECIBELS."
70   PRINT : PRINT
80   INPUT "WHAT IS THE DESIRED IMPEDANCE? ";A
100  INPUT "WHAT IS THE DESIRED LOSS IN DB? ";L
110  PRINT
120  Z = A
130  K =  EXP (L * LOG (10) / 20)
140  T =  INT (Z * ((K ↑ 2) - 1) / (4 * K) + .5)
150  F =  INT (Z * (K + 1) / (K - 1) + .5)
160  PRINT : PRINT : PRINT
170  PRINT "FOR BALANCED SYMMETRICAL PADS OF ";Z
180  PRINT "OHMS AND ";L;" DB LOSS:"
190  PRINT : PRINT
200  PRINT "SQUARE PAD SERIES RESISTORS = ";T
210  PRINT "OHMS."
220  PRINT
230  PRINT "SHUNT RESISTORS 'F' ARE ";F;" OHMS."
240  PRINT
250  PRINT "MULTIPLY SERIES RESISTOR VALUES BY 2"
260  PRINT "FOR THE UNBALANCED PAD VALUES."
270  PRINT : PRINT
280  INPUT "ANOTHER DESIGN? ";Z$
290  IF  LEFT$ (Z$,1) = "Y" THEN 70
300  END
```

SYMMETRICAL SQUARE PAD ATTENUATOR

THIS PROGRAM WILL DESIGN BALANCED
SYMMETRICAL SQUARE ATTENUATOR PADS. YOU
MUST ENTER THE INPUT AND OUTPUT IMPE-
DANCES IN OHMS AND THE DESIRED VOLTAGE
OR CURRENT LOSS IN DECIBELS.

WHAT IS THE DESIRED IMPEDANCE? 300
WHAT IS THE DESIRED LOSS IN DB? 6

FOR BALANCED SYMMETRICAL PADS OF 300
OHMS AND 6 DB LOSS:

SQUARE PAD SERIES RESISTORS = 112
OHMS.

SHUNT RESISTORS 'F' ARE 903 OHMS.

MULTIPLY SERIES RESISTOR VALUES BY 2
FOR THE UNBALANCED PAD VALUES.

ANOTHER DESIGN? NO

12.6   SYMMETRICAL H-PAD ATTENUATOR

The H-pad attenuator designed in this program (Fig. 12.6) is similar to the one in 12.3. The only difference is that this is a symmetrical attenuator. In a symmetrical attenuator, the input and output resistances are identical.

Like the former design, this one is also for a balanced attenuator. For an unbalanced design, multiply the series resistor values by 2.

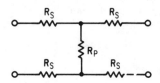

Fig. 12.6   Symmetrical H-pad attenuator

```
0   CALL  - 936
1   PRINT : PRINT : PRINT : PRINT "WRITTEN BY JULES H. GILDER"
2   PRINT : PRINT "COPYRIGHT (C) HAYDEN BOOK CO. 1978"
3   FOR X = 1 TO 4000: NEXT X
4   PRINT : PRINT : PRINT : PRINT
5   PRINT  TAB( 5)"SYMMETRICAL H PAD ATTENUATOR"
10  PRINT : PRINT : PRINT : PRINT
20  PRINT "THIS PROGRAM WILL DESIGN BALANCED"
30  PRINT "SYMMETRICAL 'H' ATTENUATOR PADS. YOU"
40  PRINT "MUST ENTER THE INPUT AND OUTPUT IMPE-"
50  PRINT "DANCES IN OHMS AND THE DESIRED VOLTAGE"
60  PRINT "OR CURRENT LOSS IN DECIBELS."
70  PRINT : PRINT
80  INPUT "WHAT IS THE DESIRED IMPEDANCE? ";A
100 INPUT "WHAT IS THE DESIRED LOSS IN DB? ";L
110 PRINT
120 Z = A
130 K =  EXP (L *  LOG (10) / 20)
140 S =  INT ((.5 * Z) * (K - 1) / (K + 1) + .5)
150 P =  INT (2 * Z * K / ((K ↑ 2) - 1) + .5)
160 PRINT : PRINT : PRINT
170 PRINT "FOR BALANCED SYMMETRICAL PADS OF ";Z
180 PRINT "OHMS AND ";L;" DB LOSS:"
190 PRINT : PRINT
200 PRINT "'H' PAD SERIES RESISTORS 'S' ARE ";S
210 PRINT "OHMS."
220 PRINT
230 PRINT "THE SHUNT RESISTOR 'P' IS ";P;" OHMS.
240 PRINT
250 PRINT "MULTIPLY SERIES RESISTOR VALUES BY 2"
260 PRINT "FOR THE UNBALANCED PAD VALUES."
270 END
```

SYMMETRICAL H PAD ATTENUATOR

THIS PROGRAM WILL DESIGN BALANCED
SYMMETRICAL 'H' ATTENUATOR PADS. YOU
MUST ENTER THE INPUT AND OUTPUT IMPE-
DANCES IN OHMS AND THE DESIRED VOLTAGE
OR CURRENT LOSS IN DECIBELS.

WHAT IS THE DESIRED IMPEDANCE? 600
WHAT IS THE DESIRED LOSS IN DB? 3

FOR BALANCED SYMMETRICAL PADS OF 600
OHMS AND 3 DB LOSS:

'H' PAD SERIES RESISTORS 'S' ARE 51
OHMS.

THE SHUNT RESISTOR 'P' IS 1703 OHMS.

MULTIPLY SERIES RESISTOR VALUES BY 2
FOR THE UNBALANCED PAD VALUES.

12.7 SYMMETRICAL LATTICE-PAD ATTENUATOR

The symmetrical lattice-pad attenuator (Fig. 12.7) is a balanced attenuator with identical input and output resistors. In addition, the position of the X and Y resistors may be interchanged.

This attenuator is only for balanced lines. An unbalanced version cannot be formed by multiplying the series resistors by 2.

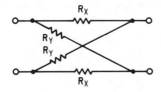

Fig. 12.7 Symmetrical lattice-pad attenuator

```
0   CALL  - 936
1   PRINT : PRINT : PRINT : PRINT "WRITTEN BY JULES H. GILDER"
2   PRINT : PRINT "COPYRIGHT (C) HAYDEN BOOK CO. 1978"

3   FOR X = 1 TO 4000: NEXT X
4   PRINT : PRINT : PRINT : PRINT

5   PRINT "    SYMMETRICAL LATTICE PAD ATTENUATOR"
10  PRINT : PRINT : PRINT : PRINT

20  PRINT "THIS PROGRAM WILL DESIGN BALANCED"
30  PRINT "SYMMETRICAL LATTICE ATTENUATORS. YOU"

40  PRINT "MUST ENTER THE DESIRED IMPEDANCE"
50  PRINT "IN OHMS AND THE REQUIRED VOLTAGE"

60  PRINT "OR CURRENT LOSS IN DECIBELS."
70  PRINT : PRINT

80   INPUT "WHAT IS THE DESIRED IMPEDANCE? ";A
100  INPUT "WHAT IS THE DESIRED LOSS IN DB? ";L

110  PRINT
120  Z = A

130  K =  EXP (L * LOG (10) / 20)
140  F =  INT (Z * (K + 1) / (K - 1) + .5)
145  S =  INT ((.5 * Z) * (K - 1) / (K + 1) + .5)
150  M =  INT (2 * S + .5)

160  PRINT : PRINT : PRINT
170  PRINT "FOR BALANCED SYMMETRICAL PADS OF ";Z
180  PRINT "OHMS AND ";L;" DB LOSS:"
190  PRINT : PRINT
200  PRINT "THE LATTICE PAD RESISTORS 'X' ARE "
210  PRINT F;" OHMS AND RESISTORS 'Y' ARE ";M;" OHMS"
230  PRINT : PRINT
240  INPUT "ANOTHER DESIGN? ";Z$
250  IF  LEFT$ (Z$,1) = "Y" THEN 70
260  END
```

SYMMETRICAL LATTICE PAD ATTENUATOR

THIS PROGRAM WILL DESIGN BALANCED
SYMMETRICAL LATTICE ATTENUATORS. YOU
MUST ENTER THE DESIRED IMPEDANCE
IN OHMS AND THE REQUIRED VOLTAGE
OR CURRENT LOSS IN DECIBELS.

WHAT IS THE DESIRED IMPEDANCE? 300
WHAT IS THE DESIRED LOSS IN DB? 3

FOR BALANCED SYMMETRICAL PADS OF 300
OHMS AND 3 DB LOSS:

THE LATTICE PAD RESISTORS 'X' ARE
1754 OHMS AND RESISTORS 'Y' ARE 52 OHMS

ANOTHER DESIGN? YES

WHAT IS THE DESIRED IMPEDANCE? 600
WHAT IS THE DESIRED LOSS IN DB? 6

FOR BALANCED SYMMETRICAL PADS OF 600
OHMS AND 6 DB LOSS:

THE LATTICE PAD RESISTORS 'X' ARE
1806 OHMS AND RESISTORS 'Y' ARE 200 OHMS

ANOTHER DESIGN? NO

12.8 SYMMETRICAL π ATTENUATOR

The symmetrical π attenuator (Fig. 12.8) is for unbalanced lines. It has identical input and output impedances.

The balanced equivalent of the symmetrical π is the symmetrical square-pad attenuator.

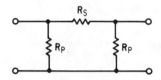

Fig. 12.8   Symmetrical π attenuator

```
0   CALL  - 936
1   PRINT : PRINT : PRINT "WRITTEN BY JULES H. GILDER"
2   PRINT : PRINT "COPYRIGHT (C) HAYDEN BOOK CO. 1978"
3   FOR X = 1 TO 4000: NEXT X
4   PRINT : PRINT : PRINT : PRINT
5   PRINT  TAB( 7)"SYMMETRICAL PI ATTENUATOR"
10  PRINT : PRINT : PRINT
20  PRINT "THIS PROGRAM WILL DESIGN BALANCED"
30  PRINT "SYMMETRICAL PI ATTENUATOR PADS. YOU"
40  PRINT "MUST ENTER THE DESIRED IMPEDANCE"
50  PRINT "IN OHMS AND THE REQUIRED VOLTAGE"
60  PRINT "OR CURRENT LOSS IN DECIBELS."
70  PRINT : PRINT
80  INPUT "WHAT IS THE DESIRED IMPEDANCE? ";A
100 INPUT "WHAT IS THE DESIRED LOSS IN DB? ";L
110 PRINT
120 Z = A
130 K =  EXP (L *  LOG (10) / 20)
140 S =   INT (Z * ((K ↑ 2 - 1) / (2 * K)) + .5)
150 P =   INT (Z * (K + 1) / (K - 1) + .5)
160 PRINT : PRINT : PRINT
170 PRINT "FOR SYMMETRICAL PADS OF ";Z
180 PRINT "OHMS AND ";L;" DB LOSS:"
190 PRINT : PRINT
200 PRINT "SERIES RESISTOR 'S' FOR THE PI PAD IS"
210 PRINT S;" OHMS."
220 PRINT
230 PRINT "SHUNT RESISTORS 'P' ARE ";P;" OHMS."
240 PRINT : PRINT
250 INPUT "ANOTHER DESIGN? ";Z$
260 IF  LEFT$ (Z$,1) = "Y" THEN 70
270 END
```

SYMMETRICAL PI ATTENUATOR

THIS PROGRAM WILL DESIGN BALANCED
SYMMETRICAL PI ATTENUATOR PADS. YOU
MUST ENTER THE DESIRED IMPEDANCE
IN OHMS AND THE REQUIRED VOLTAGE
OR CURRENT LOSS IN DECIBELS.

WHAT IS THE DESIRED IMPEDANCE? 300
WHAT IS THE DESIRED LOSS IN DB? 12

FOR SYMMETRICAL PADS OF 300
OHMS AND 12 DB LOSS:

SERIES RESISTOR 'S' FOR THE PI PAD IS
559 OHMS.

SHUNT RESISTORS 'P' ARE 501 OHMS.

ANOTHER DESIGN? NO

12.9 SYMMETRICAL T ATTENUATOR

Another attenuator designed for unbalanced lines is the symmetrical T attenuator (Fig. 12.9). It is composed of only three resistors, two series and one parallel.

The balanced equivalent of the symmetrical T attenuator is the symmetrical H.

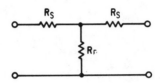

Fig. 12.9 Symmetrical T attenuator

```
0    CALL  - 936
1    PRINT : PRINT : PRINT : PRINT "WRITTEN BY JULES H. GILDER"

2    PRINT : PRINT "COPYRIGHT (C) HAYDEN BOOK CO. 1978
3    FOR X = 1 TO 4000: NEXT X

4    PRINT : PRINT : PRINT : PRINT
5    PRINT  TAB( 7)"SYMMETRICAL 'T' ATTENUATOR"

10   PRINT : PRINT : PRINT
20   PRINT "THIS PROGRAM WILL DESIGN BALANCED"

30   PRINT "SYMMETRICAL 'T' ATTENUATOR PADS, YOU"
40   PRINT "MUST ENTER THE INPUT AND OUTPUT IMPE-"

50   PRINT "DANCES IN OHMS AND THE DESIRED VOLTAGE"
60   PRINT "OR CURRENT LOSS IN DECIBELS."

70   PRINT : PRINT
80   INPUT "WHAT IS THE DESIRED IMPEDANCE? ";A

100   INPUT "WHAT IS THE DESIRED LOSS IN DB? ";L
110   PRINT

120  Z = A
130  K =  EXP (L *  LOG (10) / 20 )

140  S =  INT (2 * (.5 * Z) * (K - 1) / (K + 1) + .5)
150  P =  INT (2 * Z * K / ((K ↑ 2) - 1) + .5)

160   PRINT : PRINT : PRINT
170   PRINT "FOR SYMMETRICAL PADS OF ";Z

180   PRINT "OHMS AND ";L;" DB LOSS:"
190   PRINT : PRINT

200   PRINT "'T' PAD SERIES RESISTORS 'S' ARE ";S
210   PRINT "OHMS."
220   PRINT
230   PRINT "THE SHUNT RESISTOR 'P' IS ";P;" OHMS.
240   PRINT
270   PRINT : PRINT
280   INPUT "ANOTHER DESIGN? ";Z$
290   IF  LEFT$ (Z$,1) = "Y" THEN 70
300   END
```

SYMMETRICAL 'T' ATTENUATOR

THIS PROGRAM WILL DESIGN BALANCED
SYMMETRICAL 'T' ATTENUATOR PADS. YOU
MUST ENTER THE INPUT AND OUTPUT IMPE-
DANCES IN OHMS AND THE DESIRED VOLTAGE
OR CURRENT LOSS IN DECIBELS.

WHAT IS THE DESIRED IMPEDANCE? 600
WHAT IS THE DESIRED LOSS IN DB? 6

FOR SYMMETRICAL PADS OF 600
OHMS AND 6 DB LOSS:

'T' PAD SERIES RESISTORS 'S' ARE 199
OHMS.

THE SHUNT RESISTOR 'P' IS 803 OHMS.

ANOTHER DESIGN? NO

12.10 UNBALANCED MINIMUM-LOSS PAD

Very often it is desirable to connect two circuits of different impedances with a minimum amount of loss. This can be done with the help of a minimum-loss pad.

This pad is designed for unbalanced lines and is composed of only two resistors (Fig. 12.10). It is also known as an L pad.

In addition to selecting the resistor values, the program will indicate the minimum loss in dB.

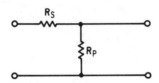

Fig. 12.10 Unbalanced minimum-loss pad

```
0   CALL  - 936
1   PRINT : PRINT : PRINT : PRINT "WRITTEN BY JULES H. GILDER"
2   PRINT : PRINT "COPYRIGHT (C) HAYDEN BOOK CO. 1978"
3   FOR X = 1 TO 4000: NEXT X
4   PRINT : PRINT : PRINT : PRINT
5   PRINT  TAB( 5)"UNBALANCED MINIMUM LOSS PAD"
10  PRINT : PRINT : PRINT : PRINT
20  PRINT "THIS PROGRAM WILL DESIGN A MINIMUM LOSS"
30  PRINT "UNBALANCED MATCHING PAD. TO USE IT YOU"
40  PRINT "MUST ENTER THE INPUT AND OUTPUT IMPE-"
50  PRINT "DANCES IN OHMS."
70  PRINT : PRINT
80  INPUT "WHAT IS THE INPUT IMPEDANCE? ";A
90  INPUT "WHAT IS THE OUTPUT IMPEDANCE? ";B
92  PRINT
95  IF  A > B  THEN   GOTO  100
96  PRINT  CHR$ (7); CHR$ (7): PRINT "INPUT IMPEDANCE MUST BE LAR
       GER THAN"
97  PRINT "OUTPUT IMPEDANCE.":  GOTO  70
100 PRINT
110 PRINT
120 K5 = (A + SQR ((A ↑ 2) - (A * B))) / B
130 S =  INT (A * (1 - (B / A)) ↑ .5 + .5)
140 P =  INT (B / (1 - (B / A)) ↑ .5 + .5)
150 L5 =  LOG (K5 / SQR (A / B)) / ( LOG (10) / 20)
155 L5 =  INT (L5 * 100 + .5) / 100
160 PRINT : PRINT : PRINT
170 PRINT "FOR UNBALANCED MINIMUM LOSS MATCHING "
180 PRINT "PADS WITH A ";A;" OHMS INPUT RESISTANCE"
190 PRINT "AND A ";B ;" OHMS OUTPUT RESISTANCE"
210 PRINT : PRINT : PRINT
220 PRINT "THE SERIES RESISTOR 'S' IS ";S;" OHMS."
230 PRINT
240 PRINT "THE SHUNT RESISTOR 'P' IS ";P;" OHMS."
250 PRINT
260 PRINT "THE MINIMUM LOSS IS ";L5;" DB."
270 PRINT : PRINT
280 INPUT "ANOTHER DESIGN? ";Z$
290 IF  LEFT$ (Z$,1) = "Y" THEN 70
300 END
```

UNBALANCED MINIMUM LOSS PAD

THIS PROGRAM WILL DESIGN A MINIMUM LOSS
UNBALANCED MATCHING PAD. TO USE IT YOU
MUST ENTER THE INPUT AND OUTPUT IMPE-
DANCES IN OHMS.

WHAT IS THE INPUT IMPEDANCE? 300
WHAT IS THE OUTPUT IMPEDANCE? 75

FOR UNBALANCED MINIMUM LOSS MATCHING
PADS WITH A 300 OHMS INPUT RESISTANCE
AND A 75 OHMS OUTPUT RESISTANCE

THE SERIES RESISTOR 'S' IS 260 OHMS.

THE SHUNT RESISTOR 'P' IS 87 OHMS.

THE MINIMUM LOSS IS 11.44 DB.

ANOTHER DESIGN? NO

12.11 BALANCED MINIMUM-LOSS PAD

Very often it is desirable to connect two circuits of different impedances with a minimum amount of loss. This can be done with the help of a minimum-loss pad.

This pad is designed for balanced lines and is composed of only three resistors (Fig. 12.11).

In addition to selecting the resistor values, the program will indicate the minimum loss in dB.

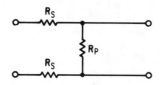

Fig. 12.11 Balanced minimum-loss pad

```
0    CALL  - 936
1    PRINT : PRINT : PRINT : PRINT "WRITTEN BY JULES H. GILDER"
2    PRINT : PRINT "COPYRIGHT (C) HAYDEN BOOK CO. 1978"
3    FOR X = 1 TO 4000: NEXT X
4    PRINT : PRINT : PRINT : PRINT
5    PRINT  TAB( 6)"BALANCED MINIMUM LOSS PAD"
10   PRINT : PRINT : PRINT : PRINT
20   PRINT "THIS PROGRAM WILL DESIGN A MINIMUM LOSS"
30   PRINT  "BALANCED MATCHING PAD. TO USE IT YOU"
40   PRINT "MUST ENTER THE INPUT AND OUTPUT IMPE-"
50   PRINT "DANCES IN OHMS."
70   PRINT : PRINT
80   INPUT "WHAT IS THE INPUT IMPEDANCE? ";A
90   INPUT "WHAT IS THE OUTPUT IMPEDANCE? ";B
92   PRINT
95   IF  A > B  THEN   GOTO  100
96   PRINT  CHR$ (7); CHR$ (7): PRINT "INPUT IMPEDANCE MUST BE LAR
     GER THAN"
97   PRINT "OUTPUT IMPEDANCE.": GOTO  70
100  PRINT
110  PRINT
120  K5 = (A +  SQR ((A ↑ 2) - (A * B))) / B
130  S =  INT ( .5 * A * (1 - (B / A)) ↑ .5 + .5)
140  P =  INT (B / (1 - (B / A)) ↑ .5 + .5)
150  L5 =  LOG (K5 /  SQR (A / B)) / ( LOG (10) / 20)
155  L5 =  INT (L5 * 100 + .5) / 100
160  PRINT : PRINT : PRINT
170  PRINT "FOR BALANCED MINIMUM LOSS MATCHING "
180  PRINT "PADS WITH A ";A;" OHMS INPUT RESISTANCE"
190  PRINT "AND A ";B ;" OHMS OUTPUT RESISTANCE"
210  PRINT : PRINT : PRINT
220  PRINT "THE SERIES RESISTORS 'S' ARE ";S;" OHMS."
230  PRINT
240  PRINT "THE SHUNT RESISTOR 'P' IS ";P;" OHMS."
250  PRINT
260  PRINT "THE MINIMUM LOSS IS ";L5;" DB."
270  PRINT : PRINT
280  INPUT "ANOTHER DESIGN? ";Z$
290  IF  LEFT$ (Z$,1) = "Y" THEN 70
300  END
```

BALANCED MINIMUM LOSS PAD

THIS PROGRAM WILL DESIGN A MINIMUM LOSS
BALANCED MATCHING PAD. TO USE IT YOU
MUST ENTER THE INPUT AND OUTPUT IMPE-
DANCES IN OHMS.

WHAT IS THE INPUT IMPEDANCE? 50
WHAT IS THE OUTPUT IMPEDANCE? 75

INPUT IMPEDANCE MUST BE LARGER THAN
OUTPUT IMPEDANCE.

WHAT IS THE INPUT IMPEDANCE? 75
WHAT IS THE OUTPUT IMPEDANCE? 50

FOR BALANCED MINIMUM LOSS MATCHING
PADS WITH A 75 OHMS INPUT RESISTANCE
AND A 50 OHMS OUTPUT RESISTANCE

THE SERIES RESISTORS 'S' ARE 22 OHMS.

THE SHUNT RESISTOR 'P' IS 87 OHMS.

THE MINIMUM LOSS IS 5.72 DB.

ANOTHER DESIGN? NO